Popular fiction in mid-Victorian Britain was regarded as both feminine and diseased. Critical articles of the time on fiction and on the body and disease offer convincing evidence that reading was metaphorically allied with eating, contagion, and sex. Anxious critics traced the infection of the imperial, healthy body of masculine elite culture by "diseased" popular fiction, especially novels by women.

This book discusses works by three novelists – M. E. Braddon, Rhoda Broughton, and "Ouida" – within this historical context. In each case, the comparison of an early, "sensation" novel against a later work shows how generic categorization worked in the context of social concerns to contain anxiety and limit interpretive possibilities. Within the texts themselves, references to contemporary critical and medical literatures resist or exploit mid-Victorian concepts of health, nationality, class, and the body.

CAMBRIDGE STUDIES IN NINETEENTH-CENTURY
LITERATURE AND CULTURE 11

# DISEASE, DESIRE, AND THE
# BODY IN VICTORIAN WOMEN'S
# POPULAR NOVELS

CAMBRIDGE STUDIES IN NINETEENTH-CENTURY
LITERATURE AND CULTURE

General editors
Gillian Beer, *University of Cambridge*
Catherine Gallagher, *University of California, Berkeley*

Editorial board
Isobel Armstrong, *Birkbeck College, London*
Terry Eagleton, *University of Oxford*
Leonore Davidoff, *University of Essex*
D. A. Miller, *Harvard University*
J. Hillis Miller, *University of California, Irvine*
Mary Poovey, *The Johns Hopkins University*
Elaine Showalter, *Princeton University*

Nineteenth-century British literature and culture have been rich fields for interdisciplinary studies. Since the turn of the twentieth century, scholars and critics have tracked the intersections and tensions between Victorian literature and the visual arts, politics, social organization, economic life, technical innovations, scientific thought – in short, culture in its broadest sense. In recent years, theoretical challenges and historiographical shifts have unsettled the assumptions of previous scholarly syntheses and called into question the terms of older debates. Whereas the tendency in much past literary critical interpretation was to use the metaphor of culture as "background," feminist, Foucauldian, and other analyses have employed more dynamic models that raise questions of power and of circulation. Such developments have reanimated the field.

This series aims to accommodate and promote the most interesting work being undertaken on the frontiers of the field of nineteenth-century literary studies: work which intersects fruitfully with other fields of study such as history, or literary theory, or the history of science. Comparative as well as interdisciplinary approaches are welcome.

A complete list of titles published will be found at the end of the book.

# DISEASE, DESIRE, AND THE BODY IN VICTORIAN WOMEN'S POPULAR NOVELS

PAMELA K. GILBERT

*University of Wisconsin, Parkside*

CAMBRIDGE
UNIVERSITY PRESS

CAMBRIDGE UNIVERSITY PRESS
Cambridge, New York, Melbourne, Madrid, Cape Town, Singapore, São Paulo

Cambridge University Press
The Edinburgh Building, Cambridge CB2 2RU, UK

Published in the United States of America by Cambridge University Press, New York

www.cambridge.org
Information on this title: www.cambridge.org/9780521593236

First published 1997
This digitally printed first paperback version 2005

*A catalogue record for this publication is available from the British Library*

*Library of Congress Cataloguing in Publication data*

Gilbert, Pamela K.
Disease, desire, and the body in Victorian women's popular novels / Pamela K. Gilbert.
p.    cm. – (Cambridge studies in nineteenth-century literature and culture; 11)
Includes bibliographical references and index.
ISBN 0 521 59323 9 (hardback)
1. English fiction – 19th century – History and criticism.
2. Women – Great Britain – Books and reading – History – 19th century.
3. Literature and diseases – Great Britain – History – 19th century.
4. Literature and society – Great Britain – History – 19th century.
5. Women and literature – Great Britain – History – 19th century.
6. Popular literature – Great Britain – History and criticism.
7. English fiction – Women authors – History and criticism.
8. Sensationalism in literature.    9. Body, Human, in literature.
10. Diseases in literature.    11. Desire in literature.    I. Title.
II. Series.
PR878.W6G55    1997
823'.8099287–dc21    97-7584    CIP

ISBN-13 978-0-521-59323-6 hardback
ISBN-10 0-521-59323-9 hardback

ISBN-13 978-0-521-02207-1 paperback
ISBN-10 0-521-02207-X paperback

# Contents

# Acknowledgments

I am happy to have the opportunity to thank some of the many people who have made this book possible. James Kincaid, its first reader, has given ample encouragement and profoundly useful criticism. Ronald Gottesman has also been a sharp-eyed and helpful critic. My colleagues at the University of Wisconsin, Parkside have been generous in their support of my research. Of my email and conference correspondents, I would particularly like to thank Talia Shaffer, Devoney Looser, and Marlene Tromp. Many more public fora of collegial discussion have contributed also to my thinking; I would like especially to thank all the participants in VICTORIA-L and the participants in Mary Poovey's summer seminar at West Virginia in 1994. After the principal work on this project was completed, there was also the material, emotional and intellectual support of the NEH, the Center for Twentieth Century Studies, Michael Levenson and the participants in the 1995 NEH seminar, which helped me through the demanding process of readying the work for publication; in this, I would also like to thank Ann Cvetkovich and Gillian Beer. Finally, family and friends have all kept me healthy and happy, including Angela Geitner, Dana Loewy, and John Whalen-Bridge. Thank you all, and especially Meryl Strichartz.

Portions of this book have been published elsewhere in different form. Part of chapter 3 appeared in *Essays in Literature* (1996) and passages from chapter 1 appeared in *LIT: Literature/Interpretation/Theory* (1997).

# Introduction

Hayden White, among others, observes that the narration of history is determined more by the needs of the historian than intrinsic properties of historical data.[1] Regarding the burgeoning critical fascination with transgression and boundaries, as evidenced by the work of Peter Stallybrass and Allon White, Donna Haraway and many others,[2] it is justifiable to ask, not only why boundary transgression is such a central metaphor in the periods we study, but why it is such a central – almost obsessive – concern to us now. We see it, most obviously, in the discourse on AIDS. Yet it is prevalent everywhere, from abortion rights (where does the individual body end and the social body begin?) to information security (in what consists the boundary between private and public?). In the rapidly shifting international political climate, as in the multicultural US, we see it in the obsessive attempts to categorize and rename, adding strings of adjectives in an attempt to "get it right," only to discover that identity is fluid and multiple, and resists naming. From national boundaries under dispute to the attempts of multinational corporations to disentangle their agendas from other interests, from feminist attempts to speak for "all women" to the efforts of women of color and lesbians to be heard as distinct, but still collective voices, identity politics consist of a quest to distinguish the Self from the Other, only to discover a multitude of others and a myriad of selves. In a global economy and ecology, wherein cultural and communicative structures become ever more immediate and diffuse, the terms "national" and "individual" lose meaning as rapidly as do terms like "private" or "woman." Perhaps this is why such labels are so highly charged. In the loss of these "clear" definitions (which after all were never really all that clear), we fear the loss of an identity that, however inadequately, *worked* for many of us. As these easy distinctions are divested of their perceived clarity, and therefore, their utility, they are invested with all the energy of a nostalgia for a loss not yet fully actualized, but dimly foreseen.

We are and have been in the midst of a paradigm shift. As boundaries between constructed categories (self/other; man/woman; history/fiction; near/far) become more permeable, and therefore more visible, our attention is drawn to those boundaries. Their very insubstantiality buttresses their importance, calls forth our anxiety. Our need to define is driven by their insusceptibility to definition. We poke obsessively at the walls we have erected in order to test their strength, and are both thrilled and appalled when all that was solid melts into air. From metaphors of depth, we move to metaphors of surfaces, a fascination with transgression. The body, our most basic cultural unit of enclosure and difference between self and other, is a text in which this drama of colliding and blending surfaces is written and read. The attention given in recent films to interracial and other "forbidden" sexual relationships demonstrates this, as does the concern with image and substance, body and machine in films as diverse as the *Terminator* series and *Sex, Lies, and Videotape*. These are hardly new themes; indeed, it is their very centrality to contemporary cultures that makes them effective. They are basic concerns which are periodically foregrounded, coming into sharper focus in periods of particular tensions. This very current interest focuses historians' critical attention on earlier cultures' perceptions of boundaries, their constructions of transgression and its gains and costs.

Mid-Victorian imperial Britain often constructed its identity as active, healthy, and masculine versus foreign identities which were passive, fevered, or feminine. Yet Britain, in order to define its culture in this way, required Others: its colonial possessions and its ancestral continental rivals. Imperial ambition coupled with nineteenth-century capitalism, however, created a trans-class and transcultural "circulation" which threatened to break down the barriers of secure distinctions between upper and lower classes, British and foreign, colonizer and colonized. Like Rochester in his relation to the Creole madwoman, the upper class Englishman faced the terrifying prospect of difference, not merely in the West Indies, but in his own home, perhaps in his own mirror. The rhetoric of inviolable British domesticity becomes both the parent and opponent of sensation fiction, drawing together concerns of national identity, the inviolability of the body, and the clarity of gender and class distinctions.

Central urban space is often perceived by Victorians as a space of "promiscuous" intercourse between the classes, even as, for example, London's outlying areas to the east (and southeast) such as Whitechapel and Southwark are marked by industrial abjection, racial Otherness and crime, and suburbs to the west like Chelsea represent an uneasy blend of respectability and petty-bourgeois transgression. Mrs. Gaskell, Charles Dickens, George Gissing, and many other novelists carefully map the classed trajectories within this urban space only to disrupt those careful boundaries with the deadly collisions of characters such as Eugene Wrayburn and Bradley Headstone in *Our Mutual Friend*. The blurring of class-distinctive space takes on new meaning under the pressure of sanitary and personal safety concerns. Literacy, no longer itself a clear indicator of class, is redefined as prose fiction becomes a major and largely urban industry, marketing across the class spectrum. The classed topography of genre nostalgically reproduces the imaginary classed geography of pre-industrial rural space; the hierarchy of "taste" which anticipates modern day "canonical" discussions replaces the apparently simpler distinctions of literate versus illiterate. The blending of boundaries and the shrinkage of previously "inviolable" spaces heightens – as conflict always does – awareness of boundaries: contact becomes associated with contagion, which, as Stallybrass and White write, "become[s] ... [a] trope ... through which city life is apprehended."[3] The equally promiscuous exchange of intellectual and cultural material in literature, especially the movement of periodical literatures across a mixed-class audience, provokes a similar anxiety regarding the contagion of ideas, dangerous infections in the body politic. The domestic space comes to represent an isolated enclosure, a "pure," closed, middle-class English body and mind embattled against the encroaching forces of disease, revolution, and worst of all, in George Eliot's words, "Silly Novels by Lady Novelists." This body was female, but as a male possession represented a point of entry through which the patriarchal body might suffer disease and ultimately emasculation, just as the erring wife represented a threat to the purity and control of the patrilinear transfer of name and wealth.

In the 1860s, the sensation genre, and the novelists and novels identified with it, provides one clear and historically well-documented instance in which the movement of these anxieties and the rhetorics which encode and create them can be traced in the construction of genre and the gendered and classed author, reader, and text. This movement can be traced both within the novels themselves and other cultural discourses which parallel and interpenetrate them (critical reviews and general literary discussions as well as non-literary articles concerned with the body and health, both individual and cultural). Genre is a category that has less to do with intrinsic properties of particular texts than the needs and concerns of readers reading those texts – a particular era and cultural group, its concatenation of fears and desires and market forces which take shape from and feed those trends. Generic categorization and slippage between categories mark a particular point of interest since the act of naming is also an act of reading the bodies of authors and readers by whom the text is produced and consumed. The sensation genre is a category of readings particularly concerned with violation of the domestic body, with class and gender transgression, and most importantly, with the violation of the privileged space of the reader/voyeur, with the text's reaching out to touch the reader's body, acting directly "on the nerves." The subsequent evolution of popular genres related to the sensation genre and its authors reflects a set of beliefs about femaleness, reading, the fiction market, and a host of related constructs.

In the following pages, I follow a "top-down" approach, beginning with an investigation of the role of the middle-class popular novel and attitudes toward reading, a broadly ranging discussion of attitudes toward the book, the body, the industry of culture, and cultural health, as they are discernable in popular middle class journals such as the *Athenaeum*, *The Spectator*, and *Blackwood's*. The theories of the body which I have found most productive are those of Bakhtin and Foucault, as developed by feminist and poststructuralist thinkers – fundamentally a social-constructionist view of the body as a text and gender as a reading. Some readers may find incongruous, then, my references to Julia Kristeva or even to George Lakoff and Mark Johnson, whose "emergent metaphors" may seem suspiciously essentialist, or my frequent borrowings of psychoanalytically based frameworks for the discussion of Self and Other. However, I find these frames not basically incompatible. The body and its gender are texts which have been read in certain ways for a very long time in what we loosely term "Western culture"; psychoanalytic thought has provided compelling and profoundly useful bases for meta-commentary on that reading. If that reading has become so powerful an institution as to acquire the privileged status of "nature," then so much more does such a reading demand our attentive critique. The status of ontological truth-claims of any theoretical perspectives, no matter how much or how little we cherish them, should not distract the feminist from her or his bricolage, from the quest for the perspectives, however multiple, most presently productive. In a work and era that celebrates transgression, there is some latitude for theoretical miscegenations and their odd progeny.

Moving on to issues of content, as with any limited project, this one leaves more out than in. Specifically, I am focusing on urban, white, middle-class, British writers. The classed, gendered, and colonized body is seen always from that vantage point. However, the texts that I do examine represent a market both devalued (as feminine and trivial) and economically dominant. The influence of the middle-class popular novel industry was far reaching, extending anywhere English and German (and to a lesser extent French and Italian) were read. It is therefore with these texts, and their construction of the body that I begin.

Within modernity, the body has been our most basic text for the reading of self, and the boundaries of our bodies are our primary *loci* for distinguishing self from not-self. Ingresses and egresses of the body are points of contact between self and not-self, places where we interact with Otherness in the dangerous process of becoming self, or vice versa. Other, less concrete, kinds of contact – the exchange of ideas, for example – are figured forth as and metaphorically aligned with the transgression or crossing-over of the body's boundaries. Since bodies are gendered, aged, classed, and so forth, these metaphors participate in these entailments; thus, for example, if reading provocative articles for pleasure is made analogous to promiscuous casual intercourse with delightful, seductive partners, the other entailments of this metaphor (moral judgments, for example) may be quite different if the reader is envisioned as a young, aristocratic man from the way they might be were the reader seen as a young, unmarried, middle-class woman. It is almost impossible to imagine a mid-nineteenth-century critic portraying a young woman reader favorably as the central figure of this analogy.

Having explored a discursive arena within which the spectacle of the body and the body reading may be interpreted, I define transgression, its relation to disease and the metaphors of space and movement which order it. I then place the social construction of genre within this arena, examining its power to produce readings consonant with the demands of a particular cultural moment, through its actualization of powerful discursive structures (metaphors of disease, for example). If the definition of a genre, and of certain texts as generic, is a social construction, i.e., a reading, then it participates in all of the entailments of readings as defined in chapter one – genres, like texts, authors, and readers, are gendered, classed, and so forth. A genre is a meta-reading, or a set of reading instructions, that coexists with a text and limits the range of its multiplicity. One productive way to expose both the imperatives of a genre and their roots in social values and concerns is to seek a different generic reading of the same text; an extended example is given in chapter 3, in the section dealing with *Lady Audley's Secret*. Impossible though it may be to read beyond or "outside" of *any* set of reading instructions, nevertheless, by shifting to another set of instructions – in effect, an alternative subject position – while maintaining awareness of the difference between that reading and the reading framed by the original genre, the reader enables her/himself to see that other set of instructions at work, much as one brings to view the normally hidden formatting commands in a word-processed text file.

We move from the general discussion of genre as concept and social phenomenon to a discussion of three very diverse sub-genres of the sensation period, three novels and authors which particularly exemplify them, and to questions of why and how this was so. Through close analysis of each of these novels and the ways in which they are positioned within their discursive environment, it is possible to discern the social forces which constructed the sensation movement, and the ways in which issues of "high" versus "low" culture (or canonical versus non-canonical texts) are defined on bases other than "intrinsic" textual properties. Analysis of one later (post-sensation) popular novel by each of the three authors provides both opportunities for comparison and examples of how authors who made their debuts in the sensation genre and were defined by their association with it later attempted to control the positioning of the texts within the marketplace. In each of these texts and sub-genres, the female body as the contested site of representation and consumption is ostentatiously foregrounded, as the status of a primarily woman-representing, woman-produced, and woman-consumed popular culture is in the process of determination.

The sensation genre, a category of reading which spanned the decade of the 1860s, is a topic of growing interest to literary scholars and feminist scholars across the disciplines today. Dominated by women writers, as much of the popular fiction market in the Victorian period was, the sensation novel generated a great deal of critical opprobrium and reader interest in its time. Many sensation novels written for the middle class audience became runaway bestsellers. Overnight successes like *Lady Audley's Secret* had also the distinction of remaining bestsellers over time. Yet they were designated "trash" by critics then and that apellation stuck. The process by which these texts have been rendered non-canonical has, in fact, much to do with the perception of their genre as a "feminine" one.

In choosing particular authors, I have a number of aims in mind.

Rhoda Broughton and Ouida (Marie Louise de la Rame or Ramée) are writers who exemplify Victorian popular literary tastes, and who are underread. M. E. Braddon is finally getting more critical interest, but while *Lady Audley's Secret* has been elevated to the level of para-canon, the rest of Braddon's impressive and worthwhile *oeuvre* is sadly neglected. These novels offer a rich complexity and intelligent commentary on the culture they represent and create, and one of my aims is to offer readings which situate the novels within the constraints of the market which they enter without reducing the texts to mere exempla of generic formulae created to describe and contain them, formulae which were never identical with any of these texts, and which were cannily invoked, subtly mocked, and opportunistically disregarded by turns by authors and readers seeking to define themselves against or within the market (or both). However, my aim is also not just to recoup part of what Elaine Showalter identified as a "Literature of Their [Our?] Own" (and Showalter is notoriously hard on "minor" authors),[4] although I think such a project entirely worthwhile, nor is it to indulge in the revisionist process which consists of discovering feminist foremothers in unlikely places; my focus is not biographical. One of the most serious failures of feminist criticism as a corpus is its tendency, even today, to focus principally on authorial biography, a practice which unintentionally replicates the traditional sexist tendency to read canonical male-author-ed texts as self-contained "art" and female-authored texts as simple extensions or reflections of personal experience. However, I am interest-ed in the "author function" associated with these women, a function whose gender, not incidentally dependent on the biological sex of these authors, was implicated in the construction of their readership, their market position, their generic placement, and finally their position outside the "canon" – and the construction of the canon itself. Hence, the fact that these are female authors makes, as well as is, a difference. That these are three very different authors writing six very diverse novels dramatizes the power of the construction of both sensation as a genre and the concept of the "popular" in the reading of culture, then and now, to contain them in a structure of kinship. These authors, all with long-term, extremely successful contemporaneous careers, to-gether provide an exemplary survey of work in women's popular novels in this period outside the realist domestic and industrial novels legit-imated by George Eliot, Mrs. Gaskell and others who have maintained a tenuous, but continuous place, at least in a feminist canon if not a mainstream one. Each novel herein examined was successful, in most cases, extremely so, and each represents key points in the novelist's career and her relation to the genre(s) she was marketed principally within. Part of the value of examining this women's popular literature, submerged in literary history even if buoyantly afloat on the market in its own time, is the opportunity for a clearer evaluation of the function of gender in articulations of the "body" of culture in the context of an emerging "popular" fiction, as object of consumption, representation of identities (national, authorial, class, and otherwise) and "subject" of discourse – puns intended.

M. E. Braddon is the author most familiarly identified with sensation. Rhoda Broughton and Ouida, each writing very different kinds of novels, had first successes in this same period (i.e., the 1860s), and were lumped together with other novelists deemed "sensational" because of similarities which today would strike readers as quite superficial, but which then were seen as definitive shared traits: setting which was both domestic and local and/or a perceived emphasis on women as actively desiring, for example. After the sixties, Broughton and Ouida were perceived as working in two separate genres, still recognizable today: the romance (love story) and the society novel, also known as the novel of high life. Braddon's *Lady Audley's Secret* (1862) is the novel conventionally credited with launching "sensation," and, although it is possible to debunk the perception of that novel as the "start" of the new genre, let alone its quintessence, the fact that it has been perceived that way has a certain significance.[5]

In fact, *Lady Audley's Secret* is primarily composed of three narratives: the moderately "sensational" narrative of Lady Audley's rise and fall; the traditional male coming-of-age story of Robert Audley's rise to adult status, and the detective plot which connects the two "main" narratives. By shifting the generic focus to read as primary the second of these narratives, we are able to trace an ironic revision of *The Odyssey*, and the suggestion that the coming to manhood of the male character is mediated and made possible by the often unremarked destruction of female power and subordination of women's sexuality to the homosocial (and homosexual) male bond. The first of the narratives is a "low-culture" genre, as is the third; the second is a "high-culture" genre. Sexuality, represented as a contagious disease, is the force that draws the narratives together and causes them to lose distinctness. The public's reading of *Lady Audley's Secret*, therefore, as a sensation novel works in exactly the same way as the multiple plot does – it provides a clear working example of how interests, issues, and themes gendered female are subordinated and sacrificed in order to maintain a classed and gendered hierarchy: Lucy's values are repudiated in order to allow Robert to adopt "appropriate" adult male values; the masculine-genre coming-of-age novel, with its implicit self-critique, is elided in favor of the less complicated reading of a feminine-genre low-culture sensation novel by a "hack" lady-novelist.

In *The Doctor's Wife*, an adaptation of *Madame Bovary* published only two years after *Lady Audley's Secret*, Braddon deliberately attempts to establish the novel, and herself as its author, in the high-culture genre of realism by positioning the novel, through internal textual cues, against sensation fiction.[6] In typical Braddon fashion, however, the novel critiques the legitimacy of the very distinctions which Braddon is seemingly attempting to use. Although the authorial voice bluntly states "this is not a sensation novel," and a character in the novel, who is himself a sensation author, repeatedly defines sensation in order to contrast it with the "real life" of the characters in the novel, Braddon uses Isabel, her protagonist, to collapse the borders between low-culture novels (which Isabel reads), the "realism" in which Isabel lives, and the superior degree of reality in which the reader exists. As in *Lady Audley's Secret*, female sexuality is the magnetic force which causes worlds to collide and to blend, which blending is always damaging and draining, though strangely appealing. Isabel becomes a vampiric figure living in the borderlands between life and art, high and low culture, upper and lower class – a diseased space which is fatal to the men drawn into that space by their attraction to her, but in which space only, like Rappacini's daughter's, Isabel's existence is viable. Within that space, Isabel, defined as a "reader," meets up with the "real reader" of the novel; within that same space, the reader of the novel must reorganize her or his perceptions of reality and fiction just as Isabel is struggling to do. Because of her "readerliness," Isabel is both more naive and more sophisticated than the other characters in the text: naive, because she fails to read her reality by cues other than those of popular fiction; sophisticated, because she refuses to be read on those other terms, and ultimately is the only survivor of the multiple misreadings which surround her. *The Doctor's Wife*, as a popular novel, inverts and comments upon social "reality" as well as "realism," transforming both into texts to be read from within the text-world of popular fiction.

Rhoda Broughton, a writer who seemed comfortable with her career-long identification with the genre of romance, was also first identified as a sensation novelist in the 1860s, largely because the protagonists of

*Cometh Up As A Flower* and *Not Wisely But Too Well*, her first bestsellers, described their passion in terms of its physical effects upon them – which evidently caused a corresponding shock to the decorous reader's nerves.[7] In retrospect, it is difficult to see any similarity between these stories, generally dealing with conventional romance thwarted in merely conventional ways, and the hidden-body, switched-identity stories of sensational magazines. But Broughton's heroines were bold and bad (within limits), and that aligned them with "lovely furies" like Aurora Floyd. One of these bold, and almost-but-not-quite-too bad women is Kate Chester of *Not Wisely But Too Well*. Kate's exploration of her own sexuality and surrender to strong attraction has disastrous consequences, as her attraction to big, bold and really-bad Dare Stamer is foiled, unconsummated, by the traditional Victorian inconvenience of a previous wife still living. As Kate works to control or eliminate the passion within herself, she undertakes a series of activities, finally ending her days as a Sister of Mercy. Again, as in Braddon's *Doctor's Wife*, passion is represented as a disease, here literally as fever, which spreads throughout the community and to which Kate is drawn. Kate's status as ministering angel is complicated by the metaphor which links disease to the sexual passion figured as resident in her own body. Kate, as passionate female body, becomes a vector for disease, which is figured as foreign invasion, class blending, and the subversion of high-culture literature by popular forms, such as the romance novel itself. Her victories over her sexuality and closure of her own body by overcoming her sexual attraction are undermined by Broughton's presentation of her as a danger to the community in which she attempts to expiate her "sins" through service. The dualism that is present in Kate is disruptive; through it, Broughton suggests the presence of that dualism within all cultural forms – just as Sister Kate carries with her the seeds of passionate "fever," the religious tracts which Kate drops into the gutter when she is frightened by rude men making sexual comments carry their own critique – they are created in reaction to the "low" and therefore cannot exist without that context. Like Isabel, Kate is a liminal creature, an inhabitant of in-between spaces, who refuses to be contained, even within the fairly impassable boundaries of the novel-world itself. Through the agency of a narrator given privileged status of someone "more real" than the characters he describes, who refers to but does not explain "another story" that involves a relationship between himself and Kate, she escapes the containment of the "story" to inhabit, however partially, the privileged space which the reader shares with an omniscient narrator who addresses the reader directly. Perhaps the most sensational element of Kate's story is that it, like the Braddon novel of domestic subversion, makes the reader less sure of or comfortable with her or his own personal boundaries and classed and gendered space.

In *A Beginner*, twenty-seven years later, the love story is subordinated entirely to a critique of the publishing industry, and the roles of gender, class, and sexual politics within it.[8] By this time, Broughton's genre conventions are so well established that she need only include a few textual cues for the novel to be "placed" generically within the class of "love stories," thereby giving her complete freedom to virtually ignore the love story in favor of a witty, sharp satire on the roles of popular fiction and the pretensions of high culture. By the end of the novel, the transgressive elements have all been eliminated – to no one's satisfaction – stripping the reader of any comfort in the assumption that the boundaries threatened and then reinforced are valid or worthwhile. By calling into question the integrity of the culture industry, Broughton simultaneously undermines the claims of the "body of culture" to represent and legitimate social concerns. The body, she suggests, is a deceitful signifier, and its doctors are too preoccupied with their own desires and needs to read its symptoms aright anyway. The subversive quality of the novel is centered in precisely its plot-level upholding of ideological standards as the reader's confidence in those same standards is destroyed.

Unlike Braddon, whose protagonists are women preoccupied with carving out and maintaining a social identity, or Broughton, whose almost entirely female group of protagonists focus on pursuing love and defining meaningful labor (writing, charity work, etc.), Ouida's protagonists are just as likely to be men as women, who are focused on maintaining a position which is initially given to them but must be perpetually earned and defended. The "good" women work against an erosion of power, as the "bad" women work to accrue and maintain power; men work against the social (and often specifically female) forces which conspire to place them in a false or compromised position. The values which work for these characters are a strong sense of gender and class status which guides them in their reactions and actions as this status is constantly attacked and undermined.

*Under Two Flags*, like Braddon's *Lady Audley's Secret*, pits different genres against each other.[9] The novel of high society intrigue abruptly becomes an adventure–war story, which is in turn used as a setting for a *Bildungsroman*. Romance completes the cycle and allows the hero to return to the domestic space; the catalyst for this generic transformation is another adventure story – one in which the ending is tragic because the "hero" is the wrong sex. However, this "unsexed" hero makes a triumphant return both to woman's estate and to the heroic status by becoming the sacrifice which enables the male hero to complete his quest and marry the more eligible domestic heroine. The containment of the masculine adventure drama within the encircling feminine narratives of the romance and high-society story provides an ironic commentary on what it takes to produce "good husband material." Within this panorama of genres and settings, the characters engage in a constant struggle to maintain an appropriate position in respect to one another, a struggle that is marked by gift offering and refusing, surreptitious bestowals of favors and goods, and other attempts to manipulate or affirm identity through patronage. The exchange of capital in its many forms represents a kind of dangerous intercourse, in which uneven or inappropriate exchanges can infect or damage the participant, metaphorically defined in explicitly sexual terms. Capitalism, in short, is figured as the disease which attacks the autonomy of classes and genders, through compromise of the boundaries that should exist between categories. The fragility of these roles and the boundaries between them is underscored by Ouida's displacement of identity – and the work of maintaining it – to the realm of capital exchange, in which one's identity can be irredeemably undermined if one becomes the victim of a chance bestowal. The relentless demand placed on the characters to attend to the maintenance of their identity highlights identity's socially constructed status, its delicacy, and ephemerality.

As if in response to the need to explore the limit of the subject's capacity to maintain itself in the world of capital exchange, Ouida wrote *Folle-Farine* in 1871.[10] Folle-Farine, a woman, is systematically stripped of all power to maintain her own identity. Her integrity as a self – both in the social and personal arena – is made dependent on her ability to defend her physical chastity. Ouida's use of this theme mirrors, and then parodies, the traditional melodramatic seduction plot. The reader, as voyeur, is drawn into the ranks of the social forces that wish to transform Folle-Farine into a commodity, thus stripping her of her identity separate from the realm of exchange – that is, her *essential* identity. Ouida shifts from melodrama to tragedy, however, in order to both destroy Folle-Farine's physical chastity and leave her identity intact, while calling upon the reader to confront her or his own sadistic alliance with the forces of capital. Folle-Farine's ability to elude the reader's rape of her identity, however, paradoxically rests on her status as abject – as having no identity and no measurable worth and therefore remaining outside the realm of the commodity. This abjection is based on her existence as a woman, who can find an appropriate and heroic role by sacrificing herself for the man she loves. Her triumphant assertion of identity in the cold chastity of death, therefore, is problematized by her status as an identity based on the absence or denial of identity – a self of selflessness. For the reader, already indicted as implicated in the realm of exchange, from which s/he can only take on a partial identity, entirely constructed by and dependent upon capital – and therefore false – this character holds out little real hope for the possibility of constructing an identity beyond exchange, in the realm of the absolutist moral framework that tragedy depends on. Folle-Farine may live (or at least die) there, Ouida seems to imply; ours, however, is the world of the partial, the socially constructed, and the economically interested, and we either must construct an identity within and from it or die trying. In both works, women's heroic sacrifice of the physical body and successful struggle to remain essentially outside the realm of exchange even as their bodies are inexorably drawn into it enable the male heroic quest. However, since that sacrifice is, in a sense, bestowed upon the hero, his victory is tainted by the patronage of these women. The woman's body, in death and in sex, becomes a conduit through which male identity is connected with and made vulnerable to the forces which surround it, forces which he rules but must also be ruled by.

All of these novels feature women characters whose bodies are defined by degrees of openness and contamination, whose identities are defined by mystery and mutation, whose locations, within the logic of the text and in setting, are marginal and indeterminate. As their identities are defined and redefined, as the boundaries of gender, race, and class, of author, text, and reader, are demolished and rebuilt, undermined and reinforced, we see the cultural work of identity politics collide with the personal work of self-construction. The critic-reading-woman-reading-woman-writing-woman's-body becomes the body of culture, observing itself clinically for signs of disease, voyeuristically for signs of pleasure, censoriously for signs of rebellion, above all anxiously for signs of vulnerability. Reading becomes a quest to define and extend surfaces – to take into the self while still asserting impermeable invulnerability – a quest which is enacted with and on and through the levels of discourse in and around the popular novel. The appeal of the novel lies precisely in both its promise and its evasion of that promise to confirm the boundaries of the self, in its ability to evoke desire and anxiety while sustaining the illusion of fulfillment.

CHAPTER I

# *"In the Body of the Text": metaphors of reading and the body*

The police and soap ... were the antithesis of the crime and disease which supposedly lurked in the slums ... [but policing is effected through the gaze of the bourgeoisie, which is then implicated in its object:] If the dominant discourses about the slum were structured by the language of reform, they could not but dwell upon the seductions for which they were the supposed cure ... Thus, even as a separation of the suburb from the slum established certain class differences, the development of the city simultaneously threatened the clarity of that segregation ... and the fear of that promiscuity was encoded above all in terms of the fear of being touched. "Contagion" and "contamination" became the tropes through which city life was apprehended.[1]

## SENSATIONAL BODIES

The body – despised, adorned, represented, medicated, ignored, dissected, and desired – is ineradicably entwined in subjectivity. What we do, feel, believe, know is as embodied beings. The body, uncertainly poised between nature and culture, practices and signifies identity. It is the fundamental trope of human experience.

The body as it has been represented is unlike the lived body in that it is almost never individual. From early anatomies to modern portrait painting, it refers, whether explicitly or implicitly, to a generalized body-template tied to its contemporary notions of health, gender, race, aesthetics, and social position. This tendency is exacerbated whenever one makes reference to "the" body – as in "the" female reader – who, by implication, is embodied as "the" female body, a body with all the characteristic weaknesses and strengths implied in an abstract, non-particularized notion of femaleness. Unspecific, it tends to resist contradiction or analysis. (Only recently, for example, has "the human (white, male) body" of much Western medical research been challenged by women and minorities who find themselves misrepresented in it.) Through these abstract constructions, conclusions are drawn, laws are made, practices born which affect real bodies, real people who differ dramatically from "the" body which represents them.

Bodies are signifiers, encoding and creating meaning, interacting with their environments and incompletely differentiated from their environments. As Elizabeth Grosz, among others, has noted, adornments, tools, and other items in the body's habitus can be cathected as part of the body image;[2] this is also true of the represented/representative body. Bodies are never "just themselves" in any meaningful way. Luce Irigaray has argued that the body of the woman in capitalist culture bears an additional burden of signification, the *schein* of the commodity which, floating superimposed above the material body, can come to subordinate or even replace it.[3] This too becomes a part of the projection of a representative "ideal" or "typical" body. However, as the material body is a polyvalent signifier, the representative body is a shifting one, dependent in part on the context of signification and also on the subtleties of race, gender, class, nationality, healthfulness which that context demands. "The" body is not the *same* body in every discourse, even though "the" body is never anyone's body in particular. The more highly charged the discourse, the more multiply determined the body becomes – and the more anxiety is displayed in the discussion of what the "essential" properties, including boundaries, of the body are. Disease, as an "othering" of the body from itself, provides the marginal position of a marked term (much as femininity does) from which to critique the dominant, naturalized concept of healthfulness; popular literary culture emerges in the nineteenth century as this unhealthy, feminine partner to an incompletely differentiated but healthy, masculine culture of which it is the degraded, commodified reflection.

The social body, a concept with a long history, takes an interesting turn in the nineteenth century, wherein the interest in fairly sophisticated practices of social representation and measurement (such as that exemplified in Herbert Spencer's *Social Statics*) and equally sophisticated modes of social control combined with concerns about a new mass readership. Mary Poovey has traced the development of a remarkably flexible set of representations of population "aggregates" in relation to the notion of a "social body" beginning in the 1830s.[4] What has yet to be done, and what I begin here, is a tracing of how, among these developments, this intense, anxious focus on the represented and representative body interpenetrates the discourses of literature and the differentiation of genre within an emerging popular culture.

## READING, EATING, AND SEX

Mikhail Bakhtin has defined the grotesque body celebrated in carnival as a body defined in terms of its openings and its "lower strata": digestive, excretory, genital, and reproductive.[5] In other words, it is a body defined by its liminal structures and states in which inside and outside merge. In carnival, this liminal aspect of the grotesque body is presented directly to view, challenging ideologies which privilege orderliness and authority/ownership, with their doxa of the closed and impenetrable body dominated by reason and will. In the Victorian era, two kinds of bodies definable as grotesque were the diseased body and the body of the prostitute – often one and the same. Both were defined chiefly by their permeability, and both became the objects of the gaze. However, they did not do so only in the context of carnival, but in the context of policing and the reinforcement of the boundaries they threatened; in lock hospitals, *cordons sanitaires*, blue books and clinics, the grotesque body was segregated from society, measured and weighed, sometimes destroyed.

Bakhtin asserted that the carnival was a transgressive action, challenging the authority of class divisions and affirming liberty. Yet, as many have since argued, the carnival's reversals of class roles depend so heavily on the order they parody that they may simply serve to reinscribe those boundaries while providing a "safety valve" for class tensions. Victorian portrayals of disease and prostitution among the poor do not simply act as carnivalesque denials of order and control; they desperately seek to assert the boundaries of the classes which, through various media of exchange, sexual, intellectual, and monetary, have been eroded at the same time they have become more outwardly visible than ever.

In the literary marketplace, the carnivalesque popular cultural forms of the broadsheet and the ballad begin to give place to half-penny and penny-dreadful literature which cannot be separated in content from the circulating library novels of the middle classes, although the packaging remains ostentatiously distinct. The carnival of the folk and the high culture of the aristocracy are both displaced in favor of a proto-mass cultural form for the bourgeoisie – a form which has always existed, but which now is accorded economic and cultural preeminence across most class boundaries, from the aristocracy through the literate working classes. This promiscuous literary intercourse gives rise and expression to anxieties which can be discerned in the fascination with the grotesque body and the disease which is disseminated by it; the "body of literature" – indeed, of culture – becomes grotesque, permeable, and the popular novel is carefully monitored and evaluated as the product and the outward and visible sign of disease. In the metaphors of reading and authorship which were current in the literary journals of the day, and, less subtly, in the concern for the capacity of the actual commodity to spread infection, we can trace the movement of this anxiety, and the desire which engenders it. Finally, when the grotesque body itself becomes the object of policing, rather than the symbol of liberatory potential, the transgressive act that remains is to seduce the reader by offering the body up to the gaze as an object without resistance, and then to remind the reader that s/he is implicated in the medium of exchange – that is, that s/he is "touched" by the object in the process of objectifying it. In other words, in getting the commercialized "formula" novel the reader desires, while being reminded that this novel is the result of the reader's manipulations of the modes of production, the textual voyeur is also reminded that s/he has created the object of his or her gaze, in the same way the middle class who polices the prostitute's "product" provides, so to speak, the context of production.

Catherine Sheldrick Ross describes two dominant metaphors of reading, both of which are very much in evidence in the nineteenth century: reading as eating, and reading as a (moral and intellectual) ladder. The reader is to "climb the ladder" repudiating "sugary" romances and "highly spiced" fictions and developing the discriminating palate necessary to appreciate better imaginative works such as poetry and nonfiction histories and scientific treatises.[6] Although Ross does not observe it, other related ways that reading is figured forth are as sexual intercourse and as the ingestion of drugs, particularly the reading of novels. Books, then, are presented alternately as food and poison, medicine and illicit drugs, and finally the erotic body and the contaminated body. In all of these metaphors, the text is a substance that enters the reader and has an effect on him or her. The text is not an inert thing to be merely manipulated, it is active – even opportunistic. In the context of the nineteenth century's twin terrors – epidemic disease and revolution, the disintegration of the physical and social body – these metaphors took on a particular role, one in which they were able to body forth the Victorians' fear of biological and social dissolution. Metaphors of ingression and ingestion rebounded upon the aggressor, emphasizing the reciprocity of the boundary transgression implied. The reader who devours the text is in some sense inhabited by that text.

The metaphor of reading as sexual intercourse is related to the eating metaphor most crucially in that it deals with the transgression of physical boundaries, just as eating itself often is a metaphor for sexual activity. It is convenient in this case to use Ross' example:

> The reader of novels only, especially if he reads many, becomes very soon an intellectual voluptuary, with feeble judgement, a vague memory, and an incessant craving for some new excitement.... . An inveterate novel-reader speedily becomes a literary roué, and this is possible at a very early period of life. It now and then happens that a youth of seventeen becomes almost an intellectual idiot or an effeminate weakling by living exclusively on the enfeebling swash or the poisoned stimulants that are sold so readily under the title of tales and novels. An apprenticeship at a reform school in literature, with a spare diet of statistics and a hard bed of mathematical problems, is much needed for the recovery of such inane and half-demented mortals.[7]

I have taken this from a larger excerpt quoted in Ross' article to show the mixture of sexual and food-oriented metaphors. Ross uses the excerpt to exemplify the hierarchy of ingestion implied by "poisoned stimulants," "spare diet," and many other food references not shown here. However, she fails to comment on the implications of references such as "intellectual voluptuary," "effeminate weakling," and "hard bed." Clearly the danger here is not merely that of becoming a gourmand, but of recklessly expending "spermatic" energy. Effeminacy, loss of intellectual powers, and intellectual and physical enfeeblement all were the hallmarks of the dreaded disease "spermatorrhea," brought on by excessive discharge of semen through masturbation or other sexual activity. (Youths of seventeen, needless to say, were among the principal victims of this complaint.) Hard beds, exercise, and study were the prescriptions then, antecedents of the cold shower, hard work, and exercise regimen even now recommended as a defense against the temptation to illicit sexual activity. Of course, there were those who took a different point of view. In an 1887 *Blackwood's* article, we are told:

> Perhaps the greatest pleasure in life is an ill-regulated passion for reading. Books are the best of friends, the most complacent of companions. In that silent, though eloquent and vivacious company, there can be no monotony as there are no jealousies and indeed inconstancy becomes a duty and a virtue, as with the sage King Solomon among his hundreds of wives.[8]

Although the moral argument is precisely the opposite of the previous passage, the metaphors are identical: reading is equal to sexual activity, and reading for pleasure is equal to illicit and promiscuous sexual activity.

Eating, as Maggie Kilgour has noted in a different context, is, psychoanalytically speaking, an aggressive move, but one not without certain dangers in that eating is the activity which first demarcates the boundaries between inside and outside, and yet perennially destabilizes them. The child first becomes aware of the non-sufficiency of the self when s/he cries for the breast and it does not appear. One eats to incorporate that which one lacks into oneself, to become sufficient to oneself, unified once more, but what one eats then is not only changed into one's own substance, but in fact changes that substance in turn. With every attempt to make ourselves whole, therefore, we make ourselves other, not self-identical, and therefore merely succeed in affirming our neediness as we satisfy our desire. As Kilgour puts it:

To imagine knowledge as tasting or eating is to set up an epistemology in which subject and object are strictly differentiated and yet finally totally identified. As it seems most people would rather be a subject than an object ... such total identification is seen with a great deal of ambivalence... Intellectual taste is associated with choice and control, the mastery of what is eaten by the eater.[9]

Using Kilgour's insight as a point of departure, we may see that in the case of the nineteenth century popular fiction market, the expression of that mastery is the intellectualizing discourse surrounding the body of culture. Food is primarily associated with the female body and breast; in this case, desire for an "uncomplicated" gratification is mediated by fear of subjectivity of the text, the capacity of the female body to transform its consumer. A hierarchy of literary taste emerges in which the most female-identified is considered the most dangerous and degraded. This marginalizing strategy is deployed through a veritable *cordon sanitaire* of critical discourse in journals, reviews, and the like which surrounds and contains the body of popular literature, and which defines literary "food" as healthy, unhealthy, sweet, highly spiced, and so on.

In the mid-nineteenth century in particular, the concern with ingestion became a matter of public spectacle to British Victorians as the food adulteration issue took center stage in the popular press. Food and water contamination became an even more central issue as the terrifying and inexplicable outbreaks of epidemic disease were traced to such contamination as well as to waste disposal. In this way, the desirable, socially acceptable, commercially and culturally reified substance of food was brought both literally and figuratively into proximity with the undesirable, socially unacceptable, end product of consumption. The primary concerns of the food adulteration investigations were twofold: foodstuffs adulterated with additives for gain (poisonous colorings added to tea, for example) and filth-ridden substances added either for gain (to add bulk) or inadvertently, through carelessness. One principal focus of the parliamentary investigations in this matter was the domestic production of milk and its adulteration with water, the condition of which would depend on its source. Several engravings in *Punch* target bake-shops, particularly in terms of bread and sweets. Bread, milk, and tea were staples, of course, which is one reason they received so much attention, but the connection of the adulteration of foods and the image of women unknowingly poisoning their young children with adulterated milk and sweets is very strong in much of the journalistic treatment of the subject. The juxtaposition of mother-love/nurturance with the threat of harm was particularly poignant because it hinged upon the fascinated fear of what was lurking beneath the smooth surface of angel-in-the-house-ism – an interest which M. E. Braddon would parlay into a fortune with *Lady Audley's Secret*. In any case, food became the focus of anxieties about the invasion of the body by dangerous substances through the wife and mother, the principal food preparer/overseer of the household. These associations became negative entailments of references to food, just as pleasure, community, domesticity, and wealth were positive entailments.

The metaphor of reading as eating or ingestion has a special significance in this era of preoccupation with the boundaries of the body and their violation. The *Temple Bar* asserts: "people are not satisfied even with reading worthless novels; they must then read still more worthless notices of them in the papers. It is the drunkard, not only draining his glass, but *licking it out*".[10] Not only is the text here to be devoured, it is a drug (alcohol) which has a specific negative moral effect – that of rendering the consumer bestial, like an animal in his or her consumption. A common opener for articles on literature in general or review articles about particular books or authors was to bemoan the proliferation of "worthless" literature, following the disclaimer with a statement of this sort: "But, for good or evil, the novels we read are becoming as important to us as the water we drink or the food we eat. It is as desirable that we should be supplied with the best possible quality, and protected, by all legitimate means, from the danger of adulteration."[11] In 1870, when this particular essay was published, the food adulteration scare was much in the press; the author's reference to it once more invokes the anxiety of "poisonous" physical invasion in which an unwitting "consumer" gets more than s/he, literally, bargained for. The apparent mismatch in the analogy is, of course, that one "sees" what one is getting in a text in a way that one might not be able to "see" arsenic in a cake; however, the repeated use of similar images makes quite clear that these writers (and presumably their readers) saw texts as potentially deceptive, slippery substances which could affect the reader without the reader's knowledge or consent, like a poison – or a disease.

Reading "bad" texts, thus, consists of a self-poisoning which can become addictive. In "The Vice of Reading," a *Temple Bar* essayist compares indiscriminate reading with dram drinking and condemns it in the terms of strongest opprobrium:

Reading, so long a virtue, a grace, an education, and, in its effects, an accomplishment, has become a downright vice, – a vulgar, detrimental habit, like dram drinking; an excuse for idleness ... a cloak thrown over ignorance; a softening, demoralizing, relaxing practice, which, if persisted in, will end by enfeebling the minds of men and women, making flabby the fibre of their bodies, and undermining the vigour of nations.[12]

A number of shallowly submerged concerns collide (and collude) in this passage. Reading is "vulgar," i.e. common, plebeian, like dram drinking, a habit principally associated with the lower classes. Like dram drinking, it is addictive, and has a degenerative effect upon the organism. It also softens and relaxes – that is, feminizes and even castrates. Finally, it enfeebles both mind and body of men and women, making them unfit for the business of production and reproduction, lastly undermining the readers at a national level – reference here perhaps both to evolutionary theories of degeneration and Britain's uneasy consolidation of power over her empire. In the reading process, then, the text is seen as actually entering the body (like alcohol) and corrupting it from within ("relaxing the fibers"), causing a sort of decomposition in the reader as the text is "digested" or decomposed by the reader. It also may contaminate the class characteristics of the reader, causing him or her to revert to lower class, degenerate practices. It also "excites" and "stimulates" the body, appealing, even in the "intellectual" pursuit of reading, to our bestial selves. A *Quarterly Review* essayist advises against reading "trash" such as H. Rider Haggard, warning that,

[although] the "aboriginal democratic old monster," not by any means extinct in the classes which wear silks and broad-cloth ... likes sensation; strong waters, not diluted, to warm his digestive apparatus and make his eyes blink, [be warned that] Plato has observed that every man keeps a wolf within him. It is advisable to hold that sanguinary beast by the ears, but not to charm and excite him until his teeth begin to glisten.[13]

Of romances, the reviewer's opinion is harsher still:

The "everlasting pantomime" of rose-pink virtue squinting across the pages of its Prayer book at vice, while it gambols within the measure of police-morality, is very laughable ... should we not send for the "common hangman" if his hand be not entirely out, and bid him make an auto da fé in front of Mudie's, with the feminine public looking on, agonized and much sobbing, but learning in this wholesome manner their first profitable reading lesson?[14]

This pits an image of "masculine" light reading as something that excites the beast within – a beast, the author implies, unworthy of the upper classes – to hunger, against an image of "feminine" light reading as associated with sexual vice, vice unnatural enough to warrant burning as a witch or a heretic. The critic collapses eating and sex metaphors into the larger metaphor of reading as consumption. In each case, the text becomes a (female) body, either to be devoured by the wolfish reader or by the "purifying" flames.

## A COMPLICATED AFFAIR: GENDERED AUTHORS, TEXTS AND READERS

In addition to the fear of "contamination" and the attempt to legislate against the diseased erotic body that marked the latter portion of the nineteenth century, gender issues surrounding the interaction of author, text, and reader must be considered. The excerpts above display a relatively uncomplicated scenario including a male reader and a female text. This posits a masterful and exploitive reader who need only be careful not to allow the wanton text to drain his virility through overindulgence. However, the typical novel reader was female. So was the typical novel writer. Indeed, as Catherine Gallagher argues, two principal competing metaphors for authorship in this period are those of the male inseminating the text with his ideas, and the woman who prostitutes herself. The female reader on the other hand, complementing the "lascivious" male, is the "passive" reader who is "drugged" or seduced by literature – literature which can figuratively "enter" her imagination and corrupt her.[15] It is not coincidental that gender becomes a site of particular contention in the mid-1860s, a period Gaye Tuchman identifies as the period of "male invasion" of the novel writing market, marked by the emerging separation of the male-authored "high-culture" novel from its "popular" female-authored contemporary.[16]

Sandra Gilbert and Susan Gubar have certainly amply demonstrated the association of authorship with paternity, of the pen with the penis.[17] Gallagher points out, however, that this metaphor coexisted with many competing ones; one in particular with which female authors struggled in the nineteenth century, was the metaphor of the author as whore. Gallagher notes that this metaphor was particularly debilitating to women precisely because prostitution was female-identified, therefore allowing male authors to remain personally untouched even when defined by this metaphor, whereas women were, both as authors and as individuals, essentially defined thereby:

The whole sphere to which usury belongs, the sphere of exchange as opposed to that of production, is traditionally associated with women. Women are items of exchange, a form of currency and also a type of commodity ... the prostitute never makes this transition from exchange to production [as wife and mother]; she retains her commodity form at all times. Like money, the prostitute, according to ancient accounts, is incapable of natural procreation. For all her sexual activity, indeed because of all her sexual activity, she fails to bring new substances, children, into the world. Her womb, it seems, is too slippery. And yet she is a source of proliferation. What multiplies through her is not a substance but a sign: money. Prostitution, then, like usury, is a metaphor for one of the ancient models of linguistic production: the unnatural multiplication of interchangeable signs.[18]

Thus, explains Gallagher, the paternity metaphor involves itself in the production of worthwhile substance, the privileged text, and the whore metaphor with the proliferation of useless signs.

The question remains, how can literature as food be reconciled to an image of the male author, since food and nourishment are traditionally the purview of the female breast rather than the penis? However, just as parenthood is appropriated to the male and the name of the father, and the mother becomes merely a "midwife" to the child, nurturing and giving rebirth to the male's substance, food is provided (produced), in the patriarchal family structure, by the male "breadwinner" and then prepared (reproduced) by the mother. We may speculate, then, that the good mother and bad mother who provide good food and poisonous food (or withheld food) are split, the role of the good mother being either usurped by the patriarch as the artist that generates literary children/ nourishment or by the "domestic" female author who (re)produces ideologically correct family-oriented literature, often for children, leaving the bad mother to be the prostituted author of the commercial novel, who produces only filth and falsehood. The male imagination produces true ideas, the female "fancy" reshapes those ideas and impressions as the housewife reshapes the substance that the male brings home, nourishing her family with male substance through her female artifice. Naturally, as we move away from the privileged origin of thought and imagination and into the sphere of replication and reproduction, there is an increasing potential for contamination and distortion. Further, the capacity for minute description of everyday detail which was requisite in the mid-Victorian novel was supposed to be the particular strength of the woman, grounded in the body and in the concern with the ordering and reproduction of the physical world, while the male imagination was better suited to the abstract, the conceptual. Thus, male writing produces the world of ideas, in history, philosophy, and the like, whereas female writing reproduces the physical world, more or less accurately, through meticulous recording of sense impressions. And, as Kate Flint has made abundantly clear, the effect of text on the woman reader was a primary concern throughout the period.

Obviously, this is only a simple and schematic explanation of a much more complex issue. The interaction of the specific gendered text, reader, and author is rarely straightforward; when competing gendered cultural icons of the Text, Reader, and Author intrude themselves, it becomes evident that categorical analyses must be viewed skeptically. Yet, there are discernible consequences to particular constellations. As Susan Stanford Friedman notes of the metaphor "writing is giving birth," the gender of the writer using this metaphor – one which has been used by authors of both sexes throughout literary history – does affect the use to which the metaphor is put. Friedman notes that men use the "female" metaphor of childbirth to express the "ethos of their times" whereas women use it to reflect their personal experiences and concerns. Extending this analysis, we can see precisely why the image of the author–prostitute was so crippling to women, and why the concept of paternity excluded them so effectively.[19] In either case the text is an extension of the woman's body – either the prostitute's or the nameless mother's – in either case it is the physical substance of a woman that is exposed in the marketplace. Thus, when Frederic Harrison cautions, "we forget the other side to ... literature: – the misuse of books, the debilitating waste of life in aimless promiscuous vapid reading, or even, it may be, in the poisonous inhalation of mere literary garbage and bad men's worst thoughts. For what can a book be more than the man who wrote it?"[20] we might substitute "bad women's worst sensations" and gain a good sense of the subtle difference in audience perceptions of the gendered author. The authority of the woman is based on her feelings, her intuitions, her connection with the earth and nature,[21] in short, on her reproductive body; the authority of man is based on his will, his reason, his name which both identifies him with the patriarchal god and distinguishes him from other men, in short, his productive mind. Note that the thoughts of bad men are "poisonous inhalation[s]", miasma, and morally contagious. In both cases, it is important to note the equation of the book with the author; here, the male author's mind, by extension, the female author's body.

Novels, as the popular "mass market" literary form, fall into this metaphor of literary production – authorship as prostitution, the text as commodified body – almost automatically, and as Gallagher notes, "Silly Novels by Lady Novelists" are almost sure to be devalued as illegitimate – often with particular severity by the women authors struggling to distance themselves from the commercial metaphor, like George Eliot. (Margaret Oliphant has perhaps the most troubled relationship with this metaphor, alternately railing at women authors like Eliot, whom she perceives [erroneously] to have been free of financial need as "kept" women, for their freedom, and money-hungry "hacks" like Braddon, for catering to "low" public tastes.) Both Oliphant and Braddon are examples of authors who were frequently told that their immense production disallowed them from writing any truly great work, and both apparently accepted this verdict while excusing themselves from greater efforts by stating that they had to value quantity over quality to support their families, thus both emphasizing the financial nature of their authorship, and deprecating their desire for it in favor of a domestic, non-competitive image.

Gallagher does not, however, mention the other substance that prostitutes are charged with proliferating in the nineteenth century, another intangible sign multiplying itself into infinity and attacking and contaminating the sacredness of paternity and the social body: disease. Disease enters the body through intercourse, sexual and economic, multiplying itself inexplicably and invisibly. The intangible substance of syphilis eventually yields the sign of its presence upon the body of the consumer of the adulterated and adulterous body of the prostitute – and upon those of his wife and children. The danger of diseased text – the apparently innocent book carrying a hidden dose of "moral contagion"

– bears vigilant scrutiny. Of all the harsh criticisms Braddon's work received, none stung her so as the charge, levied by an anonymous assailant later identified as Mrs. Oliphant, of indecency. Through all the murders, bigamous unions, and forged identities of her sensation novels, she indignantly claimed, there could not be found one hint of an *illicit* passion. Charles Mudie based his considerable fortune on his claim that, as patrons of a "select" circulating library, his readers could feel safe from the exposure to immorality usually associated with such libraries since the eighteenth century. In George Colman's *Polly Honeycombe* (1760), a character states that he would rather expose his daughter to Covent Garden, a gathering place of prostitutes, than to a circulating library.[22] Even in the late nineteenth century, the faint scent of impropriety lingered on; in Braddon's *Joshua Haggard*, a minister states his belief that only married ladies and elderly spinsters could "safely" read novels. Sometimes, also, the precise nature of the transgression is vague; it is a discriminating critic indeed who can safely "diagnose" the problem. Nineteenth-century critic A. Strahan quotes a story from a "family paper" to illustrate the subtlety of the symptom:

"While Lutie and the young trustee were together in the little parlour, they had no end of fun about something – laughed till Madame, in desperation, opened the door and found them confronting each other so gravely, that she apologized and went away."

We do not know anything more ingeniously prurient than this, and yet where is an indecent word? The last few sentences are very vulgar, and that is all. The pruriency is to be felt, rather than defined.[23]

The critic-as-doctor or critic-as-policeman here indicates his superior "sense" of what is wholesome and what is prurient – itchy, unhealthy. A pruriency such as this one is very dangerous precisely because it cannot be defined or diagnosed through reason, it must be felt, experienced – contacted or contracted directly to be noticed at all. By that time, the damage is done. The critic sets him- or herself up as a buffer between the law-abiding, healthy but vulnerable public and the subtly adulterated goods of the criminal, diseased vendor of popular fiction.

A perpetual drain on the spermatic economy of inspiration, as well as on the economic domain of legitimate (male) earnings, the independent authoress is, in effect, a "loose woman" independent through economic parasitism on the male. There is an analogy here to the sexual activity of the prostitute; two reasons drive women to such extremes: financial hardship and unnatural desire. Although women who have been "driven to" authorship by financial necessity are to be pitied, they clearly cannot claim the respect due to the properly domestic woman, and as for the woman who is financially secure and still ventures to write, no scorn is too scathing:

In the miscellaneous hosts of the novel writers, the fair sex very largely predominates . . . they have far more leisure and fewer ways of disposing of it to their satisfaction . . . They can't well carry a gun, and they have neither nerve nor inclination for the hunting field . . . There is the grand alternative of matrimony, of course . . . [but] the lady may be fastidious, or possibly unattractive.[24]

The writer goes on to note, however, that writing novels as a distraction rarely occurs to "real men":

In fact, the youth who betakes himself to poetry or novel writing, is likely to have a strong dash of the feminine in him. He wears his hair long, taking exquisite care of it in its studied disorder . . . it must be confessed that he shows his appreciation of the suitable and of the essential elements of the art of dress. For he shrinks with a womanly sensitiveness from the rougher masculine nature; he is scared by the stories which enliven the smoking room . . . though there may really be no great harm in them . . . he gives himself effeminate airs of intellectual superiority.[25]

It would seem that the novelist cannot win; the male who writes is an "invert" who shuns masculinity, yet the woman who betrays knowledge of masculine nature is indelicate and lower class: "At the very best, her range of actual knowledge must necessarily be extremely limited . . . or if she be better informed than we are willing to believe, her delicacy binds her to a double measure of reserve, unless, indeed, she have the shameless assurance to unsex herself."[26] The woman who writes is shameless, unsexes herself – which, paradoxically, defines her primarily by her sexuality. Naturally, no novel can be excellent without that knowledge of human nature which decent women perforce lack, and which the male novelist described above understands even less. In a somewhat contradictory passage, the critic laments that novel-writing "must long ago have made its way even below the middle strata of the middle classes. At least it would be difficult otherwise to account for the repulsive coarseness of style, and the grosser vulgarity of thought, which would shock any woman with the slightest pretensions to refinement" ("Contemporary Literature," p. 326). An angry *Temple Bar* writer responds tartly to this sort of criticism, repeated *ad nauseam*:

you are gravely told that it is absolutely impossible that a woman can know anything about a man – about his habits, his thoughts, his life. As the majority

of men spend a full half of their time in the company of women, the consequence which follows from this statement is a little curious, and must create a
vague and horrible doubt in the minds of women which it is uncomfortable to
contemplate. They are taught to believe that they never see their brothers, their
fathers, their husbands, or their friends, without the covering of a mask so
artfully constructed that it suffers no indication of the features beneath it to
appear... We can imagine the possibility of doubt arising in the feminine mind
whether that particular part of a man's life which is so carefully concealed from
her, does always furnish the noblest materials for Art. But of course this is a
profane thought, and one which a critic could never entertain for a moment.[27]

Apparently very few critics did entertain these profane thoughts.
Throughout this period, feminine literature – particularly the "romance" – is associated with ill health and passivity, whereas morally and
ideologically correct literature is "thoroughly healthy and masculine."[28]
Masculine literature is "wholesome physic"; feminine literature is comprised of "poisonous sweets." The novel in general is feminine, effeminate; this perception did not change until the advent of modernism.

Indubitably, therefore, a great portion of the hostility toward literature as a commodity stems from ambivalent attitudes toward imaginative literature (particularly the novel) as art on the one extreme, and
effeminate perversity on the other. Art, like domesticity and other
fundamental values, was not compatible with commodification; it inhabited a separate sphere. On the other hand, there was such a thing as
wholesome "rational" amusement, which was masculine and therefore
could safely inhabit the realm of commerce. Critics seemed to largely
agree that the novel was entertainment rather than art, and could not be
compared with, say, the epic as a literary form. On the other hand, there
were clearly some rather good novels and novelists, and that must be
recognized. And finally, there were some critics, particularly toward the
end of the century and the beginning of modernism, who recognized the
novel's potential and that the novel, for good or ill, was the peculiar
hallmark of the nineteenth-century period. Victorians denigrated
novels, execrated their proliferation – and read them constantly. In
1891, the *Quarterly Review* speculates on the role of the novel as literature:

The Novel might amuse, might serve as a pastime to make the idle crowd
laugh, and, in general, play the merry-andrew to our earnest energetic strivings
of every day; but mount the throne and assume the robes of heroic literature? –
not until we had forgotten our Chaucers, Miltons, and Shakespeares!... [Yet]
When literature is called upon to balance the conquests of science, must we not
understand by literature the novel?... [But] there are eight hundred Novels a
year published in England! Of which, how many survive the year after?... The

staple English commodity which circulates in three volumes is a conventional product, an institution like Saturday excursions to Brighton and Margate for half-a-crown, a refuge for distressed needlewomen, a thing as native to our shores as Britannia metal and afternoon tea. The Homeric epithet, dedicated by long custom to its service, is "trashy".[29]

Thus begins the review of the collected novels of H. Rider Haggard, Robert Louis Stevenson, and George Meredith. It is interesting to note exactly what these reviewers felt were these multifold dangers of novel reading *per se*. Over and above the censorious concern over particular kinds of content which we might expect and which persists in our culture today, there is anxiety over the effects of reading for entertainment at all. Many felt that it would cause people to dislike more difficult, intellectually engaging reading. There were outcries against the lack of physical exercise encouraged by "unhealthy" novel-reading. Most seemed concerned about the passivity of it, and its addictive quality – arguments reminiscent of twentieth-century indictments of television. The *Temple Bar* accuses:

Novels intensify and encourage all the other foibles of the time. We are passionately addicted to excitement, and novels excite us... Akin to this craving is a preference for quantity over quality, and our novelists strive to load the palate rather than to stimulate its tasting and discriminating power. There exists a marked tendency in favour of pleasure that shall be unintellectual and even lazy, and novel-reading is for the most part the idlest and most vacant of pastimes... This quality of narrow curiosity, which is the paralysis of all wide and noble interest ... the novel stimulates and feeds... Other and nobler branches of literature necessarily catch the infection, or are doomed to neglect for want of the interesting malady.[30]

There is a kind of despairing admiration, a fascinated panic in the way some reviewers refer to the proliferation of the novel. "One half of the world..." begins one reviewer "has now been written over."[31] In a thirteen-page (favorable) review of Rhoda Broughton's work, four full pages are devoted to a harangue against novels and novels' readers, who are, as the article explains, absolutely everybody:

It is the age of novels. Novels, Monday, Tuesday, Wednesday, Thursday, Friday, Saturday; aye, and Sunday too; novels, not only every day of the week, but every week of the month, and every month of the year, every year of the decade, and then da capo; novels, morning, noon, and night, novels here there and everywhere... They come out in bits, in parts, in chapters, in serials, in one volume, two volumes, three volumes. They are thrown at our heads, they are stumbling blocks ... they abolish thought, and even compete with slumber...

The world is one big circulating library (to us), and the circulating library is the novel.[32]

There is a mesmerizing quality to this tirade which can be only faintly suggested in this brief excerpt, a schizophrenia which can be only partially dismissed by the author's humorous transition, wherein, after asserting that novels are causing the rapid decline of the British empire, s/he urges "let us hasten to recognize the fact that there are novels and novels, and that there exists the widest distinction between them." (Frederic Harrison, in a different article, helpfully quantifies this distinction: "as much as diamonds differ from sand on the seashore, as much as our living friend differs from a dead rat."[33]) Miss Broughton's novels, we are told in this review, are "fresh and sweet" and presumably may therefore be enjoyed without endangering the nation. Still, there is never any attempt to identify them as art, merely as a more wholesome consumable commodity. If masculine literature, such as the history, the epic, etc. represent the mind of the age, the romance, indeed, the popular novel as a genre, represents the body of culture, a female body, to be alternately viewed with horrified fascination and obscured by a compulsive analytical discourse.

It is the conflicted understanding of the novel, its value and purpose, that characterizes many pieces of general criticism published in this era. If the novel aspired to the status of art, was the primary purpose of the novel to please (feminine) or to teach (masculine)? And whom was it to please or teach? Should it aspire thus? This confusion is exemplified in the *tendenz* novel controversy toward the end of the century, some critics praising a novel for being obviously written to a moral, others condemning the same work for that very characteristic. General within this discussion of the purpose of *belles-lettres* is a strong awareness of the potential of the novel, serialized or otherwise, as a medium for propaganda. For such critics, novels were measured largely against a standard of ideological confirmation. The purpose of the novel, therefore, was ultimately to reconcile dissonance and to laud conformity.

### THE COMMODIFICATION OF THE TEXT

In our time the material facilities given to production have multiplied mediocrity as heat multiplies carrion flies; it should have no quarter shown to it; it is a ravaging pest.[34]

Nineteenth-century critics perceived their era as a turning point in terms of the commodification of literature, and their denunciations of commercial literature pit the hack or prostituted author who writes to order (and therefore seldom well) against a Romantic image of the bardic artist who writes only when he (and I use the pronoun advisedly) has something he must communicate, a literary paternity gestating irresistibly. Many essayists felt that there had been a recent and radical reduction in the value of reading, and that this shift could be traced to the production of literature as a commodity by "hacks." "The author who refuses to spice his dish for the jaded palate of the multitude has usually the satisfaction of finding that it remains untasted" complains a *Temple Bar* essayist. Mark Pattison writes:

Literature is a commodity... Certainly authorship is a profession ... demand creates supply, and prescribes its quantity and quality. You see at once how vital to literature must be the establishment of this commercial principle as its regulator, and how radical must have been the revolution in the relation between writer and reader which was brought about when it was established.[35]

The three assumptions that most commonly surface in reference to the commodification of literature are first, that proliferation indicates inferior quality; second, that the "professional" status of the author causes him or her to create texts to suit the taste of the consumer, rather than the author's own; and third, that this creation to order, inevitably, leads to a decline in quality. The first assumption rests on the conviction that art cannot be forced without reducing its quality, and more obliquely on the belief that art is something that the author has within him (or her) in a certain amount – if expended too profligately, it will be exhausted early in the author's career. This assumption links artistic inspiration squarely with the metaphor of capital that dominated the perception of both the social and the physical body (e.g. the spermatic economy.)

The second assumption rests on the conviction that the "mass" public has, collectively, degraded tastes. Certainly, critics evidence a distaste for the financial issues surrounding authorship which do not seem to extend to any critique of the old patronage systems under which earlier authors labored. Yet, the question remains, why would the "tyranny of the consumer" be so much more repugnant in this case than it is in any other? No one debates the buyer's right to demand that his or her furniture be made to certain specifications; why should the buyer not dictate the specifications of the literature he or she will read? The reasons behind the devaluation of the reading public's taste are complex. Part of it no doubt stems from the spread of literacy across class barriers. Some critics complained that the mass public (presumably the "great unwashed") is dictating the standards for literature. Yet, if this were true, then the mass public must largely have been composed of the middle to upper-middle class, for these were the primary patrons of the circulating libraries which largely dictated the terms of novel production. Although the servant classes often were beneficiaries of the circulating library memberships of their employers, the employers were still the ones selecting the books, and thus, helping librarians like Mudie to articulate standards. Of the working classes, most apparently contented themselves with penny publications until the public library movement began to grow toward the end of the century. The penny press came under scrutiny as well, but great care was taken to distinguish it from the circulating library novel – although with rather equivocal success (perhaps this is why M. E. Braddon was never forgiven for republishing a penny-numbers thriller in the guise of a respectable three-decker). One salient change is that control of the market standards had been permanently wrested from the few who had shaped it in earlier times and delivered into the hands of the many, over whom little control could be exercised in turn. However, the real revolution is in the creation of a large class of producers and consumers of a culture industry which is neither high nor low, neither transcendental nor ephemeral, neither articulated by the supreme ruling classes nor against it by the exploited lower ones. The popular novel in the nineteenth century was a truly middle-class, bourgeois, consumer-oriented literary product, which quickly demonstrated its potential by promiscuously seducing readership across most class boundaries.

And, of course, the circulating library system was frequently indicted as encouraging a "cookie cutter" approach to the production of books, and a collapsing of critical standards by, on the one hand, encouraging publication of works of little merit, and on the other, encouraging Procrustean censorship of the new, exciting, and different in literary work. Some of the evils attributed to the circulating library characterize any mass market system, yet others were particular to the unique market conditions of the time. Guinevere Griest points out that the circulating library, with its guarantee to buy so many copies of just about anything in the three-volume form, so long as it was not offensive, provided publishers with a no-risk situation.[36] The positive side of this system is that it provided a market for young hopefuls who could not break into the demanding periodicals market. However, although these are certainly the explanations with which publishers defended or derided the circulating library system, with its stranglehold on the full-book publishing market, the fact was that even with the guarantee of Mudie and other librarians to purchase a cautious number of copies of a new novel, the publisher would be lucky to break even on a library edition of a book by an unknown author that was reviewed badly. Therefore, the young hopefuls often had to resort to a "Vanity Press" system, providing subventions for all or a large part of the production costs, in order to enjoy a percentage of possible profits later (profits that often either did not materialize or mysteriously melted into so much red ink on the left side of the publisher's ledger). Although libraries like Mudie's did "push" certain authors, recommending them to patrons, and although the public was, in fact, sensitive to critics' comments, particularly about an unknown and untried author, finally, the consumer exercised his or her right to choose. Established authors sold heavily regardless of the critics (witness Ouida's sales), and authors who were not well liked went unasked for at the library counters. Although rural customers had to accept whatever books the library chose to send, they were not forced to read them. In fact, the circulating libraries did not really account for the ongoing support of very many truly unpopular authors (as Broughton's book *A Beginner* humorously illustrates). And as George Moore's *Literature at Nurse* demonstrates, there was relatively little censorship for established authors as well; certainly the passage from Ouida that he cites is much "warmer" than anything in his banned book – but Ouida's books were bestsellers and his was not.[37] Clearly, the stipulations both on form and content applied much more strictly to new authors or authors of uncertain popularity than to authors with a following.

Still, it would be unwise to underestimate the effect of the circulating library, particularly in terms of the structure and length of novels. Broughton suffered tremendously under the stipulation that novels must be long, as her fast-paced but not heavily plotted romances were ill sorted for the long format. Her fees were significantly reduced on occasion when she simply could not stretch her story sufficiently.[38] Ouida, who loved the wide canvas, arguably improves in the tighter one-volume form, wherein her tendency to prolixity is restrained. Certainly, authors frequently elongated or foreshortened parts of their work in order to build in the requisite balance of completeness and suspense in each volume – enough to satisfy until the next volume arrived, but also to maintain interest until its arrival, the volumes being circulated separately to maximize profits.[39] In some sense, the three-volume structure was a larger, more accommodating version of serial publication; even though the volumes were published at the same time, they were rarely available at the same time to the same reader. (Of course many novels underwent both modes of publication.) In this sense, indeed, the circulating library dictated the terms of production to authors, and also provided a showcase for "first novels" and other work that would otherwise probably not have seen the light of day in a direct sales market. But for the "proliferation of worthless trash" of which the critics accuse the system of responsibility, we must look elsewhere for explanation.

In the 1890's, the three-volume "library edition" which circulated through the great commercial libraries of the nineteenth century fell out of favor with a rapidity that has startled many historians. However, the evidence suggests that the form had actually been losing readership (and therefore money) for several years, which is precisely what motivated the interdiction. Historians have cited the drop in production figures as evidence of the power of the libraries to dictate product standards; in fact, it merely demonstrates their ability to artificially extend those standards, at a crippling cost, for a brief time. It was the reading public that was no longer satisfied with the form. Although some felt that the length of the older novels was no longer appealing, in fact, many were little reduced in length; instead they were reduced in print and margin size to accommodate more text on fewer pages. The establishment of free libraries may have had something to do with a decline in the attractiveness of subscription libraries, but it does not truly explain the decline in the three-volume form. I would suggest that out of many possible reasons for the change, two stand out. First, the commodification of literature as item of mass production, so long bemoaned in the journals, had indeed finally taken place. That is, the readers, probably influenced in part by those very journal articles, had finally come to see novels as truly disposable, and demanded a cheap and disposable form for them. Second, the British finally became a book-buying public instead of a book-sharing public under the impetus of the kinds of anxieties partially expressed in the facets of the disease scare discussed below. Desiring to be less connected to other people, other bodies, in the processes of consumption, readers preferred to purchase rather than borrow, to read books which were complete rather than handle three different volumes at different times. Readers withdrew from the community of readers reading texts in process, and devoured books in solitary, sharing opinions after the fact. It is no coincidence that we see

the decline of the serial form in this period, and the rise of the short story
as a dominant literary form in periodicals. Readers may have been more
comfortable with a text which could be consumed in one sitting, a text
which was already finished and therefore did not require the shared
speculation of a community of readers, the contamination of ideas
shaping the reading and writing process. The new forms were complete
in and of themselves, self-contained. They do not suggest openness,
periodicity, the permeable body, the shared experience, as readily as do
earlier forms, although it is, of course, in the nature of text itself to do so.

CONTAGION AND CLASS: THE DOCTORS AND THE CRITICS

In all of the discourse surrounding the popular novel, whether savagely
denunciatory or ruefully indulgent, there is a strong sense of critical
surveillance, a need to categorize, to name and contain. Since the
rhetoric of literary surveillance and reform was motivated by precisely
the same terrified fascination with transgression as that of sanitary
surveillance and reform, it is not surprising that we find the two discourses becoming confluent. Fiction, like contagion, might become the
vehicle by which important physical boundaries were breached: distinctions between subject and object, upper and lower bodily strata, upper
and lower class, masculine and feminine, food and filth, mother and
whore.

Certain kinds of fiction were naturally targeted for more surveillance
than others; much of this was class-based and perhaps the strongest
censure was reserved for morally unacceptable literature with blatantly
"lower-class" properties which had yet infiltrated middle-class markets.
The sensation novel controversy is the most dramatic example, the
sensation story having existed for years in broadsheets and penny papers
as a lower-class amusement before Braddon was credited with introducing it in *Lady Audley's Secret.* Just as the genre's name derives from the
physical "sensation" of excitement that the story was to produce, the
condemnations of the genre are set in extremely physical language:
sensation would "breed a pestilence so foul as to poison the very
lifeblood of our nation."[40] Earlier (1863) the *Quarterly Review* wound
down a lengthy and generally hostile analysis of "Sensation Novels"
with this dark observation:

Regarding these works merely as an efflorescence, as an eruption indicative of
the state of health in the body in which they appear, the existence of an impure

and silly crop of novels, and the fact that they are read, are by no means favourable symptoms of the conditions of the body of society. But it is easier to detect the disease than to suggest the remedy.[41]

Lower-class literature, in particular, was associated with both vice and the incitement to criminal behavior (which, in turn, was often figured forth in terms of disease, as readers of *Erewhon* will doubtless recall). A. Strahan of the *Contemporary Review* writes:

Many a time have we heard a shopkeeper declare "Hard as it is to have an errand boy who cannot receipt a bill, or even read one, I would rather mine could not read at all" ... "Here is a girl of twenty, who has learnt to read at Sunday School, talks good Evangelical, and yet reads the vilest penny trash, steals in order that she may dress like a prostitute, gets into the company of young roughs who have fed full fat upon just the same kind of reading, and before she has had time to learn what household decency is, she is gone to the bad."[42]

The two types of stories offered in the penny magazines for young people were primarily "highwayman stories" – descendants of the Newgate broadsheets – and romances, usually of the *Pamela* type, but often "of high life." The *Quarterly Review* laments the existence of the penny dreadfuls, giving voice once more to the apparently general conviction that such stories were turning their young readers into criminals: "When it is remembered that this foul and filthy trash circulates by thousands and tens of thousands week by week amongst lads who are at the most impressionable period of their lives ... it is not surprising that the authorities have to lament the prevalence of juvenile crime."[43] Here we have the suggestion, with "foul and filthy trash," of a reference to the corruption of the body through improper cultural sanitation. But the *Edinburgh Review* makes the most heartrending plea against penny dreadfuls. In "The Literature of the Streets" (1887), the reviewer apologizes to his or her readers, promising not to make them "wade through such a nauseous mass" of penny literature, but "to select from the whole heap a few specimens" to illustrate the "mental diet" of poor children. The writer singles out for particular opprobrium the "small but pestiferous class of weekly publications which pander to the worst tastes of readers ... the so-called "Society journals" ... all relying on the same poisonous condiments to season every dish. . . No one scavenger could alone and single-handed contrive to amass such a wealth of unsavory refuse."[44] Although the reviewer somewhat confusingly concedes that s/he can remember finding in all these pages "no one single indecent phrase or illusion [*sic*]," s/he declares that

> the feast spread for them (poor readers) is ready and abundant; but every dish is poisoned, unclean, and shameful. Every flavour is a false one, every condiment vile. Every morsel of food is doctored, every draught of wine is drugged; no true hunger is satisfied, no true thirst quenched; and the hapless guests depart with a depraved appetite, and a palate more than ever dead to every pure taste, and every perception of what is good and true.[45]

The author asks, once again, for better penny fiction: "They ask for bread of some kind; it will not do to give them a stone. That which they now eat is of adulterate, poisoned flour, and no other is within their reach... To do this is no less than to deliberately poison the springs of a nation's life."[46] Once again the metaphor of reading as ingestion is in play, with its contemporary reference to the adulteration issue. Significantly, adulteration is linked, through subtle imagery, to the sanitary concern with "nuisance abatement," a topic of established and perennial interest to journal readers since the 1850s. (The "scavenger" that amasses a "wealth of refuse" must indeed garner his specimens from the "nauseous mass" of the dungheap: Mayhew's "pure" finders come to mind.) The suggestion is that the children are literally being fed excrement – like the waste which was often found to have leached through the soil and into the "springs," wells, and other water sources which supplied drinking water and incidentally cholera – a theory which, even as early as the 1850s, had begun to find an interested, if skeptical audience.

Obviously, for a number of reasons, this is a powerful metaphor. For the contemporary reader, each carefully chosen word would have called to mind, not merely a vivid image of the city streets around him or her, but the endless controversy, fear, and suspicion of disease and contagion surrounding human waste. Certainly the children of the poor were literally being fed human wastes in their food and in their water. But, once again, this is an unpleasant reminder of the vulnerability of the upper classes to those same wastes, and perhaps to those same poisonous influences on a mental level. Secondly, it invokes the kind of repulsed fascination that begins with the anal phase equation of fecal material with wealth which initializes the theme of class conflict so powerfully in Dickens' *Our Mutual Friend*. The fools' "gold" that the poor are getting, particularly in ersatz "society journals" and sensation novels of "high life" may foment a revolutionary attitude: first, by eroding the poor's perception of the upper classes as different from themselves in kind, rather than merely in degree, and secondly, by leading the reader to believe that it is possible for him or herself to become upwardly mobile, thus possibly leading to envy and resentment if the reader's hopes are disappointed.

A. Susan Williams comments on both the undeniable association of the poor with disease and filth and the forced recognition of the "two nations" connectedness in their human vulnerability to a disease which could be communicated "upward."[47] This consciousness was evident enough in the days of the miasma theory, but at least one could identify and take steps to avoid bad smells, and deodorization was considered tantamount to disinfection. With the germ theory, however, the enemy became invisible, unavoidable. Middle-class readers were encouraged to think of the poor and diseased not only in terms of physical proximity (Do they live close by?), but in terms of actual physical contact through microorganisms (Have they infected articles which I have purchased?). Tracts like Charles Kingsley's "Cheap Clothes and Nasty," in which the feverish sweated tailors or sempstresses pass deadly disease to rich buyers who do not even know of their existence, emphasized the human bond between the clean middle classes and the filthy and dangerous poor.[48] Germs, like literacy, redefined class boundaries. When, in his 1895 article "The Microbe as a Social Leveller," Cyrus Edson reminds his readers:

We cannot separate the tenement house district from the portion of the city where the residences of the wealthy stand, and treat this as being a separate locality ... a hundred avenues afford a way by which the contagion may be carried from the tenement to the palace ... This is the socialism of the microbe, this is the chain of disease, which binds all the people of the community together,[49]

he is merely repeating a rather hackneyed commonplace. What bears noting is that it depends more obviously than most on the motif of socialism and revolution and, as Williams argues, the social violence of the "dangerous classes" was a common association with their capacity for spreading disease – an association inseparable from the guilt and responsibility of the upper classes for the condition, both sanitary and economic, of the poor. The association of cleanliness with morality (and dirt and disease with immorality) is still too much a current part of our culture to require much proving. Dirt was not only thought intrinsically immoral, but would cause an otherwise moral person to degenerate. Both the conditions of mortality and morality which afflicted the poor and made them dangerous to the rich were often attributed to the inadequate Christian stewardship of the wealthier classes and their *laissez-faire* economics. Prostitution was often (inaccurately) explained as being caused primarily by the seduction of working-class women by middle- and upper-class men;[50] the myth which accounts for the fall of individual women, although generally untrue, accurately represents the larger social truth that the conditions of poverty which drove many working-class women to prostitute themselves was a direct result of middle-class exploitation. Thus the syphilis that the middle class man contracted from prostitutes was often seen as poetic justice or divine retribution for poor economic and moral stewardship. On a broader scale, the danger from the filth and fevers of the poor was similarly an ever-present reminder of not only the failure of Victorian society to care for its less fortunate members, but of its active and culpable exploitation of their weakness. The fascinated horror of the Victorian reader "insatiably devouring" endless "sanitary ramblings" in the journals, and tract after tract of harrowing descriptions of dwelling houses and rookeries seems motivated, not only by fear of the danger, but, as Williams makes clear, partially by desire to atone. The filth that is being generated is as truly a middle-class product as the commodities which the middle class also produce through the bodies of the poor in factories. Kingsley writes:

> The social state of a city depends directly on its moral state, and I fear dissenting voices, but I must say what I believe to be the truth – that the moral state of a city depends ... on the physical state of that city; on the food, water, air and lodging of its inhabitants... When we examine into the ultimate cause of a dangerous class; into the one property common to all its members ... we find it to be this loss of self-respect ... whatever may be the fate of virtuous parents, children brought up in dens of physical and moral filth cannot retrieve self-respect. They sink, they must sink, into a life on a level with the sights, sounds, aye, the very smells, which surround them... And remember, that these physical influences of great cities, physically depressing and morally degrading, influence, though to a less extent, the classes above the lowest stratum.[51]

In this passage, we see several pairings at work: the social body and the individual physical body, physical health and moral integrity, mental impressions and physical effects. The compliance of the reader with the directive of the text – to support reform – is motivated in two fairly direct ways: fear of the "dangerous classes," and fear of contamination or moral "contagion" moving upward through society, with its hint of disease (the "very smells"). The less obvious appeal is to the guilt and sense of responsibility of the reader, reminded that the antecedents of the "submerged" classes were probably "virtuous parents" who had suffered an unknown fate.

However, we must take care not to ascribe this concern with disease, poverty, and filth entirely to a sense of social responsibility, or merely to fear. In the endless and detailed accounts of sanitary "nuisances," of the appalling condition of rookeries and slums offered up to the middle-class reader in the great quarterlies and fortnightly journals, there is a sensuality and wealth of physical detail that make the strongest "sensationalism" seem pallid indeed. In fact, the rhetorical strategy of authors of articles on "bad literature" and on sanitary issues are remarkably similar: both generally start with an apology to the reader for bringing such disturbing and unpleasant material to his (or, less probably, her) attention, an encouragement to steel oneself to the unpleasant task, followed by pages and pages of detailed descriptions or excerpts, closing with a brief exhortation to support change. The object of concern becomes the subject and substance of the text. There is a pleasure being derived from the supposedly necessary scrutiny of such horrors; in some sense, these textual re-productions of the literal and figurative "refuse" of society are being packaged and sold to an eager middle-class consumership – in short, not to put too fine a point on it, shit makes good copy. Thus the misery of the exploited classes itself can be exploited and turned to account. (Writers like Dickens both exploit this market and critique it with their harrowing and graphic accounts; consider the equation of the dustheaps with gold in *Our Mutual Friend*.) The prostituted body and the diseased, contagious body have much in common; both are grotesque, that is, defined by their openings, their lower bodily strata, their discharges. One of the most "sensational" moments in the testimony of Mr. Barr, a lock hospital inspector, during the Parliamentary investigations on the Contagious Diseases Acts, was his statement that many prostitutes were so wretched that they lived in drains, and his example, "This [sixteen-year-old] young girl had only been seduced about three weeks, and was found living in a drain under the turnpike road, where she had been for a fortnight, the vermin were in myriads around her."[52] In this way the prostitute to be placed under surveillance is allied with sewage, with its connotations of fever, as well as the venereal disease for which she is admitted, and simultaneously dehumanized into a kind of sexual troll, waiting for victims beneath the roadway. Three days later, the commission was still referring to this anecdote in its examination of other inspectors: "Dr. Barr spoke to us about some of those unfortunate women who live neither in rooms nor brothels, nor public houses, but 'absolutely in drains."[53] Through this discourse, any subversive potential of the grotesque body is dissipated. The diseased body and the prostituted body are watched and regulated in lock hospitals and fever wards. The horrified delectation of the dirty details is the very conoisseurship of exploitation, a kind of abstract class sadism masking itself as humanitarian concern. As Jessica Benjamin states of the nature of sadism, it is in many ways a self-protective gesture on the part of the sadist, who wishes to exert control by eradicating the subjectivity of the Other. Regrettably, once this is accomplished, the Other ceases to hold any interest for the sadist – because, in fact s/he ceases to *be* Other.[54] In the case of *Sanitary Ramblings* or *Gatherings From Graveyards* (evocative titles!), the utter helplessness and degradation of the victim manages to maintain a *frisson* of interest in the oppressor, since the victim's powerlessness paradoxically provides the very power to retaliate, through contagion. (The possibility of actual revolution, of course, is somewhat less erotic.)

### THE BODY AND METAPHOR

The word "transgression" comes from Latin and meant a crossing, passage, or other movement across space; it also meant a transposition of words. In English, it retains the connotation of crossing over, but usually the boundary crossed is the invisible one of a rule, law, or social code. The word has come to have an association of sin or criminality; it has lost the innocence of its Latin childhood. Transgression, then, is a movement, but a specific kind of movement, one in which boundaries are crossed which are supposed to remain inviolate. If all desire is movement (of which more later), illicit desire is that which leads one to transgress, to move out of the approved space assigned and into other spaces. Braddon's novel *The Lady's Mile* is based on this metaphor; the mile-long carriage track is symbolic of the restrictive social codes that enclose middle-class women within a needlessly small space in which to move. However, those women who go beyond the boundaries of The Lady's Mile are socially condemned and lost to sight forever. Social codes of conduct are envisioned as physical boundaries ("You've gone too far – you had better watch your step"), as are class and gender distinctions, which are also codes of conduct. These codes are often metonymically identified with reified geographical or functional spaces (the East End, Angel Meadow, Belgravia, or conversely, the public versus the domestic sphere). In this manner, transgression may be assigned both physical and metaphorical spaces, so that when Nancy of *Oliver Twist* goes into the upper-middle class hotel, the significance of her entry clearly goes beyond the matter of the few feet between street and parlor; she is "out of her element." Because it is precisely at the border, or the moment of crossing, that transgression takes place, it is the liminal space that is most highly charged, particularly if the possibility of transgression is immanent but not yet actualized.

The possibility of transgression is based on duality. The notion of the boundary acknowledges that there is an Other; the notion of transgression acknowledges that the boundary between Self and Other can be collapsed, at risk to both identities. Transgression is alienating because it re-creates the transgressor as Other than him- or herself. Desire is alienating, because in desiring an Other, one moves toward transgression; therefore, desire must be "contained" by law and custom, or sublimated.

The body is constructed as the most irreducible physical space of the self. There is an inside and an outside, and various liminal structures which connect the two, and elaborate cultural rituals attend the proper utilization of those structures. Physician Jacques Sarano notes that even though Western culture is marked by self–body dualism, that dualism only becomes conscious during times of illness or discomfort; in other words, the healthy person identifies totally with his or her body, without being aware of the body as such, but pain or discomfort makes us aware of our bodies, and in those moments we construct ourselves as alienated from them. The product of this consciousness, which Sarano calls the "body-object" is also body-as-spectacle:

[One feels that] I am not my body; I have a body. It is one thing or another. I look at it; I touch it. I am the spectator of my body... The body-object is also rightly called "the-body-for-the-other," precisely because others take, vis-à-vis my body, the same position as spectator and utilizer.[55]

I would add to Sarano's analysis that the female body as commodity and the desiring (needy, incomplete) body are consistently constructed in this way. If, as Sarano argues, "the ambiguity of the subject–object body bursts out in full in sickness," then illicit desire is aligned with sickness in its effects; both succeed in alienating the healthy, complete, socially approved self from the part of the self that is unhealthy, incomplete, socially transgressive. Yet it is the body that unites all these selves; a character in a sensation novel may have multiple identities, but the body betrays their unity – a birthmark, perhaps, or the physical impossibility of being in two places at once, or, even more poignantly, a fingerprint will testify to the uniqueness of the body and the oneness of all those selves. It is, then, not surprising that we find disease used as a metaphor for other, often less avowable transgressions, and that disease is framed in the competing models of a personally uncontrollable attack from without and the direct and controllable result of sin. Often, these two are reconciled within the opposition of the individual and social body, e.g. Esther Summerson of *Bleak House* is the innocent victim of a disease which the larger social body of English society has brought on itself with its greed and callousness. (It is in this way, also, that twentieth-century moralists reconcile a reading of AIDS as a heavenly punishment on the homosexual community with the existence of AIDS-infected children.)

The body then, as a semiotic unit which encodes similarity and difference, self and other, is a metaphor. And this metaphor is extended throughout human experience of difference-within-unity. Society is a body, a community is a body, a corporation is a body, as is a family, political group, or geographical feature. So too is the complete production of a single author, reference to whose "corpus" may have an unpleasantly moribund connotation, yet serves the purpose of indicating its readiness for critical dissection. Of course an individual "body of work" is only part of the body of culture, which, like the physical human body-object, both expresses and betrays (which is to say, expresses too well) its subject, and is scrutinized anxiously for signs of dis-ease.

The cultural body "betrays" the subject when it expresses internal difference – that is, the possibility of transgression. Who is this betrayed subject, since a culture is made up of many individuals? Obviously, tastes differ, but in the body of a society/culture, there is a "head" or group wherein power is highly concentrated, and, in accordance with this metaphor, it is usually this head that speaks for the rest of the body, and interprets the inarticulate signs of the betraying body: the patient tells the doctor about the feeling generated by the ulcer within the outraged stomach; journalists and members of Parliament interpret the Hyde Park riots.

It is a cliché that the head of society in Victorian Britain was comprised of fairly conservative white imperialist males of the upper classes, and this cliché is, like most clichés, both highly accurate and egregiously oversimplified. Power in Victorian England was, of course, not solely wielded by persons fitting this description, and there was far more multiplicity of values than the "head" metaphor allows for. (The goal of all body metaphors is to collapse differences into unity.) Yet, finally, power does tend to be deployed in measures that favor its continued distribution along previous lines – that is, to preserve the *status quo* wherever it is feasible to do so, for the understandable reason that persons and groups that have power tend to deploy their resources in keeping or enhancing it. And, except in periods of severe social up-heaval, differences between members of a power group do not over-shadow the similarities that uphold this shared aim. It is in this sense that we can say, for example, that Victorian England was imperialist even though members of that society expressed widely differing opinions on the subject, or that the critical establishment expressed anxiety over the sensation novel in the 1860s, although some individuals defended it.

The growth of the popular literary market, the advent of inexpensive printing and the spread of literacy in the nineteenth century accom-plished a revolutionary feat: it gave several previously mute parts of the social body voice and an arena in which to be heard. Although popular cultural forms had always expressed the perspectives of these groups, such forms had generally been ephemeral and restricted in locality and could therefore be ignored or patronized by power groups as the situation warranted. The popular literary industry diffused the power to speak for the culture downward and outward to a limited, but significant degree, allowing the vast range of the middle classes and semi-marginal voices such as the middle-class woman and, to some extent, the foreign or religiously radical to be heard. The task of the cultural power group became, then, no longer only to express the culture, but to organize and control these other voices and determine their presentation both to the culture itself (British readers of various classes) and to others (French readers, for example). Thus, a hierarchy, built on existing hierarchies of values, is established and enforced through ideological institutions such as critical discourse or educational curricula. The criteria of such a hierarchy, then, is based on the extent to which the "head" of society feels that it is being expressed and not betrayed by the cultural produc-tion. If a cultural production is unified, "healthy," and not overtly evocative of dualism and transgression, in other words, what Bakhtin identifies as epic, it will be accorded high status as "serious" literature. Literature that betrays dualism, evokes the specter of transgression, is polyvocal and therefore "unhealthy" will be accorded low status as frivolous or even dangerous literature, which marginalizing practice will somewhat neutralize its enormous popularity – inevitable because it appeals to the concerns of the large proportion of the body of society. Most circulation library novels were a mixture of transgressive elements veneered with an epic storyline, often glued together with a moralizing narrative voice which counterpoints the presentation of transgressive events and actions with a pious "party line" interpretation of those actions. Mrs. Henry Woods' famous narrative intrusion in *East Lynne* – a plea to her reader never to consider doing what the protagonist, in fact, does – is an excellent example.

Because disease is so expressive of the dualism of the subject–object, it is both a semiotically charged phenomenon in itself and a powerful metaphor for Othering. Transgression of boundaries – which are always the boundaries between subject and object, self and other – is expressed as the parallel scission of disease, and the desire that creates it is presented as corrupt, unnatural, insane, even murderous.

## THE OUTWARD MOVEMENT OF DESIRE: COLONIZING THE BODY OF CULTURE

Let us examine for a moment the nature of the desire illustrated above. Desire is movement. It is movement toward an "object," just as repulsion or disgust is movement away from an object. Both have this in common; they depend on the existence of the object for their motive force, and in that sense they are interchangeable. Gaining or utterly losing the object have the same effect – invalidating and excluding movement. Both movements affirm the incompleteness and dependency of the subject – its non-self-sufficiency, its non-closure. In another sense, disgust is often the direct product of desire, as food is turned to excrement, exploitation of surplus value to slums, etc. In this sense, disgust is part of the process of satisfying a desire that yet affirms the separateness of the object, the non-permanency of satiety. Because the subject is dependent on the object, there is an element of repulsion in desire, and of desire in repulsion; therefore the aim of the subject is not so much to incorporate the desired object or to exclude it entirely, as to neutralize it as a source of anxiety, to exert power over it.

The body is the ultimate referent for the state of desire, permeability, non-completion. The condition of life is one of uncertainty, movement, continuation of the body with the environment, and of vulnerability as an entity to that "external" contact. The body is read as a signifier which communicates the condition of that continuation with the environment (the body looks healthy, emaciated, pregnant) and the environment itself is read as a continuation of the body through metaphors that have their roots in the way humans physically experience the world (what George Lakoff and Mark Johnson call "emergent" metaphors).[56] However, as Donna Haraway, Pierre Bourdieu and others have noted, the way we read the world is not only conditioned by our bodies, the way we read our bodies themselves is conditioned by the discursive environment in which our bodies become known to us. In that sense our bodies are not only continuous with a physical environment, but a discursive one, into which collapses other discourses – legal, political, moral, etc. The tendency to think of our bodies and our selves as distinct, even if related, phenomena encourages a sort of blindness to the powerful ways in which the discourse of the body is used to condition perceptions in discursive arenas which seem to be separate, in which the discourse of the body seems to be a "harmless" metaphor (e.g., the body of culture). As Peter Stallybrass and Allon White argue,

cultural categories of high and low, social and aesthetic ... also those of the physical body and geographical space, are never entirely separable. The ranking of literary authors or genres in a hierarchy analogous to social classes is a particularly clear example of a much broader and more complex cultural process whereby the human body, psychic forms, geographical space and the social formation are all constructed within interrelating and dependent hierarchies of high and low.[57]

Along with desire comes the need to police the object of desire – to control without simply eradicating it. Whether policing the rioting workers in Hyde Park or the contagious prostitute at the waterfront, the goal is to make possible the enjoyment of their object value without the contamination of their subjectivity – for such is what their power (to be violent, to spread disease, in short to contribute something to the act of their own consumption) comes to mean. The goal is to enjoy without being *touched*, to incorporate without being connected to, and therefore dependent on, the object. It is precisely the impossibility of this that lends piquancy to desire, and precisely the anxiety occasioned by this impossibility that creates the *cordon sanitaire* around the diseased body, the policing critical discourse around the body of culture, the panoptic gaze that contains the prisoner. Similarly, the novel must, to hold the reader's interest, contain the possibility that the reader/voyeur will be seen, touched – will be incorporated into the novel in the act of "devouring" it. D. A. Miller identifies this crucial element in the sensation novel:

Perhaps the most fundamental value that the Novel, as a cultural institution, may be said to uphold is privacy, the determination of an integral, autonomous, "secret" self. Novel readers take for granted the existence of a space in which the reading subject remains safe from the surveillance, suspicion, reading, and rape of others. Yet this privacy is always specified as the freedom to read about characters who oversee, suspect, read, and rape one another ... every reader must realize the definitive fantasy of the liberal subject, who imagines himself [*sic*] free from the surveillance ... The sensation novel, however, submits this panoptic immunity to a crucial modification: it produces repeated and undeniable evidence – "on the nerves" – that we are perturbed by what we are watching.... The specificity of the sensation novel in nineteenth-century fiction is that it renders the liberal subject the subject of a *body*, whose fear and desire of violation displaces, reworks, and exceeds his fantasy of intact privacy.[58]

Miller's brilliant analysis admits of little improvement, yet I would slightly recast his observation to note that the sensation novel was not so much capable of "doing" this as of being constructed so – as I would argue *any* novel must do precisely this: titillate the desire of the reader with that *frisson* of fear, of non-closure, of mystery wherein the reader may be constructed as open to and continuous with the text, rather than its closed and sovereign overseer. The "popular" novel (versus the "classic") is more susceptible to construction as a discourse that "touches" the body – that is, that clearly participates in discursive structures aligned with the "lower strata," the feminine, etc. In a heavily policed popular market, "light" novels are tolerated, even patronized, so long as they comply with authority – demonstrate submission to the critical gaze and compliance with certain standards, just as "light" women might be tolerated who submitted to medical examination and did not dress ostentatiously as such. The seductive/transgressive gesture that remains – and transgression must be defined as the destabilization of heavily policed, highly charged boundaries such as those between reader and text, masculine and feminine, upper and lower class, healthy and diseased, etc. – is to apparently submit to the gaze, while occasionally, rebelliously "looking back," reminding the reader of his or her desire, neediness, of his or her status as a participant rather than mere consumer. To such an end, in romances, virtue "gambols within the measure of police morality" while "squinting across the pages of its Prayer book at vice" ("English Realism and Romance," p. 470), the police in this case being the critics, the librarians, the readers, and perhaps even the litmus paper cheek of the Young Person.

Because desire is expressed in movement (the movement of a body toward food, for example), it follows that this movement takes place in space, and the measure of the movement is the distance covered, the boundaries crossed. The point at which desire intersects with fear, then, is in the crossing of the boundary, the moment of contact with the object. The movement of imperial desire is traced in countless travel articles, anthropological studies and adventure stories, and the twin tropes of exploration and conquest become dominant metaphors for understanding the movement of desire. In this way the object of desire (and of the journey) is both made central and neutralized by the clinical discourse of the scientist/military administrator who is the colonial equivalent of the urban doctor/policeman. Nancy Aycock Metz points out that the literature of sanitary reform pointed in two rhetorical directions: the literature of exploration, with its "emerging cliché of 'deepest, darkest London'" and to sensation fiction, with its sense of hidden secrets in the midst of respectability. She concludes that there was a crossover between fictive and non-fictive prose forms in terms of "vocabulary, dominant tropes and rhetorical stance."[59] Doubtless, this is true; an even more interesting question is why it was so. Certainly the lower classes and the indigenous populations of the colonies had much in common in terms of their roles in supporting the industrial capitalism of empire. What is striking is the double gesture of othering the human and geographical objects of "clinical" interest and of calling attention to their proximity, centrality, their at-oneness with the reading subject. The expression of that double gesture is the invitation to the reader to go on "expeditions" – to take "rambles", traversing distance while insisting to the reader that there is simultaneously no real distance involved. There is a desire to "go see" and a fear and repulsion that one may already be in that place.

Class, gender, and race are interimbricated with particular urgency in the late 1850s, 1860s, and 1870s as Britain moves, not without trepidation, toward an officially imperial identity. Following the revolt of popular British sentiment against Indian natives after the Mutiny of 1857, and the uncertainty about Britain's role and responsibility for the events which preceded it and the appropriateness of Britain's subsequent responses, as well as other colonial expressions of discontent, such as the Fenian disturbances, the gender stereotyping that Patrick Brantlinger traces in the British reaction to the Indians can also be traced in relationship to the British working classes in a period of reform legislation. In short, the "splitting" of the working class or colonial male into two types – one hypermasculine, sexually violent, uncontrollable, and bloodthirsty, the other effeminized, sexually perverse, irrational, deceitful, easily led, and intimidated, is evidenced in the concern for popular culture as a feminizing "infection" – a disease which not only erodes masculinity, but subverts racial integrity and makes the English (middle-class) Other to itself. Eve Kosofsky Sedgwick provides an example of this logic in her excellent analysis of *Edwin Drood*: "Colonials ... can 'go' native: there is a taint of climate, morale or ethos that, while most readily described in racial terms, is actually seen as contagious... The first chapter of *Edwin Drood* also suggests another route to becoming racially declassed: through the ingestion of foreign substances [here, opium]."[60] The "contagion" here is not through the opium *per se* – Jasper here is looking at an Englishwoman who has smoked opium until she looks like a "Chinaman." It is actually, as Sedgwick emphasizes in her quotation of Dickens but does not comment upon, viewing this racially corrupt Englishwoman which threatens to corrupt Jasper: "As he watches ... her face ... some contagion in [its movements] ... seizes upon him ... he has to withdraw himself ... until he has got the better of this unclean spirit of imitation."[61] Sedgwick focuses on the effects of the opium, by proxy, upon Jasper, but it is in fact as a result of looking at/reading the woman that an infection of imitation attacks Jasper, who must withdraw in order to regain himself and exorcise this spirit/disease which attacks the masculine body through the medium of the English-woman made foreign through ingestion, dangerous through her capacity to represent and therefore reproduce that foreignness within the body of the English, simply through her existence as a specular object. As the working classes in England come increasingly to inhabit the position of the Other within the metropole, governed by a vice-regency of middle-class cultural missionaries/police, the relationship between gender and the working-class male subject and between the middle-class Englishwoman and working-class identity increasingly develops homologies with that of the colonial dynamic.

Authors of many articles indicate a paternalistic interest in controlling the reading of the working classes, the presumed first and most numerous group of penny-fiction consumers, and obviously expect their own readers to be as concerned as they. George R. Humphery writes in *The Nineteenth Century*, "No class of the community has had such paternal and patronizing care bestowed upon it as the class of working men," but he laments that although one would think that working men would take direction in their choice of reading material, in fact "They are very suspicious of recommendations to read certain books. The librarian has to be very careful not only *what* he recommends, but *how* he suggests the advantages of reading any particular books."[62] This, although the librarian only has the working man's best interests at heart and is trying to steer him away from "lectures and articles which contain broad denunciations of other classes of society."[63] The *Quarterly Review* is even more blunt:

> The British workingman, in short, will neither buy tracts nor read them. For the first time, perhaps, a good many people saw him in his true colours during the late strikes – suspicious, haughty, jealous, irritable, and resenting above all things the very appearance of patronage and condescension. If we wish to improve the literary food that he will accept, we can only do so by offering him better things.[64]

There is an almost subterranean imagery associated with this examination of the "workingman" whom one so rarely sees, imagery that would later be more explicitly treated in novels like Wells' *Time Machine*, in which the worker became a literally subhuman, subterranean dweller. The writer invites his readers to examine the British workingman rather as an entomologist might invite a class of naturalists to inspect a rarely seen and particularly voracious locust. In each of these examples, the concern is to pacify and "improve" the workingman with "better literature" than he reads – even against his own will and better judgment. And in both, the threat that goads this manipulation is the fear of class violence and revolution. The workingman is "othered" through strategies like the one demonstrated here (W. Arens and others have noted that a typical strategy for "othering" is to accuse the target group of cannibalism; *Time Machine* readers will recall that this is precisely the charge levelled against the Morlocks.) Better literature, thus, is that which upholds and reinforces class boundaries and middle-class values.

These same attitudes are expressed in responding to the classed and generic "topography" of reading. Just as the lower classes were portrayed as alien barbarians and animals in the sanitary literature, the reading of the literate lower classes was regarded with great suspicion – even greater because literature was a definitive connection between classes. With terms such as the "Unknown Public" (of readers) and descriptions of the "nauseous mass" of penny dreadfuls, reviewers discussed lower-class literature in exactly the same terms as the literature of exploration or sanitary reform: a physical "descent" into an unknown "space" wherein the local fauna are clinically classified and described. As in the literatures of exploration, what follows description of the terrain is the impulse to "improve" it – civilize, sanitize, and regulate.

The distrust of literature's – particularly fiction's – power to seduce and corrupt is a complex phenomenon and resists a simple explanation. But some partial explanations may be tentatively essayed. In addition to the obvious Low Church distrust of the desecration of the sacred word through frivolous use, there is also an evident movement to reevaluate and protect class boundaries by the upper middle classes in the face of a growing literacy, and in a period of domestic restlessness and the threat of revolution. Text itself thus becomes the vehicle of class-boundary transgression, and thus, violence against the social body. In addition to the fear that literacy will foster discontent in the lower classes, there is also the anxiety that the literature of and for the lower classes will "flow upward," like a miasma, and contaminate the literature of the morally upright middle class. The infiltration of their own class by decidedly "lower-class" literature was therefore an important concern to the middle class. Thomas Wright of *The Nineteenth Century* notes "I have seen the penny fiction journals in the cottages of gentility. I have seen 'fashionably attired' young ladies ... reading the penny journals in sight of every passerby. I have seen the journals in parlours that were dignified with the name of drawing rooms."[65] Although Wright's notice of this phenomenon was actually indulgent, many were less so. Their anxiety is evidenced not only by the association of novels with moral contagion, but, later in the century, by the fear that library books were physically spreading disease. The association of books with contagion, always identified as a lower-class evil, reveals an interesting facet of the middle-class Victorian ambivalence toward the circulating library and also illuminates the other metaphors of reading which we have identified.

Andrew McClary speculates on the reasons behind the germ scare in America: "the older miasmic gases were inert, passive. Germs, however, were disturbingly different – they were alive... A constant war was waged between body and germ and as one writer in *Colliers* put it, we must therefore fight a great battle throughout life against invading germs, which lurk, 'ever ready to step in and take possession of the body'."[66] Many authors have noted the essential similarity of the miasma theory – the dominant theory of how fevers were transmitted – to the later germ theories. In fact, it almost seems strange to us today that there was so much resistance to the germ theory, since the difference is so slight. However, McClary's observation illuminates the one new feature that is truly significant. J. K. Crellin mentions in another context that in the late 1860s, speculations on germs tended to emphasize their invisibility.[67] In 1887 "Robson Roose" summed up the current debate in laymen's terms for readers of the *Fortnightly*:

There is strong evidence in favour of the view that these contagia are actual living things ... ordinary poisons ... have no power of increase and propagation ... the poisons of infectious disease must be something of an entirely different nature. We know that they multiply in the system to an almost infinite extent, and that every one of the myriads of atoms thus developed is as potent for evil as the atom from which it originated. The possession of this and other properties clearly indicates that the contagious agencies are independent living organisms.[68]

That notion of germs' invasiveness, with its suggestion of intentionality, and the idea that germs might somehow change the victim, "take possession" like an evil spirit, is also common to nineteenth-century writers' concern with reading material. The wrong literature, with its questionable moral intent, could plant seeds of discontent in the pleasure seeking reader – seeds which might bear poisonous fruit. In Braddon's *The Doctor's Wife*, the heroine lives her life according to notions derived from romance novels, destroying the man she loves and her own happiness. In Broughton's *A Beginner*, the silly friend of a budding novelist is inspired to infidelity by the heroine's literary efforts – an effect which the dismayed novelist little intends, but texts, she finds, have lives – and perhaps minds – of their own.

The similarity of the social concerns surrounding disease and text, and the conjunction of the key notions of invisibility and invasiveness in both make a convergence between the two rhetorics inevitable. It is instructive to examine some of the connections made by health writers between the moral and the physical in regard to the theory of disease. Germ theory, for example, retains enough similarity to the miasma theory to inherit some of its associations. Health is aligned with morality, disease and dirt with evil. The Greek root of the word "miasma" has a connotation of "evil, corrupt" and germs were perceived as "microscopic abominations." Disease is aligned with poverty, foreignness, and moral corruption. Health was not only associated with wealth, it was interchangeable with it, as we see in the title of Edwin Chadwick's popular book *The Health of Nations* (1887), the slight substitution calling attention to the equivalency of terms.

Health, of course, was not purely a physical affair. As the health of the body could be infected by contagion, the health of the mind could be harmed by negative impressions or "moral contagion." Indeed, the connection between the tangible and intangible, the mental impression and the physical, was not so neglected as we, in our rediscovery of holistic healing, would like to believe. Benjamin Ward Richardson, one of Britain's most prolific health writers for popular journals, articulates this connection forcefully in his essay "The Health of the Mind":

> We are conscious that the food of the body influences the health of the mind . . . But we do not recognize with like readiness and in the same way the effect of the foods of the mind on the mind and its health; nor is this remarkable, for the body feeds perceptibly, and by one stomach alone, whilst the mind feeds imperceptibly, by five stomachs, by every sense . . . Common foods and drinks must be healthy in order that the material of the body may be good; and the impressions which enter the body by the senses, the foods and drinks of the mind, must also be healthy in order that the mind may be good . . . the coming school of sanitarians will take up a new sanitation . . . as uncleanliness of mind is the most obvious cause of mental disease, and cleanliness the surest indication of mental health.[69]

Further, he warns the reader, the mental food taken in repeatedly or in youth will permanently shape the mental tastes of the individual. The mind must be trained to only pure and rational discourse, in order that it may detect and avoid "false and foolish" words that make for mental uncleanliness. Many writers of the period, medical and otherwise, comment on the liability of the body to disease engendered by "mental shocks" and any reader of Victorian fiction will recognize the familiar disease of "brain fever" – a disease not to be found in any modern medical book – which often attacks a character after a severe emotional shock of any kind. Books, of course, comprise this mental food in very large part.

Kate Flint provides an excellent discussion of these connections in the context of assumptions about gender in *The Woman Reader, 1837–1914*. At mid-century, in particular, Flint notes, women were believed to have more physiological susceptibility to emotion, to such an extent that G. H. Lewes argued that in "'feminine natures' there is an unusual development of the direct [neural] connection between brain and heart."[70] Flint also notes that, although Lewes does not refer to literature in this discussion, his theory coincides with the debate on the effects of the sensation novel. Often, these comparisons were couched in terms related to ingestion.[71] Although Flint's discussion does not follow up on the promising leads provided by the food metaphors, she does note in passing doctors' frequent comparisons between women's gastronomic and mental desires.[72] Mental and physical disease could clearly originate in the unnatural stimulation of novel-reading.

1879 seems to have been the first time that the question of books and physical contagion was raised in a significant public forum, at a meeting of the directors of the Chicago Public Library. W. F. Poole quickly took steps to defuse the scare, which was an immediate threat to the public library movement, with a meticulously researched report published in *The Library Journal* entitled "The Spread of Contagious Diseases by Circulating Libraries," which deprecated the danger of infection.[73] Nonetheless, the subject immediately caught the imagination of the public and by 1888, during a smallpox epidemic, many libraries in Britain were taking steps to disinfect books.[74] In 1889, the "Infectious Disease Notification Act" specified "a long list of diseases, including all fevers" which had to be reported to health authorities. The names of the sufferers were sent to the local libraries, who destroyed or disinfected all books loaned to those households.[75]

Immediately following the initial panic, experiments were begun to see if germs could indeed live inside books. Books were "inoculated" with pus and "in a short time the books were full of germs of measles, scarlet fever, smallpox and other diseases."[76] Similar experiments were made wherein consumptives were encouraged to spit upon the pages of books, the pages then being ground up, a "wash" made and injected into guinea pigs.[77] Not surprisingly, the guinea pigs languished under this treatment, confirming the public's worst fears.

More interesting is the popular reporting on the treatment of circulating books. Naturally, there were many articles on effective disinfection, the public being interested and the libraries being motivated to reassure their patrons. For a time, the most popular method was to leave the book in an enclosed space with a solution of formalin. A competing method was to expose the book to live steam, which had rather obvious drawbacks – ditto the autoclave. There is a certain Puritan spirit of vengeful glee in the descriptions of these processes; I would like to cite one particularly apt passage at some length:

a large volume of 1300 pages was selected for experiment. One of the middle pages was saturated with pus and another was soiled with fecal matter ... The volume was then placed in the disinfecting oven, and heated for about two hours and fifteen minutes to about 180 F ... Unfortunately, the treatment slightly injured both paper and binding ... In the improved process, the books first go through the beater. This machine is a long box connected at one end to an ordinary stove, and provided at the other end with a door through which open racks containing the books are introduced. Inside the box wooden rods are caused to rise and fall, alternately, by cams placed on a cylinder which is turned by a crank ... When the crank is turned, the rods strike the covers of the books and dislodge the dust. The heavy dust falls into the drawer upon a mass of sawdust, saturated with a powerful disinfectant, while the lighter dust, carried off by the air current, is consumed in the stove. After this treatment, the books are suspended singly by pincers from a series of open metal racks, the covers of the book being bent back. Thus the pages are freely separated, and give easy access to the antiseptic vapor. These racks are mounted on rails, on which they are run into the disinfecting oven ... The ovens are sheet iron boxes, hermetically closed ... In the center of the oven is a vessel filled with formic aldehyde, into which dips a strip of felt, which can be moved up and down from the outside of the oven. The ovens are heated, by steam pipes placed below them, to 122 degrees F. The irritating vapor of formic aldehyde makes its escape through a pipe at the top of each oven. The operation of disinfection is simple ... This improved process of disinfection does not injure either paper or cardboard.[78]

I have cited this passage at length because the language, a unique combination of technical and pornographic rhetoric, cannot be effectively paraphrased. To highlight, however, the dirty book is first beaten by wooden rods (Steven Marcus' comments on the eroticism of flagellation come to mind) and then hung from "pincers," the covers "bent back" to "freely separate" the pages, exposing them to an "irritating vapor." The image evoked is a cross between the rites of a penitential religious order and of the lock hospital. An article in *The American Journal of Pharmacy* in 1910 even credited several cases of gonorrhea to infected books![79] Like the "circulating" woman, the book's erotic body is a source of delight, whose commensurate danger to the patron must be controlled through medico-legal channels. Both the Act which mandated informing libraries and the later Act which imposed a fine on any diseased person who loaned a book were, of course, part of the controversial series of Contagious Diseases Acts, two of which in the 1860s mandated the registration of prostitutes and the forcible examination and imprisonment of diseased "public women." The cases of the prostitute and the book are not, of course, analogous, yet both stem from the same set of anxieties which are in turn expressed in metaphorical terms which conflate the two distinct situations; at the unconscious level, the two cases are the same: both involve the invasion of the desiring subject by an apparently passive, but secretly aggressive and dangerous object. The fear of the physical contamination of books by germs is an expression and crystallization on a physical level of anxiety related to a less specifically identifiable agency of moral contamination in the text. Text, which exists only after its enablement by the reader, which in fact inhabits a non-space between the author/other in the outer world and the inner domains of the ingesting reader, is assigned the physical space of its tangible medium – the book – and addressed in terms of a physical contagion which can be localized, measured, experimented upon, and expunged through proper rehabilitative (punitive) treatment. The book becomes a body to be cured (or exorcised), with the sole caveat that a cure which destroys the host body is undesirable. (It is interesting to note that the only defense of the three-volume form offered by the society of authors following the edict of the libraries was that there would always be a market for a small edition of the three-volume form because invalids would want them! The identification of the circulating library three decker with the sickroom was clearly, at least to this professional in the publishing industry, a matter of course.) The circulating book disease scare serves as evidence of the depth and importance of many readers' fear of moral "contamination" through "adulterated" text, and highlights the libraries' role in policing text circulation.

# CHAPTER 2

# Genre: the social construction of sensation

The strategic value of generic concepts for Marxism clearly lies in the mediatory function of the notion of a genre, which allows the coordination of immanent formal analysis of the individual text with the twin diachronic perspective of the history of forms and the evolution of social life.[1]

## GENRE

In a work of this nature, it becomes necessary to address and, to an extent, to problematize the concept of genre. M. E. Braddon, Ouida, and Rhoda Broughton are identified as the chief exponents of certain genres or sub-genres of the popular novel: roughly, the sensation novel, the novel of high life, and the domestic romance. Critics identified them as authors of books, usually early in their careers, that "fit" these definitions, and then read their subsequent works against those generic designations, often regardless of how far afield the texts themselves wandered from those definitions. Yet, upon close examination, even the early texts may be read "outside" of the genre which they supposedly, to perfection, exemplify. Consequently, a working definition of "genre," although necessary, is elusive.

Formalist definitions of genre rely on a permutation of the natural sciences model, creating a taxonomy of texts by family resemblances. These definitions rely on three assumptions: that resemblances between texts are more pertinent than differences; that there is a natural hierarchy of textual characteristics (a book is assigned its genre often on the basis of plot, rarely on the basis of a "minor" character) and genre is based on the ones at the "top" of that hierarchy; and that genre is intrinsic, rather than extrinsic, to any given text. These assumptions are all questionable, and, in addition to ahistoricizing the text, tend to force it into a critical Procrustean bed. In any text, there will be as much or more that falls outside a particular generic category as within.

My purpose, however, is not to abolish the category of genre, but to relocate and redefine it. Although genre is not an important structural feature of particular texts, it is a crucial feature of reading. Genre acts both as a topographical feature of the terrain of the marketplace and as a set of reading instructions anterior to the text itself. It is produced discursively as a social category and is aligned with other social categories such as gender and class; indeed specific genres are assigned gender and class, according to perceived author, perceived textual characteristics, and perceived readership. Like other social categories, genre is perpetuated by the tendency of subjects to re-produce themselves ideologically. Thus, once an author/text is established within a certain generic domain, that is, coming from a certain "location" within the marketplace and appealing to a certain consumership, critics, publishers, authors, and readers will enforce, through master-readings (reviews), packaging, textual references, and reading assumptions, a reading of that text which is congruent with its assigned generic pedigree. This serves both to secure the text's position within the marketplace and, crucially, to limit the play of the text's multiplicity, both "vertically" (within the social hierarchy of the marketplace) and "horizontally" (within the range of possible meanings and significances assigned to various elements of the text).

If genre serves as a set of reading instructions, a meta-text situated in social discourses, then genre itself becomes a dialogical process. Julia Kristeva poses the problem this way: "One of the problems for semiotics is to replace the former, rhetorical division of genres with a *typology of texts*; that is, to define the specificity of different textual arrangements by placing them within the general text (culture) of which they are part and which is in turn, part of them."[2] Presumably, then, this would include the historical specificity of the social discourses surrounding the text itself, which Kristeva defines as a "productivity." Confusingly, however, Kristeva accepts Mikhail Bakhtin's distinction between the epic and the dialogic text, which would seem to obviate her own definition; a text as productivity must include both epic and subversive tendencies (to oversimplify, in a hopefully productive manner, the term "dialogic"), as every utterance contains its own repressed semiotic content. The principal difference between the epic text and the dialogic text and even the carnivalesque text is merely the degree to which one ubiquitous feature is elevated and the others submerged; all are present, however, in every text, or, even more precisely, in every reading. On the level of popular generic labeling, calling a particular novel a "love story" does not mean that there is not a social-problem novel lying between the same covers; it merely means that the social-problem novel shall remain invisible. In this way, genre produces coherence within the multiplicity of the text; in some sense, it produces the text (the reading) itself. Again, the point here is not to render the category of genre inoperative, but to render its operations suspect, and to redefine it as a dynamic process in discursive production rather than a static inclusion within a product.

Tzvetan Todorov, in *Genres in Discourse*, argues that genres are "codifications of discursive properties" which are repeated in any given sociohistorical framework. Because genres, for Todorov, are "the meeting place between general poetics and event based literary history" the interesting question is why and how particular speech acts are chosen by a particular culture at a given historical moment, to be perceived as genres.[3] Todorov's purpose here is to introduce an alternative narratological code by which texts may be read, and he presents three structures, which may all be present in a particular narrative, but of which one may be in the ascendant: mythological, gnoseological, and ideological. Briefly, the first is based on temporal or causal linkage between successive events in a narrative, the second depends on the changing perception of events through the narrative as an organizing principle, and the third relies on an abstract rule or ideological principle to produce coherence within a narrative which contains diverse and perhaps even apparently unrelated events. Todorov does not intend this to be an exhaustive or rigid system of classification, but he suggests that it is helpful to "look for the qualitative or quantitative predominance of certain transformations," such falling within one of the three categories.

Although, from a narratological point of view, these three distinctions are indeed useful, in the discussion of genre as historical rather than textual category which I am advancing here, it is helpful to collapse this distinction in a way that Todorov does not exclude. All three narrative structures may be subsumed under the ideological, since the first two are organized by time, causality, and the concept of knowledge, which are all ideologically and historically determined. What is an appropriate cause, what is worth knowing and who is to know it – these are logical relationships which are naturalized within the whole discursive universe of a particular time–space of a culture. It is in this sense that all three organizations are ideological in content. What arguably changes is the way in which the reader's interest is maintained. Todorov tells us that the mythological organization keeps the reader's attention with the question "What happens next?" and the gnoseological text asks "What is the nature of what is, or what has happened?" He does not provide an explanation of the lure of the ideological text *per se*, but based on the work of Fredric Jameson and others, let us assume it is a systematic working-out of anxieties in order to achieve confirmation of the ideologically constituted subject (which of course applies to the first two categories as well), in this case by presenting a series of ideological contradictions in order to finally resolve them. Todorov's initial questions are extremely useful, although his answers are, for our purposes, less so. Interestingly, Todorov himself noted in his study of Bakhtin that Bakhtin's work moves from a "strong systematic" approach to genre which is extremely problematic to a much more clearly sustained discussion of particular sub-genres by chronotope that implies no overriding, essential system of genres.[4] As always, we return to the core problem; any taxonomy of genre can be reduced to distinctions which are social and historical, rather than "purely" formal. Although those categories may be useful as "tools" with which to handle given texts in a particular period for a given purpose, those tools are only truly useful to the extent that we keep their non-innocent, historically and ideologically specific nature in mind.

Given these cautions, it is helpful to conflate Todorov's "ideological" structure (as I have redefined it) with Bakhtin's "epic," not as a category of given texts, but as a historically determined property of all texts, which is then designated as genre. Genre, then, is determined by the topical properties of the text that provide ideological confirmation; in turn, the generic designation serves as reading instructions that occlude properties of the text that invoke ideologies contradictory to the dominant imperative of the reading. Thus a marriage plot like the one in Broughton's *A Beginner*, although a negligible feature of the novel, becomes the dominant feature of the reading (after all, it is a woman's novel, written by a woman known for her love stories, etc.) and eclipses the critique of market conditions that charts the failure of a woman novelist to transcend them. We shall trace this process in more detail below (see the second section of chapter 5, below). A text which is so aggressively multiple as not to allow its reading within its assigned genre will either be redesignated, (perhaps by an alternative readership) or simply declared hysterical or unreadable – and consequently, left unread. A high-culture novel may perhaps be distinguished from the "low" popular novel simply by the amount of play the text seems to its readership to invite, or that its readership will tolerate, popular texts traditionally being accorded a fairly narrow range.

If genre is a socially constructed category, the question then becomes, as always, a question of power, its source, its strategies, and its opposition: "Who speaks that name?" Since the system of genre categorization "works," this question rarely arises. Readers, critics, authors, and publishers in the nineteenth century (as in the present) colluded to naturalize the "boundaries" of genres. Predictably, however, these boundaries were destabilized at the precise locations that parallel discourses were disrupted: those of gender, sexuality, and class, among others. In these cases, the onus of classification devolved upon the "master-readers" of the marketplace – review critics. Different reviewers would struggle to "place" the text, and that placement might depend on such factors as the perceived sex of the author and his or her class as much as on the structure or subject matter of a novel. Yet the critic was not all powerful; after all, a critic who constantly and radically disagreed with his or her readership would lose currency rapidly. To be effective, the critic must act as the representative of an "interpretive community" of readers with shared values and assumptions. Yet within the limits of that community's values, the critic did wield some power to direct the flow of consumption by shaping reader attitudes and book-borrowing patterns (which in turn affected the sale of editions directly). One way in which such suasive rhetorical acts are accomplished is by referring to (and thus borrowing authority from) existing and highly charged discourses, such as the discourses of disease, gender, etc. The placement of a text, in other words, was (and is) constructed from existing discourses.

Genre operates not only as a way of binding the reading process, but of locating the text within the "boundaries" of a "space" within the marketplace. This is particularly important in constructions of the popular literatures, which are, as we have seen, devalued with the label "commercial," distancing them from the "aristocratic" pursuit of literature for the sake of knowledge, beauty, or social good, which is the purview of those who do not have to worry about making a living. The marketplace is commercial, and therefore, both plebeian and morally suspect, and is associated with vulgarity in language and action. The literary marketplace is textual and discursive, consisting as it does of books, reviews, serials, and salons, rather than geographic, but it participates metaphorically in many of the same processes as any other nineteenth century marketplace, both in that there is a geographical center of production (London) and distribution (e.g., Mudie's of London) and in that desirability of a given product determines and is determined by its location (in this case, metaphorical) in the marketplace and its contingency to other desirable goods/locations. In this same way, genres were, to an extent, considered spatially contingent to one another, and this partially determined their status. Thus, devotional poetry is "closer to" the religious tract (high status) than to the sensation novel, which itself is "closer to" the half-penny broadsheet (low status). Genre is often assigned according to what is perceived as the dominant (or most relevant) topic of a text, and it is no accident that topic and topology are derived from the same root.

This spatial analogy serves an important purpose. If genres are envisioned as occupying physical spaces, some contingent upon each other, others widely separated, it becomes possible to think of genres as having discrete boundaries which are either not to be crossed, or, if crossed, only to be crossed into "adjacent" areas. In a review of Broughton's *Not Wisely But Too Well*, an anonymous *Athenaeum* critic concludes, "Worse than even the immorality of the whole novel are the stupid, misplaced attempts at sermonizing throughout. They might be very well in another work, but being where they are they simply disgust. We need say no more."[5]

Although this critic is clearly offended by the perception that the sacred and profane are being inappropriately joined, there is also a sense that the "sermonizing," which, we must note, is intrinsically inoffensive, is "misplaced" (the spatial metaphor that runs through the passage is significant) – in other words, that in "another work" – in another genre, another location, it would be appropriate. It is not only that Broughton has "stepped over the line," so to speak, it is the perceived distance she has traversed that upsets the reviewer; a novel that "panders to the gross tastes of the day"[6] is, or should be, far removed from one that "sermonizes." The religious novel and the sex novel are not contingent genres, and Broughton is out of her neighborhood. Put another way, the "epic" is always central, spatially and ideologically; the further the distance of other elements in the text from the epic/center, the more that center is destabilized. When it is sufficiently destabilized (sufficiency being relative to historical, social, and individual sensitivity), the text's dialogism enters the realm of the carnivalesque.

Perhaps the reason that this crossover is so upsetting in the case of *Not Wisely But Too Well* is precisely because of the disruptive potential of sex in the marketplace. In anathematizations of "the social evil", one of the most telling points is the frequent repetition of the horrified observation that prostitutes might be seen openly practicing their trade in the best of neighborhoods. The text-trade and the sex-trade have this in common: "quality" or "purity" in the traditional sense are not indices of desirability – in fact, there is often a negative correlation. In this way, they both violate the spatial norms of the classed marketplace; lower-class wares, perhaps repackaged, perhaps not, are unabashedly vended in upper-class neighborhoods. This violation of space takes place on the metaphorical level as well. The sensation novel was said to be offensive partly because it located crime – traditionally located in the margins of society – in the heart of the middle-class neighborhood and even the family itself. In the anti-Papist pamphlet wars, the most devastating insults to the Roman Catholic Church figured the church as a whore; what is horrifying is the proximity of degraded sexuality and religion, because these are traditionally considered "widely separated," even opposite concepts. Broughton attempts to reconcile these opposites to make *Not Wisely But Too Well* a "moral" novel (the heroine never does run off with her lover, but becomes a Sister of Mercy and decorously dies a virgin); the reviewer finds their proximity intolerable and indefensible.

It is, of course, precisely this proximity of the hierarchically (spatially) opposite that constitutes the carnivalesque. Ironically, the purpose here is apparently, in the Bakhtinian sense, epic, or normative (the heroine is "reclaimed"), yet the critic usurps the epic purpose to him/herself:

The great object of books like these is apparently to teach immorality by representing it in an interesting and seductive form ... If this is not their object, we can assure their authors that it must inevitably be their effect... It is time, then, for critics to speak out boldly, and to declare in plain language what they think of the tendencies of these books, and see if by so doing whether they cannot put a stop to their production.[7]

The critic reserves to him/herself the role of master-reader and moral censor for the public good; amusingly, the critic admonishes, "If any one doubts this [opinion], let him take the book we are now reviewing and read it coolly and critically, and ask ... what impression on the mind of an ordinary reader it is calculated to produce."[8] Since the *Athenaeum* is precisely the type of survey that "ordinary readers" went to in order to make their reading choices, this distinction between the review's reader and the ordinary reader whom the critic must protect is somewhat unclear. Clearly, however, the intention is to leave nothing to chance – if the reader insists on reading the novel, the reading is to be dictated by the critic. The critic seeks to distance the reader from the carnivalesque, turning her or him into a spectator rather than a participant, thus "sanitizing" and domesticating the text within a *cordon sanitaire* of surrounding critical text – through which the reader only experiences the novel as a sort of Blue Book example. Notwithstanding, *Not Wisely but Too Well* became one of Broughton's most popular novels. (Perhaps there was even a causal connection; many critics spoke of their fear of condemning a particular novel by name, since it was "as good as an advertisement.") Yet, the critical interdiction may have had its effect after all; such novels became popular precisely as "improper" novels, readers taking delight in transgression just as we do today (consider the success of *The Satanic Verses*).

Ironically, in many ways, such criticism depended symbiotically on the existence of such texts to denounce, just as the "Water Police" depended on prostitution for their own livelihood. Often, in these essays, Cato seems to play Pandarus. For example, Mrs. Oliphant's 1867 denunciation of sensation novels declines to name the titles of certain books, in the interest of leaving the very "objectionable still untouched";[9] these same titles are helpfully provided in the footnotes, a practice which arguably draws more attention to them than if they were simply mentioned in passing in the text! Yet even if the critics did not stem the popularity of these novels, they determined how the books should be approached, which may be an even more effective censorship. If the carnivalesque reconciliation of opposites in Broughton's novel is seen as blasphemous and disgusting, even if intriguing as a result of that perception, then it is effectively contained as spectacle.

### GENRE AND THE BODY

If Victorian critics were concerned about the intake of the generic, gendered text into the gendered body of the reader, they were also concerned about the reader's body as text itself – as constituted by, as well as constitutive of narrative. Peter Brooks has argued that the activity of reading within modernity is motivated by the "epistemophilic" urge, often figured as the urge to know the body of the woman who is the archetypal object of desire. Thus, we are brought to the end of narrative: the absence represented by the woman's genitals, in response to which the subject experiences terror and desire.[10] The subject position of the reader is gendered male. In Brooks' formulation, the aesthetic of modernity thus eliminates the polysemy of the body, which comes passively to mean, or be one thing. The possibility of subversion is the repressed awareness of the subject whose gaze constructs the body in the process of knowing, a process, which as Michel Foucault tells us, is intimately mediated by structures of power.[11] However, genres gendered and addressed to a female reading subject complicate this dynamic. The recuperation of the material repressed in the process of the privileged subject's seeing/knowing is exactly what is at stake in the consumption and production of a popular culture by women. As we have discovered, the text becomes lesbian, or perhaps reflective of a narcissistic subject (or both). This narcissism is not uncomplicated, simply revealing an existing reality, an existing body. Instead it constitutes the body of the reader as female, textual, and therefore identifiable with the insufficient, the diseased, and the mutable. The act of mirroring the female body, therefore, can distort not only its reflection but the original itself; whereas the male spectator confronts only the fear of castration in the Other, for the female, the mere act of reading constitutes a potential (pleasurable!) violence done to the self. The body, then, as the ultimate cultural referent of the "natural" ("Old Adam" – or Eve), also exists as the type of nature mediated and inscribed by culture – for good or ill – in which reading may be seen as a continuous and dangerous process of new inscription which may enhance, deface, or distort the old. Even now, most histories of the body focus on the histories of women's bodies as objects of representation; as Brooks points out, no such history of the male body-object yet exists. Histories of the embodied subject, however, with a few notable exceptions such as the efforts of French feminists in the 1970s to find an *écriture feminine*, have tended to position the subject as male. For the Victorians especially, because women are seen as closer to nature than men, civilized women are more heavily inscribed by culture than men – and thus, more vulnerable to revision.

In her excellent recent work on Victorian representations of the sick body, Athena Vrettos states, "Persistent attempts by Victorian writers and physicians to define the terms of human physicality, to locate in the body the source of sexual and social divisions, to create a physiological blueprint that would explain the meaning of racial difference and restore a sense of social and material order provided a means of controlling potentially disturbing cultural issues by relocating them in questions of physiology."[12] Vrettos is most interested in narrative portrayals of the body, but her observation, based on the considerable recent work on the body as text (Peter Brooks, Helena Michie, Elaine Scarry, etc.) offers us a way of thinking about genres of bodies.[13] In fact, the move that Vrettos traces, in relocating social issues in the physiological, becomes only a stopgap measure, as the physiological, the essential, is subject itself to revision, as readers' bodies, infected by their intake of narrative, become narrative themselves. Instead of the body stabilizing ideology and narrative, ideology and narrative destabilize the body.

Although Charles Darwin's *The Descent of Man* is often seen as a point of origin for degenerationist theories of the body which came to be deployed in discourse about both colonial and domestic working-class subjects, these theories were current, if fragmented, for at least a decade and a half earlier. The word "genre" itself comes from biological systems of taxonomy, from the same source as the Latin word for family. Families are the fundamental social constructions hiding under the cover of "nature." Biological taxonomies and the scientific gaze have, of course, never been innocent, as Thomas Laqueur and Londa Schiebinger have demonstrated; they have always been freighted with cultural constructions of gender and race.[14] What is perhaps most interesting in the period of the 1860s is the entanglement of class and race and of class and gender (gender and race having long been so entangled). The sixties and seventies were a period in which many believed that bodies were not merely developed or decorated according to a certain social class, but were biologically classed, in the same way that phrenology located character in anatomy. Class could be read as an essential trait, in the way that gender was (and sex still is). This reading emerged out of an active essentialist/social constructionist debate, of course; it was never wholly accepted, perhaps even by a majority. But its currency was widespread enough to have far-reaching consequences, and its metaphors penetrated the discourse, and in turn the thinking, even of people who may not consciously have accepted the theories themselves. (By the end of the century and the emergence of nationalist rhetoric across Europe, the racialization of class, at direct odds with concepts of national unity, provides for constellations of physical descriptors which become convoluted almost to unreadability, such as the simian genius of Holly in Rider Haggard's *She*.)

More than a clever metaphor, the notion of genres of bodies is productive precisely because it is hidden in the very structure of the ways in which science, especially popularized science from the mid-nineteenth century onward, "thinks about" bodies. More importantly for our purposes here, it is the other pole of the analogy between texts and bodies which enables a kind of two-way traffic between the two; i.e., if texts were a little like bodies, but bodies really not, at some deep level of awareness, analogous to texts, there would not be so much anxiety about their interaction. Genre provides a means to make texts (bodies) legible – highlighting some readings and hiding others – but, perhaps more importantly, it also contains texts (bodies) within a certain family grouping, with all the limitations that implies. Like the geographical metaphor outlined above, these entailments of the text as body metaphor provide models for and act to manage the text in ways that Victorians already knew to manage commodified bodies; they also raise the anxiety about the adequacy of these management techniques which is evident in health legislation throughout the period. Genre slippage not only destabilizes a particular text or reading, or worse, a particular reader, it calls the whole structure of containment into question. If genre (and thus genre slippage), is in the eye of the reading community, as I have argued, then the textual cue that is most likely to initiate the reader's uncertainty is that which calls upon the vexed, fluctuating discourses surrounding the gendered, classed body and its non-natural, non-essential slipperiness and opacity.

The bodies of women, being more permeable, more mutable, more *textual* than those of men, depended more on context for their meaning, and were vulnerable to rereadings – or rewritings – through experience which could change them essentially. In short, a gentleman, however degraded in his experiences, remains a gentleman; a lady degraded is a lady no more. Even a lady who lost only her familial economic status and not her innocence might be referred to as a "decayed gentle-woman," an apellation perhaps more descriptive than it was intended to be. Characteristics which are supposed to be essential become surprisingly mutable in portrayals of women characters and readers, and the whole dynamic is exacerbated when the author function which helps define genre also contains this radical feminine mutability. The woman reader and the woman character were both vulnerable to revision, and it bears noting that, although reading could theoretically be ennobling, it was far more likely that consuming text would cause degeneration, a kind of genre slippage initiated in the reader by the corresponding slippage "in the text," the results of an infection which not only inscribes the signs of its presence on the body but transforms it.

SENSATION

The nineteenth-century sensation novel has attracted a good deal of critical and historical attention in recent years; the two first long studies were written by Winifred Hughes and Thomas Boyle. Hughes sees the sensation novel as a "literary upstart" that arose in the 1860s, and, although she acknowledges its indebtedness to the Newgate genre, recognizes it as a thing unto itself: "What distinguishes the true sensation genre, as it appeared in its prime during the 1860s, is the violent yoking of romance and realism, traditionally the two contradictory modes of literary perception." It is based on "propinquity," that is, the setting is in the time and place of the intended reader.[15] Hughes argues that the sensation novel is a sort of antidote to the stodginess of Victorian respectability, and that it is radically subversive by virtue of its deconstructive "yoking of opposites." Boyle, however, finds less distinction between sensation fiction and its contemporary discourses of reality. He writes of his surprise, in the early stages of his research, to find that the average Victorian newspaper "was sensational to say the least, [and] certainly not supportive of an image of domestic tranquility."[16] His work documents what Reade and his contemporaries insisted – that the sensation novels were, to an extent, "studies from the life," extending from the discourses of the newspapers. If so, these novels hardly owed their attractiveness to their status as the sole respite from mid-Victorian respectability.

One must question why a genre of literature that was a mere extension of existing news items gained such popularity. I would suggest that, rather than the directly subversive purpose that Hughes assigns it, a primary purpose was to shape and provide coherence for that barrage of information. Far from bringing the terrifying into the midst of the middle-class neighborhood, as Hughes asserts, the sensation novel's purpose was to remove it and frame it, so that it might be perused safely and at some distance. A novel about a bigamist or a child-murder in a fictional middle-class neighborhood is far less immediate than a newspaper which places such events a block and a day away. Also, whereas news items appear without prior warning, with limited explanation and often, without resolution, the novel provides all of these, bounding the uncanny within the conventional strictures and structures of plot development and denouement, in which conventional values are, at least nominally, upheld. Yet perhaps this is the real outrage to which the critics were reacting. It may very well be subversive to suggest that there can be order and reason within such "pathological" social dysfunctions. Perhaps in the very act of providing a structure within which such actions are naturalized and explained, the sensation novel provided a radical critique of a society in which such actions *could* be explained and assigned motive.

Where the sensation novels are most subversive, however, is in the reading practices which they support. Hughes remarks this:

the threat to literary standards is only exceeded by the threat to social ones. Reading sensation novels becomes a subversive pursuit because it brings the middle and lower classes together over the same printed page ... The blurring of social distinctions, remarked in actual life in the mild form of a shared literary taste, becomes more flagrant and disquieting in the world of the novels themselves. Not only do the middle- or upper-class characters mingle a little too freely with their inferiors, they begin to imitate lower-class behavior.[17]

Jonathan Loesberg argues that the defining characteristic of sensation fiction – a phenomenon he correctly argues to have been constructed by critical reception in the 1860s – is the loss of class identity on the part of the characters, a concern which he relates to the Reform Bill debates. I would shift the grounds of his argument to suggest that the Reform debates and the class anxiety displayed in the novels emerged from and expressed the same complex set of anxieties; however, the fact is that popular literature continued to be attacked long after the 1860s for exactly those same concerns after "sensationalism" ceased to define the sub-genres of literature which evolved from it (for example, the novel of high life). However, the emphasis on the blurring of class boundaries in reading is an important feature of the popular novel, sensational or otherwise.

The emphasis on proximity correlates to the metaphor of genre as topography. On the level of content, the truncation of distance is a key feature in the mid-nineteenth-century popular novel. As Hughes notes, earlier "romance" (not to be confused with the later, more restricted use of the term to mean "love story") was distinguishable by setting. Usually, it was displaced in time and set in some exotic location. The local, the mundane was reserved for the more privileged realist novel, generally novels of what Northrop Frye terms the high mimetic mode.[18] To import the extraordinary events of romance into the ordinary reality of quotidian existence was generic miscegenation of the worst kind. Had the content of sensation fiction remained marginal to the central and domestic concerns of middle-class society, it might well have been permitted much more outrageousness, just as Ouida's sexually liberated European characters were permitted to circulate through Mudie's while George Moore's tamer but more localized fictions were firmly declined. Precisely because it is domestic in its content, the genre is figured forth as a foreign invader, both of the body (as a disease) and of the nation (as a foreign plague). In her excellent study of Wilkie Collins, Jenny Bourne Taylor notes that the appetite for sensation was linked to anxieties about cultural degeneration, observing that the physiological referents of sensation operated "to articulate anxiety about imminent cultural decline by referring to an image of an explicitly 'feminine' body that was at once its product and metonymic model" marked by a neurotic susceptibility to excitement that was specifically a reaction to modernity.[19] In fact, this body was not only feminized, but racialized. Boyle notes that sensationalism was aligned both with disease and racial "blackness," but does not pause to elaborate on these interesting observations:

There is a racial undercurrent near the surface of many of the discussions of sensationalism throughout the 1860s. Images of disease, bestiality, and sex occur and recur in the context of "blackness" ... [Boyle quotes an 1866 Westminster Review article:] "as those diseases always occurred in seasons of death and poverty, so does the Sensational Mania in Literature burst out only in times of mental poverty and afflict only the most poverty-stricken minds." Now the mania for Sensation seems to have changed from "epidemic" to "endemic."[20]

Boyle does not remark at length upon this disease imagery, and, although Hughes observes that the "imagery of disease becomes prominent as critics of sensationalism describe the unnerving progression by which this 'virus is spreading in all directions, from the penny journal to the shilling magazine, and from the shilling magazine to the thirty-shillings volume,'" she does not pursue this observation either.[21] However, the quoted reference to epidemic and endemic in conjunction with race is extremely meaningful within the context of the medical concerns of the 1860s. The sixties saw a determined, even a desperate attempt to control the ravages of cholera which had repeatedly decimated urban England. Cholera was particularly associated with impoverished immigrant workers (since they were most frequently the principal residents of the poorest, hardest hit areas), and was considered by most medical experts to be not native to Britain. In 1867, the *Quarterly Review* published an article on "The Cholera Conference," which principally concerned itself with tracing the progress of the disease from various other locations, most notably India and the Mediterranean, to "the present year [in which] it has overrun the whole of the continent, and has attacked England."[22] Fixing responsibility for cholera seems to have been a primary concern: the French are said to have blamed the English for its presence in India, but the English disproved this to their own satisfaction, pronouncing it, with relief, endemic to the region: "[T]he whole odium of being cholera producers has been thrown on our Indian possessions."[23] Although cholera was supposed to have come originally from India, many physicians believed that the disease lived in "the subsoil" while it raged, and if active long enough in a given location, could establish itself permanently in its subsoil and thus become endemic there. Naturally, the English wished to prevent this, although some feared it had already happened. The rest of the article evaluates the Conference's recommendations for containment, using specifically military terminology, planning to "attack" the "enemy" "at a distance" – in the Red Sea, in fact.[24] (Parliamentary Records confirm this preoccupation with the "naturalization" of the cholera in Britain. It continued to be a frequent topic of discussion for some time.) The disease is an alien enemy from the colonial lands which attempts to "penetrate" and lodge itself in domestic soil. Literary critics, by referring to sensationalism as an epidemic which threatens to become endemic, align the sensation novel with the foreign, with disease, with filth and refuse, with poverty, and with invasion – in fact, with the unpleasant underside of industrial empire.

It is curious how frequently popular literature is constituted as a risk specifically to the imperial subject. An 1874 *Temple Bar* review sermonizes:

Indeed we have been, since the Romans, the only truly imperial people. We have embraced the globe with the arms of our ambition; we have scoured every sea; we have colonized every sphere. But the insularity with which we were once unfairly rebuked is at last becoming ... our characteristic and opprobrium ... We are determinedly insular, and we find even the island too big ... "our neighborhood" is the most delightful and absorbing thing in life ... It is this quality of narrow curiosity which is the paralysis of all wide and noble interest, which the novel stimulates and feeds ... these are the main concerns of a once imperial people.[25]

And the *Edinburgh Review* refers to Newgate novels as a deliberate attempt "to poison the springs of a nation's life."[26]

The great danger of such fiction, according to these critics, is that it renders the reader passive and of narrow interests. The imperial subject is active, masculine, and moves outward; the novel reader is passive, feminine and receives inward movement, is female and colonial rather than male and imperial. Particularly in the 1860s, 1870s, and 1880s, when the appropriate role of the British civil servant was contested within an emerging awareness of and sympathy for the subjectivity of the colonial Other, the imbrications of the discourse of empire in the discourse of gender bear close scrutiny. The feminized and infantilized "Aryan little brother," for example, must be reconciled with the hyper-masculine Indian soldier of the still clearly remembered Mutiny of 1857, just as middle-class women are becoming disturbingly visible in traditionally masculine public spaces in the metropole, as Judith Walkowitz has recently made clear. The disruptive power of these changes is clearly visioned as a threat to empire through the integrity of the imperial subject's masculinity. Mark Pattison identifies novels as a sort of sedative to ease the transition from imperial to non-imperial subject:

The mind of the English reader is not, as in the southern man, torpid, non-existent; it is alive and restless. But it is not animated by a curiosity to inquire, it is not awakened to the charm of ideas, it is only passively recipient of images. An idea is an excitant, comes from mind and calls forth mind. An image is a sedative... There must be no reflex mental action. Meditation is pain. Fresh images must flow as a continuous douche of tepid water over the mind of the reader, which must remain pleased but passive. Books must be so contrived as to produce and sustain this beatific self-forgetfulness.[27]

The drugging of the mind produces a self that is defined as a passive body, and this self, like the lotos-eaters of *The Odyssey*, is a self that forgets its duty and obligation to a "restless" journeying. The definition of sensation novels as a stimulant, as a "hot and strong ... dram or ... dose," would seem to contradict Pattison's characterization of popular literature as an opiate, and perhaps we should separate the anaesthetized mind from the body of the reader. Indeed, the whole notion of a sensation is a physical one, and the effects of sensation fiction are generally defined in physical terms. The *Quarterly Review* defines sensation novels as novels which produce "excitement, and excitement alone" by "preaching to the nerves," that abound in "action, action, action!"[28] The effects of this action upon the reader are physical:

A great philosopher has enumerated in a list of sensations "the feelings from heat, electricity, galvanism, &c." together with "titillation, sneezing, horripilation, shuddering, the feeling of setting the teeth on edge, &c.;" and our novels might be classified in like manner, according to what sensation they are calculated to produce. There are novels of the warming pan, and others of the galvanic battery type – some which gently stimulate a particular feeling, and others which carry the whole nervous system by steam.[29]

The tone here is satiric, of course, but the treatment is fairly consistent across a number of reviews; the core of the sensation novel is the activity of the text in producing a physical sensation, an activity which is complementary to the passivity of the reader in whom the sensation is "produced."

Not surprisingly, then, sensation novels as a genre are perceived as feminine, despite their murders, plots, and generally very active characters, which would seem to align them with the "masculine" adventure novel. And, also unlike the adventure novel, the sensation novel generally features a female protagonist. As Hughes points out, "Even the sensation novels written by men focus on the feminine point of view; both Reade and Collins draw effortless portraits of mature, sophisticated, sexually aroused women, heroines as well as adventuresses."[30] *Blackwood's* is very clear on the point that sensation novels are written primarily by women. Ironically, after lambasting sensationalism for no less than nineteen pages, Oliphant holds up as two models of excellence in literature, presumably comparable to one another, Anthony Trollope and Charles Reade! It would surely be pardonable to think of Reade, as Hughes does, as the purest distillation of sensationalism, in whose work madmen, murderers, and mistaken identities congregate with a kind of baroque density, yet we are told by this despiser of sensation fiction that Reade has

become one of the greatest artists in the realm of fiction . . . His power is of the kind which will always seem coarse to a certain class of minds unable to discriminate; for he is very apt to call a spade a spade; and among the minikin performances of the day, his strong and genuine mastery over human characters and passions shows out with a force of outline which may possibly, in some cases, look exaggerated.[31]

Possibly. Yet, even a cursory study of Reade's work will reveal that the sexuality demonstrated by his rather remarkable women (see *Hard Cash*) makes Broughton and Braddon seem tame indeed. Still, it would seem that, in Reade's case, it is not only not coarse, but not sensational either. Clearly, the fact that the critic defends Reade from "misunderstanding" demonstrates that this is not a unanimous opinion. Yet, just as clearly, for Oliphant, what is sensational and reprehensible in a novel written by a woman becomes realism in the case of a man, especially a man whose central characters are often male. The critic attacks Braddon, Broughton, Ouida, and Mr. Yates – a diverse group of novelists, but all ones with active, aggressive heroines, and lionizes Trollope and Reade. (Strangely, of Wilkie Collins, there is no mention.) Kate Flint argues that the primary source of anxiety about sensation novels has to do with their primarily female audience, but notes that the female author is implicated in this equation as well: "critical attention ... makes no bones in showing what it was about these fictions which gave cause for alarm. Its frames of reference are drawn from familiar suppositions about women's affective susceptibility ... [sexual] disruptive potential was greeted with particular anxiety when it was located in novels written by women."[32] Subsequent to Oliphant's jeremiad, another *Blackwood's* piece asserts that the sensational writers are "for the most part, feminine, and their pens go dashing along with true feminine volubility."[33]

Perhaps more importantly, sensation novels undermined conventional notions of causality and motivation; in their dependence on incident and "surprise" or chance happenings, they rely on associative (il)logic that is often defined as specifically female. Loesberg identifies the "nonseriousness" of thematic connections as the disruptive element of the sensation novel:

Characterizing sensation fiction as emotional evocation without thematic correlative is not merely a judgment upon it but also a virtual description of how it operates. The plot operates through various forms of transference and reversal to isolate the moments when it produces the sensation response apart from any thematic readability, insisting almost on the nonseriousness, even the illicitness, of the response it calls forth.[34]

It is disruptive because it treats serious matters – like the loss of class identity – in a "nonserious" manner. In essence, I agree with Loesberg's assessment, but I take exception to his use of the term "nonserious." The notion that "sensational" occurrences might happen without clear, and therefore controllable causality may indeed have been terrifying, but it is anything but nonserious. Nancy K. Miller argues that plots which lack plausibility – defined as the "effect of reading through a grid of concordance" with social doxa of "appropriate" causalities, defined as masculine linear logic – are labeled as "arbitrary narrative" – women's literature, and largely excluded from the canon on that aesthetic basis.[35] With Miller's argument in mind, we may return to Loesberg's analysis to see, not a readership that perceived "nonseriousness," but a critical readership that was highly motivated to reject any alternative logic in addressing "serious" issues, and to marginalize it as nonlogical and feminine.

Another nineteenth-century critic, somewhat less idiosyncratic than Oliphant in his/her delimitation of the genre, argues that the sensation novel is, in fact, a disease arising out of market conditions and lower-class refuse:

A commercial atmosphere floats around works of this class, redolent of the manufactory and the shop . . . There is something unspeakably disgusting in this ravenous appetite for carrion, this vulture-like instinct which smells out the newest mass of social corruption, and hurries to devour the loathsome dainty before the scent has evaporated . . . [Penny publications] are the original germ, the primitive monad, to which all the varieties of sensation literature may be referred . . . In them, we have sensationism [sic] pure and undisguised, exhibited in its naked simplicity, stripped of the rich dress which conceals while it adorns the figure of the more ambitious varieties of the species.[36]

This critic moves through a dizzying number of images, touching on the commercialism of the novel, linking it to refuse (implying that commercialism produces "carrion"); as carrion produces disease, so social corruption produces sensationalism, which is a lower-class commodity at its root, but, like the lower class prostitute, it can be given a "rich dress" to lure the upper-class consumer. Although these metaphors may be, on a literal level, "mixed," on a logical level, they are rather perfectly coherent within the discursive frameworks of 1860s social concerns. Dangerous refuse was linked primarily to poverty stricken neighborhoods with high population and poor sanitation, and to industrial areas, particularly those with slaughterhouses and tanneries. Such areas produce disease both directly and through the commodities they export into better neighborhoods – cheap clothes and nasty women, to name a few; in fact, the critic compares sensation novels to cheaply produced fabric, "so many yards of printed stuff, sensation pattern [which] . . . rank with the verses of which 'Lord Fanny spins a thousand such a day.'"[37] The association with cheap fabric aligns sensation to the production of impoverished, "sweated" women, who were associated both with disease because of their unhealthy working conditions, and with seasonal prostitution which received attention during the 1860s investigations of the Contagious Disease Acts (see William Acton for more on this). Surveying these denunciations of sensation fiction, recent critics have understandably tended to read the perception of Victorian critics as a Manichean one: the critic is the force of good sent out to fight a (losing) battle with the evil sensation novel. I would argue that Victorian critics' perception of their own role was less naive and more in tune with the sense that popular fiction, like alcohol and prostitution, was a fact of modern life less to be eradicated than carefully managed. The critic aligns him/herself with the sanitary inspectors whose purpose it is to police consumption and make the commodity safe for the middle classes.

The sensation novel is in a most peculiar position. Having a female author, text, and reader, it is similar to the romance. However, in the romance, the heroine is generally active only in the luring of the male, whereas in sensation novels, the protagonist often takes on very "masculine," active traits. Hughes sees this content as subversive, as do most current feminist critics, and Natalie Schroeder notes that these women characters often use their sexuality in their bids for power, power being the real subject of the narratives.[38] Yet although these critics see the sexuality of the content of this fiction (which is, after all, generally punished or at least contained, at the level of plot if not theme), they do not concern themselves with the more threatening sensuality of the reader–author–text interchange, an interchange which is as homo- as auto-erotic. Boyle points out that "the 'referent' of the author of 'Philosophy of Sensation' [a critic who denigrated the sensation novel] is his personal terror of a female sexuality that is both voracious and bestial . . . women are seduced by the stories into inattention to the would-be dominant male, or they are metamorphosed into man-eaters."[39] It is not the rivalry of another male that produces the monstrous female, with her characteristically fishy extremities. Whether lesbian or heterosexual nymphomaniac, the transformative seduction of the middle-class woman comes about through her association with another corrupt female – the prostituted hack paid to produce a sensation.

Very recent feminist criticism of sensation fiction has evinced more interest in the reader than earlier studies which were more focused on establishing authorial feminism. Lyn Pykett's work is an excellent example. Working off Annette Kuhn's observations about soap opera, she gives the intriguing suggestion that, "By being positioned as the spectator (especially of a female character) the female reader is offered a culturally masculine 'position of mastery' . . . in sensation fiction this mastery is also an effect of the specularity of the melodramatic style [which offers the female body as object while simultaneously inviting an identification of reader and protagonist] . . . It is this contradictory process . . . which opens a space for oppositional readings."[40] As readers of early feminist reader-response theory will recall, however, this is the process of "immasculation" which Patrocinio Schweickart persuasively traces in readings of Joyce's *Portrait of the Artist* by female students; it is not necessarily liberatory or oppositional, although with "resisting reading," as Judith Fetterly terms it, it can become so.[41] However, Pykett's argument locates the opportunities for resistance in the structure of sensation fiction, which seems to have ontological claims of its own in this study; although she acknowledges that sensation must be read in its cultural and market context, she does not articulate the ways in which the play of "oppositional" reading might be limited or dictated by that context, or even evoked by that context in order to engage a spectacle of opposition – and containment. Anne Cvetkovich's excellent recent work is also more concerned than most with the reader, and her possible investment in the notion of a transgressive expression of affect, a confession that by "telling" pain evokes the fantasy of social change. As Cvetkovich astutely notes, denunciations of the sensation novel constructed the reader/consumer as a body, experiencing affective states "in physical terms."[42] However, the direction of her work on the social construction of affect and the reader's identification with protagonist or situation leaves little room for the discussion of the desire that drives *and determines* the reading process itself, a desire whose significance may transcend the significance of the content of a particular book in question in favor of the context of its production and cultural consumption – the reputation of its author, the quality and tenor of its reviews, the possibility of interaction with others of its readers. Cvetkovich's focus on affective responses to particular content, while important, leaves unexamined the process by which the reading of that content is socially constructed, how a sensation novel *becomes* a sensation novel – or something else.

The sensation novel, then, is a novel which was believed dangerously and inappropriately to excite its readers, appealing to the "lower" tastes (feeding the lower mouths/openings of the body, which are supposed to be, in the upper- or middle-class woman, closed and impermeable). It is defined in opposition to the discourse of the master-reader/critic, the critical struggle being not to abolish the carnivalesque, as many current critics have apparently assumed, but to reduce it to an object for the consumption of the middle-class gaze, rather than an opportunity for participation and exchange, so that the novel's subversive potential is effectively contained by the discourses of the marketplace which define it as a commodity/spectacle. And it is so defined, precisely within the terms of parallel medico-legal and journalistic discourses.

What novels, then, fit this category? After all, given that any success-ful novel must interest the reader, and that any interesting event might be said to cause a sensation, why is not all literature sensational? And, even if those interesting events are limited to those of a sexual, violent, or criminal nature, many novels not normally considered sensational would fall under this designation. Certainly Hetty's last minute rescue from the gallows in *Adam Bede* is sensational, as are, earlier still, any of the Brontës' books. And of the *Scenes From Clerical Life, Janet's Repentance* is clearly sensational through and through. Why did these authors escape the charge so entirely, and why were Charles Reade and Mrs. Henry Wood sometimes included in this category and sometimes not? The critics who excuse the last mentioned authors generally do so on the grounds of their morally irreproachable message. Yet Braddon gen-erally included the appropriate obeisance to middle-class values; in-deed, Ellen Miller Casey sees it as her worst weakness as an author. Oddly, although both Ouida and Broughton are identified by Mrs. Oliphant as sensational, few other reviewers defined Broughton that way, and Ouida was rarely identified as sensational by reviewers after the 1860s. Ouida and Broughton both dealt with women's passion, often straining or, in Ouida's case, ignoring altogether the bounds of middle-class propriety. Yet Braddon is the most traditionally sensational novel-ist, especially in reference to *Lady Audley's Secret* and *Aurora Floyd*, neither of which refer directly to sexuality. Instead, they portray their female protagonists as aggressive and capable of unexpected, even criminal action. Interestingly, although contemporary critics tended to agree that the sensation novel was founded on incident and abounded in murders, crimes, secrets, etc., in each of these two novels there is only one murder and one secret – and Lady Audley's bigamy is a "secret" which is known to the reader almost from the novel's inception. These aggressive female characters seem to be the real key in defining the novels as sensational, and it is indeed this element that current critics identify as the subversive feminist appeal of these novels.

In addition to blurring the distinction between passive heroine and active villainess, these female texts, like prostitutes, circulate freely across the boundaries between the lower and middle classes. Braddon wrote penny dreadfuls, and at the height of her popularity, republished one as a three-decker for the circulating libraries (*The Trail of the Serpent*). Several critics refer to both Braddon and Ouida as authors who main-tain a following in both the lower and middle classes. In "Concerning the Unknown Public" that is, the penny serials readers estimated at five million people, Thomas Wright identifies the chief readers of these serials as the "young lady" classes (shop girls and the like), a kind of grey area of working women between the servant and middle classes, refuting the often repeated statement that such journals were mainly read by domestic servants and barely literate laborers. This article was published in 1883, and Wright notes that while Braddon was "first favourite" with this readership until "the last few years" and that

One (presumably) favourite novelist of the Known Public there is who holds a place apart in relation to the unknown public. And that novelist is Ouida! ... Their belief in her is not a matter of reason but of faith ... Though it does not appear in penny serials, Ouida's writing is essentially the acme of penny serial style ... The difference between the serials and Ouida's works, though great, is one of degree only, not of kind. The transition from one to the other is easily made, and the writings of the author of *Moths* do the State some service in that they materially help to bridge the gulf between the generally inane fictions of the penny serials and the better classes of fiction.[43]

This was two decades later than the 1860s denunciations of sensationalism, and Wright is an open-minded and favorable reviewer of penny fiction who confesses to reading it himself as a youth. He sees the bridging of the classes as a "service" to the state. But even in the late eighties, this was not a majority or even a common opinion; in fact, even in the nineties, the *Quarterly Review*, *The Edinburgh Review* and *The Nineteenth Century* were bewailing the corruption of the lower classes with "penny trash" and, to the extent that they believed such literature was being read by the middle classes, they denounced the overlap heartily.

In short, we are left with two questions about the sensation novel in the 1860s: why did it spring into being at that time, as many critics argue it did, and why was it labeled in the way it was? The answer to the first question is that it did not. There have always been novels with aggressive heroines, novels with sex, novels with crimes, etc., although they may have taken a particular turn toward the setting of everyday middle-class domesticity at this time, partly because of the "boom" in journalistic information from which the sensation novel took its substance, as Boyle argues. The second answer, I would suggest, is that the qualities of sensation literature mentioned above, which have always been characterized as "trash" literature by gender and class characteristics, collided head-on with the discourses of disease and contagion which they had paralleled for some time. "Sensation" became a thinly veiled literary euphemism for the action of disease upon the body; spurred by economic and social anxieties, women's popular novels became re-presentations of the grotesque social body and critical discourse became the speculum with which to achieve surveillance and containment.

The mid-Victorian period was a time of large contradictions. The balance of the age of equipoise may well have been maintained by the tension of these contradictions. This was an era which saw an increasing fear of the lower classes, and an increasing concern for their well-being. The upper classes resisted contact with the laboring classes and yet mingled with them in the Crystal Palace and other public amusements. Denial of lower bodily function and obsessive interest in sanitary improvements flourished simultaneously. The expanding crinoline both grotesquely exaggerated the lower bodies of women and prevented casual contact by mandating a clearly defined circular space between the wearer and the nearest person or object. The cultural production of this period is profoundly evocative of the interrelationship of this contradiction in several discursive fields. Genre arises out of particular confluences of discourses emerging out of certain historical conditions; in this case, imperial and domestic economic and sanitary concerns combined with public and critical response to literature to produce the category "sensation." Although in the 1870s and 1880s the category continued to be used, it was restricted to include principally the domestic crime melodrama, whereas in the early 1860s, the category was often used as an indiscriminate label for popular literature, usually by women, that seemed in any way transgressive. By the mid-seventies, the sensation genre was redefined with more specificity, and other sub-genres that previously were lumped in with it gained their own identities and were each targeted for critical surveillance by different issues (class, sexual transgression), which yet contained the trace of the ineradicable connection of those issues in the permeability of the body.

## GENERIC "TRANSITION"

Ouida provides us with an interesting example of this transition. We have said that Ouida was, at one time, considered sensational, yet later this gives way to her placement in the slightly less uncertain and shifting category of the novelist of high life. Indeed Ouida's early novels included a little of everything: adventure, romance, intrigue, and sentiment, just as her later novels privileged a mixture of sentimentalism and political critique similar to Dickens, although without his humor. However, her wildly successful early novels, including *Strathmore* and *Under Two Flags*, were notable for their improbable aristocratic heroes, heroines, villains, and villainesses living large with an opulence and an utter disregard for middle-class values as unlikely as their Herculean strength and their fierce adherence to an aristocratic code of Ouida's own manufacture. Her characters are sexually active, and the males (good, bad, or indifferent) and the villainous females are adulterous and promiscuous as well.

From the very beginning, critics showed at least equal concern with Ouida's representation of the upper classes as with her dubious morality. 1860s reviews were amusedly patronizing, pointing out the flaws and errors in her already thoroughly unbelievable characters, or they were furious with her attribution of amorality to the aristocracy. In 1873, Vincent E. H. Murray somewhat contradictorily denounces Ouida's novels for their lack of fidelity to social reality and then states that their principal danger is that they both reflect and encourage a licentiousness that is a social truth. For Murray, they are dangerous precisely because they are read, not by "those whom it is customary to call 'the people'. . . These books are issued by one of the first houses in the trade; they are written for and read by society." Ouida's novels, Murray informs his readers:

throw an evil light on the social corruption of which they are an exhalation . . . Precisely as certain diseased conditions of the body give rise to a craving after unnatural food, so do certain morbid conditions of the mind produce an appetite for literary food which a sound mental organization would reject . . . we believe further that the society which reads and encourages such literature is a "whited sepulchre" which, if it be not speedily cleansed by the joint effort of pure men and women, will breed a pestilence so foul as to poison the very life-blood of our nation.[44]

Murray's denunciation of Ouida uses the combination of offal and food imagery typical of the critical treatment of sensation literature ("unnatural appetite"), although he does not classify her novels specifically in this way. It shifts, though, at the end (this is, by the way, the conclusion of the article) to incorporate contemporary imagery from another area of the sanitary crusade – that of the graveyard. Articles abounded on inadequately interred bodies that bred pestilence, church walls that oozed pus, and other interesting images. By shifting from the image of drugged or adulterated (unnaturally stimulating) food to the parallel threat of the diseased cadaver, Murray identifies Ouida's readers as subhuman, literally ghoulish, and a threat to an entire nation of "pure" men and women who must prevail in purging their society of its degenerates.

This is strong "medicine" indeed, but Murray addresses his directive to a class/body which shall purge/medicate itself. He is quite clear on the belief that this is a problem internal to one, classed readership, which is to be handled within that social body. Yet not all reviewers were as comfortable with Ouida's supposed containment within middle-class markets. By the late seventies, as Ouida's novels grew less admiring of her own creations and more censorious of their behaviors, some critics began to see real danger in her portrayal of a decadent aristocracy. Of Ouida's novels, *Blackwood's* says:

The mischief they must answer for is likely to survive the unnatural excitement and the extreme absurdity which were their redeeming virtues... Stories written for the gratification of the ordinary subscribers to Mr. Mudie, are passed on in due course to be devoured by the milliners' apprentices and lawyers' clerks. There seems no reason why the young lady who admires her *beauté du diable* daily in the looking-glass should not make the acquaintance of one of these noblemen... Whether she may have to make away with him afterwards or no is a question she may postpone for the present... These stories are circulated or imitated in the columns of the "penny dreadfuls" [and are dangerous like] the demagogues who get a living by stirring strife between classes.[45]

In the passage above, we see that the danger is not only that the lower-class woman may prostitute herself or be seduced through her vain ambition, but that she shall become murderous if she does infiltrate that higher class. There is the underlying threat of revolution and sexual transgression in that "unnatural excitement." The critic moves on to make this connection explicit, imagining a working-class reader coming to his own conclusions after reading stories like Ouida's:

You see that they are not only effete but rotten to the core; they batten on the sweat and blood of the people. Depend on it, the only things to agitate for are abolition and confiscation; and if we don't send these curled heads of theirs to the guillotine, by – , Sir, they may be grateful to the clemency of the people![46]

Confusingly, in this 1879 review, Ouida's work is referred to both as "sensational" and as "novels of society that are as frivolous [as sensation] though less harmless."[47] The distinction is already being made between the two genres, but they are clearly contingent, perhaps even overlapping.

Why the emphasis on class tensions is foregrounded in this period is uncertain. Certainly such tensions always existed, but were less visibly in evidence in the late 1870s than they had been in the Reform Bill period of the late 1860s. On the other hand, we do see an emerging tendency toward sustained surveillance of class boundaries at this time; in the absence of the threats of continental revolutionary activity and Reform Bill riots which had plagued Britain a few decades earlier, and which called for event-specific action, we see the emergence of the detective division of the metropolitan police, partly under the impetus of Fenian activity.[48] The preventive visibility of the street patrolman and the definition of the police's role as "keeping order" on the streets evolved into one which privileged clandestine surveillance and more active covert operations as well. S. J. Davies also notes that a "basic change took place in policing in the 1870s. This was the final shift away from preventative policing to detection."[49] Whether this is seen as a response to the political climate, as Phillip Thurmond Smith argues, or as an outgrowth of the consolidation of wealth during the prosperous seventies, it is clearly significant in terms of class attitudes. Smith also notes, in an unrelated passage, that before the 1880s property offenses (theft, etc.) tended to be more prevalent in times of economic depression, whereas after the 1880s, the opposite was true – more property crimes occurred in periods of economic strength,[50] which would also seem to indicate a difference in class relations. Again, the causes are less important to this argument than the fact that such a change occurred. The "criminal" or "deviant" classes – which were discursively aligned with the so-called "dangerous classes" of the 1840s, that is the impoverished, the casual laborer, etc. – were constructed as the object of a discourse of surveillance in much the same way that Foucault identifies sexuality as being constructed. Like the discourse of sexuality, this, too, offers opportunities for intervention, and those opportunities existed in the classed geographical spaces between the criminal and the upper classes whom the police protected (the protection of other members of the underclass being a sort of by-product of this action): "The heaviest concentrations of police seem to have been in those 'border' neighborhoods that separated rich and poor areas... There was more than a little truth to the police axiom 'You guard St. James by watching St. Giles.'"[51] Critics were equally vigilant in their surveillance of the classed borders of fiction; the lower orders were ever likely to be incited to some desperate deed by fiction that either presented the upper classes as too accessible (to the sexuality of the lower-class female) or as physically or morally vulnerable to the lower classes (through the infiltration of false heirs, blackmailing lower-class witnesses to upper-class crime, or direct revolutionary action). The "bridges" that Ouida was building between classes of readers not only threatened to breach those borders, but also offered the uncomfortable possibility of the object of surveillance "looking back" by taking such an intent interest in Ouida's fictive upper tenth. If such promiscuous reading habits were not bad enough, there was also the actual content of the novels – the characters and their actions. In Ouida's early work the successful border-crossers are of two types: the lower-class woman who becomes a courtesan and ensnares a noble, but erring man of "race" (the nobility), or the artist, who alone is allowed to transcend the restraints of class and gender through creative genius. (Although not infrequently, the penniless peasant artist is also discovered to be a displaced scion of "race.") Conversely, her aristocratic women occasionally succumb to the influence of less than blue blood in their family trees and degenerate to the vulgar. The men, however, never do; heroes and villains alike take lower-class mistresses, marry out of season, and misbehave themselves in a host of other lighthearted ways, and yet even the villains remain ineffably noble in their fastidious villainy. Ouida's outrageously bald exploitation of the double standard for sexual conduct drew shocked condemnation, as did her portrayal of aristocratic women taking lovers and living lives of pleasure, especially since, no matter how much she condemns these women, they remain among her more lively and appealing female characters. In this way, she both exposes the upper classes to criticism for their sexual morals and seals them off from such criticism (they are members of "The Order"; they are not comparable to or understandable by other mere mortals). In the troubled 1860s, when upper-class Britons were being circumspect with their displays of wealth, Ouida set her characters in absurdly lavish scenes of conspicuous display. Interestingly, in her later novels, although she never quite loses her sense of the mystical *je ne sais quoi* of the aristocracy, she turns to savage denunciation of the morals of the wealthy and takes up the cause of the abused peasantry in Italy, exchanging, in the words of one *Spectator* critic, "the role of an Ovid for that of a Juvenal."[52] Regardless of this critique, though, Ouida never loses sight of the need to preserve class distinctions. Her virtuous peasantry are always those who keep their place, and social ambition in the lower classes is always criminal. The same Ouida who defended the peasants came out vigorously against socialism, fighting for the rights of the wealthy to their property even as she died of starvation. She repudiated her own British, middle-class roots and claimed a continental, aristocratic identity (in fact, she often dressed as her characters, apparently assuming their roles for months at a time).

Her radicalism was aesthetic; beauty, and the artist's capacity to create it, was the one characteristic that could transcend class and national boundaries, conferring natural aristocracy on anyone. Ouida refused any identification with commercialism. She saw herself as an artist, constitutionally above such petty concerns, and let her mother handle the bills. In contrast to Braddon, who saw herself as a professional businesswoman attempting to supply a demand, and who accepted criticism on those terms, Ouida's self-mystifying celebrity refused to acknowledge the critics' charges of crass commercialism, aligning herself instead with the icon of artist-as-bard, dispensing truth through art. Her residence on the continent probably also lent itself to glamorous interpretation; it certainly made it harder for her critics to attack her personally in the absence of a concrete presence in England. Although it is not clear that her imitators in this genre presented the same persona, their identification of themselves as writing from within the wealthy aristocratic milieu (and implicit generic identification with Ouida herself) may have communicated, particularly to the penny audiences, a disregard for the commercial aspect of publishing. This may have made the truth-claims of the genre seem more potent for evil to the watchful critics, who wished to disassociate it from privileged literary forms and realign it within the discourse of the popular, which was inextricably tied to the image of the novel as commercial article of (domestic) manufacture.

Also in contrast to Braddon, who attempted to control critical discourse from within by editing her own journals and contributing reviews like everyone else, Ouida refused to play by the rules, responding directly and imperiously to her critics rather than using the usual circuitous countermove. Ouida, in other words, aggressively claimed the space of high culture while exploiting the marketability of the popular; her "very fine and nasty books" (Oliphant) were critically deported from that high-cultural space by force, and under protest from the author, and it is not clear to what extent the critics' opinion was the one that prevailed among Ouida's multiple readerships. At the end of the century, appropriate tribute to Ouida may be found in the gorgeous but short-lived *Yellow Book*. G. S. Street takes her on her own terms, very appealing to the decadents:

I acquit myself of impertinence in stating what I find to like and to respect in the novels of Ouida. For many years, with many thousands of readers they have been popular, I know. But ever since I began to read reviews, to learn from the most reputable authorities what I should admire or avoid, I have found them mentioned with simple merriment or a frankly contemptuous patronage. One had, now and then in boyhood, vague ideas of being cultivated, vague aspirations towards superiority: I thought, for my part, that of the many insuperable obstacles in the way of this goal, this contempt of Ouida's novels was one of the most obvious ... [yet] the two qualities, I think, which underlie the best of Ouida's work, and which must have always saved it from commonness, are a genuine and passionate love of beauty, as she conceives it, and a genuine and passionate hatred of injustice and oppression.[53]

Beauty of medium and quality of message – these are the characteristics of high art. In view of these pretensions, it was doubly intolerable that Ouida should appeal so persistently to the *hoi polloi*.

Additionally, most novels of high life, especially as they appeared in penny and sixpenny numbers, were either love stories or, less frequently, crime stories. Yet, although Ouida's novels often contained a love-interest, they frequently focused on adventure; in her best-selling *Under Two Flags*, her focus directly recalls the adventure novels of Dumas *père*, as she tells of the triumphs and travails of a British aristocrat displaced into the French foreign legion in Africa. Her lead characters in these early stories are always male, and she follows them where no lady should have dared go. To facilitate realism in this process, Ouida gave all-male parties for members of the Guards, at which her guests were required to smoke cigars, in the belief that they would speak freely in front of her if they were smoking. In regard to her highly irregular conduct, Ouida's defense was that she was an artist, and, as an artist, transcended her sex. Her mother, who chaperoned at such gatherings, helped Ouida in her note-taking, out of which she was able to create the slang and sporting references that gave her characters distinctiveness, if not complete credibility.

Ouida flouted gender conventions openly, both in her "personal" (public) life and her writing, and the critical countermeasure categorized her, first as a sensationalist, then as the chief example of another existing genre (the romance of high life, descended directly from *Pamela* and *Clarissa*) which represented only one facet of the stories she was actually writing. In fact, her writing is much closer to what we refer to today as society novels, by Danielle Steele or Harold Robbins, blending sex, romance, political and economic intrigue with elements of mystery and adventure – what John G. Cawelti identifies as social melodrama.[54] She violates the boundaries of the romance of high life in that love is not necessarily the dominant force in the story, she often focuses on action in preference to character, and even when love is a key feature, the good heroine often fails to get the hero (as in *Two Little Wooden Shoes* or *Folle-Farine*, for example).

Ouida's work is quite different from Braddon's or Broughton's, in that the setting is displaced from the middle-class urban or suburban domesticity characteristic of the latter two authors. Perhaps because of this, Ouida had no trouble gaining entry to the circulating library market, despite her characters' explicit improprieties. (Ironically, it would be the public libraries at the turn of the century, who were more free from market pressures than the private ones, who would fail to stock Ouida, probably on moral grounds. Simon Eliot found that fully one-third of public libraries excluded Ouida, although her sales were still very strong.) These novels could never be accused of re-presenting the middle classes to themselves; they were clearly about the fatal attraction of the Other. In all Ouida's range of characters, from the fabulously wealthy to the starving Breton peasant, the middle classes and the urban poor are conspicuously absent. Even Britain itself rarely appears and then is scarcely recognizable. Indeed, the opposite of the sensation stories of Braddon and Wood is not, as is usually stated, the realist novel; it is the novel of high life by Ouida.

If the sensation novel may be seen as a structuring container for anxieties focused on the domestic, perhaps the novel of high life was indeed a sort of adventure story for women, in which the reader could vicariously experience the joys of being, in a couple of senses, an adventuress, while comfortable in the knowledge that it was acceptable to enjoy this sort of behavior, because it belonged to a different world with different standards – and one that was in no danger of intruding on domestic reality. Ouida's evil adulteresses are rarely punished, as sensation villainesses always are, while the "good" women are as often sublimely martyred as rewarded. Sensation stories provoked "horripilation" because they were stories about the dark side of real life; Ouida's stories, no matter how heartrending, always had the glow of fantasy. Their radical component was the way they structured the reader's interest around class tensions, evoking envy, admiration, disgust, and even hatred by turns.

Rhoda Broughton is best known as a writer of romances, usually concentrating on the love-interest of a middle-class woman. The stories are told in a lively and humorous style, with much *badinage*; the plots are simple and the stories usually focus on the development of the primary character. Whereas Braddon and Ouida may employ a whole unpredictable range of plots, characters, and motivations, often multiple, Broughton's choices were more limited. Although more unpredictable than today's Harlequin-style romance (Broughton's did not always end happily), there is an essential similarity of concerns at some level of the plot (although these concerns may be only a minor focus at the thematic level): a woman is in love with a man; there is some obstacle to their union; a final resolution takes place. Broughton's stories were always set in the world she knew – the world of middle- to upper-middle class domestic life, and her main characters were conventional young women who sometimes lapsed into unconventional behavior. Broughton's pages are conspicuously devoid of the swashbuckling aristocrats of Ouida or the calculating criminals of Braddon, and the most devastating secrets her characters conceal are unhappy or illicit past love-interests.

Broughton's initial generic "placement" was firmly in the sensation genre, apparently because of her female characters' rather frank acknowledgment of desire and physical stimulation. Her work, however, shows none of the other trademarks – secret marriages, changes of identity, or class slippage – that show up so abundantly in Wilkie Collins or Braddon. A reader today would have some initial difficulty determining how Broughton came to be placed in that category at all. I would argue, however, that Broughton's work is consistent in that first decade with one overriding concern shared with other sensation novels – that its "feminine" nature as romance written by a woman author and its focus on the bodies of young women characters allow readers to construct those bodies as vehicles for the exploration of desires and anxieties regarding class, gender, and national identity expressible in terms of contagion. After the anxious 1860s, Broughton was redefined as a writer of love stories, a move which elided the social content of her novels from critical commentary, even though many of her later novels were organized around specific social questions.

Broughton's especial trademark was the use of the third person present tense in her narratives, a feature that was much imitated by her followers. Critics who admired her wrote of the "lightness and vivacity" of her touch and her charming if rather wayward female characters. Those who disliked her found her stories "coarse," largely because her heroines confessed to passionate feelings for men, and often came close to what the *Temple Bar* called "the abyss."[55] *Blackwood's* elaborates:

Now it is no knight of romance riding down the forest glades, ready for the defence and succour of all the oppressed, for whom the dreaming maiden waits.

She waits now for flesh and muscles, for strong arms that seize her, and warm breath that thrills her through, and a host of other physical attractions, which she indicates to the world with a charming frankness ... were the sketch made from the man's point of view, its openness would at least be less repulsive. The peculiarity of it in England is, that it is oftenest made from the woman's side – that it is women who describe these sensuous raptures – that this intense appreciation of flesh and blood, this eagerness of physical sensation, is represented as the natural sentiment of English girls, and is offered to them not only as the portrait of their own state of mind, but as their amusement and mental food.[56]

Curiously, the point that the critic returns to over and over in this article is that such representations are not unusual, but frequent, that they have been adopted rather than denied by the classes whom they supposedly represent (i.e., middle-class women readers), and that they are yet utterly untrue. (Oliphant is adamant on this point, adducing support from her own knowledge of the middle class to assert that this is so.) The critic's concern is not merely with the misrepresentation of English-women to Englishwomen, however; the real issue is that other nations, most notably the French, will consider Broughton's work representative of the best in English fiction: "We confess to having felt a sense of injury in our national pride when our solemn contemporary, the 'Revue des Deux Mondes,' held up in one of its recent numbers the names of Miss Annie Thomas [Broughton] and Mr. Edmund Yates to the admiration of the world as representative novelists of England."[57]

Here we see, once again, the reference to books as food, but perhaps more importantly, the notion of fiction as something that shapes the nation through its representation of the nation to itself and to others; clearly, a woman's fiction that does not reflect reality has the power to corrupt that reality, creating a new and worse one, especially through women readers – the seduction of the wife and betrayal of the family patriarch is equal to the traducing of the state:

It is a shame to women so to write; and it is a shame to the women who read ... Women's rights and women's duties have had enough discussion ... we have most of us made merry over the Dr Marys and Dr Elizabeths [*sic*]; but yet a woman has one duty of invaluable importance to her country and her race which cannot be over-estimated – and that is the duty of being pure. There is perhaps nothing of such vital consequence to a nation ... There can be no possible doubt that the wickedness of man is less ruinous, less disastrous to the world in general, than the wickedness of women.[58]

It is clearly the sexual purity of Englishwomen with which the critic is concerned, that the representation of sexual activity in the text will be "ingested" (as contaminated food) and, like a germ, reproduce itself within the reader, who will in turn reproduce the text as an "illegitimate" national reality. The metaphor of reading as sexual activity is not overt here, but the critic's sense that such texts would be less offensive if written by men strongly suggests that sexual activity represented to women by women is a dangerous liaison indeed. A subsequent comparison to the fall of Rome (which Oliphant, somewhat inexplicably, blames on the impurity of Roman women) "cinches" the connection – imperialism depends on the impermeability of women's minds and bodies to subversive sexual forces, on their attraction to the "wholesome" rather than the "hectic", sexual fever being comparable to that caused by contagion.[59]

Broughton, of course, never allows her women to go over the edge of that "abyss"; they die, realize their errors, become social workers, or marry the "right" man who has been patiently waiting in the sidelines for the demise of the more glamorous but morally inappropriate suitor. Always, finally, traditional values are reaffirmed. Yet, the refusal or interrogation of those values which takes place in the unfolding of the story leaves its trace, even if the heroine herself is brought to a problematic acceptance. Broughton uses current events and popular discourse to highlight her thematic concerns; in *Not Wisely But Too Well*, she uses the current concern with fever and sanitation to underline her treatment of Kate's sexuality, and in *A Beginner*, the publishing market itself becomes a vehicle for the implication of the reader in the suppression of women's creativity in the very consumption of the commodity of women's writing.

# CHAPTER 3

# M. E. Braddon: sensational realism

M. E. Braddon (1835–1915), certainly one of the most prolific authors and editors of the period, is central to any understanding of the Victorian novel. Although she came to the middle-class public's attention with *Lady Audley's Secret* and *Aurora Floyd* in 1862, in fact she had been writing for six years. Braddon's production encompasses over seventy novels, many short stories, plays, essays, and the editorship of several journals, most notably *Belgravia* and *The Mistletoe Bough*.

Braddon's understanding of the book trade in which and by which she lived is clear-eyed, canny, and comprehensive. Unlike Rhoda Broughton, who had a comfortable social position independent of her literary earnings, Braddon supported herself, her family, and her lover's family by her literary activities. After being "typecast" as The Sensation Novelist after her early two bestsellers – a designation which itself is open to inquiry – Braddon found herself in active competition with the public and critical construction of her and her early work for control of the generic designation and market placement of her many other novels. In the sensation novel, the woman's body is clearly foregrounded. However, in her later novels of any genre, Braddon's constant rewriting of her own position in the marketplace and use of multiple genres to manipulate her placement brings her inevitably back to the woman's body as a site of reading and generic designation. Her reading of the place of the woman's body, as reader, author, and text, forms the substance of her rewriting of *Madame Bovary*, *The Doctor's Wife*, in which she comments on the place of literature, literary genres, the market, and reading practices.

In fact, Braddon produced in many genres, most deliberately in sensation/melodrama (especially after *Lady Audley's Secret* and *Aurora Floyd* were so successful under that designation) and in the realist tradition, which Braddon viewed as the "high" culture novel, in com-

mon with the critical view emerging at that time. (She also wrote ghost
stories, which are beginning to garner a fair amount of attention now, as
the Victorian short story and gothic both receive the attention due
them.) Realism comes to be understood as a genre which constructs
itself on the basis of difference from the popular, and thus, as a genre
which relies on framing the body in more careful, more nuanced and
less spec(tac)ular ways.

Braddon, like Charles Dickens, is less interested in character *per se*
than in social situations, although she comes to have more interest in
character and interiority in her later works. Her work is carefully
plotted, and plot, rather than character, tends to motivate the action
and support the story. Braddon's exploitation of the trope of woman's
body as text and text as body within her novels as part of an ongoing
dialogue with the critical commentary surrounding popular fiction
blurs, while seeming to reinforce, the boundaries between commodity,
artistic statement and critical policing. The epic task is always closure of
the woman's body, whose openness creates danger for those around her
and, if she is a "good" character, for her as well. Contradicting,
reinforcing, or subverting that narrative line run other tales, other
genres embedded in the same text, sometimes the same flesh: Lady
Audley's body is contained, but the social circumstances which produce
her are not controlled – rather the opposite. Protean, Braddon as editor,
critic, artist, and purveyor of highly successful commodities vanishes
behind and manipulates her various personae in public life and their
spokescharacters within her texts to create and maintain a space in
which she attempts to direct reading practices.

## LADY AUDLEY'S SECRET[1]

*Lady Audley's Secret* is often accused of or credited with laying the foundation for the sensation novel, and yet the text undermines that foundation
at the same moment. Lady Audley, her secret, and her deeds form the
sensational story that mark the novel's genre, yet the forced growth of
Robert Audley and the masculinization of his character constitute an
equal and complementary counter-narrative to Lady Audley's tale,
which itself subverts the "return to order" which marks the sensation
genre and relocates the source of sensation from the disordered and
alien individual female body to the male social body of the patriarchal
socio-legal institutions. These elements coexist in the text, yet only the

former structure was "selected" by readers as a generic property; critics expressed outrage over the portrayal of the alienated woman and entirely missed the much more subversive portrait of alienated patriarchy. Robert Audley, the Temple Bar lawyer who has never submitted a brief, Lieutenant Maldon, who sells his daughter to the highest bidder and drinks the proceeds, George Talboys, who abandons his wife and baby son, and even Sir Michael Audley, whose love-"fever" drives him to take a wife who admittedly does not love him – these are the aristocratic and generally privileged men who set the events of the story in motion. Robert Audley finally rouses himself from his habitual lethargy to pursue the "madwoman" and himself becomes mad in the process. This madness is "healed" when he takes as a wife Clara, George's sister. The mad wife is replaced by the mad husband, whose madness is more acceptable to society, but it is made perfectly clear that the social order is both artificial and a mere mask for the chaos or "madness" beneath. Thus the story is less one of Lady Audley's disguised madness (as Dr. Mosgrave says, "There is no madness in anything she has done" [*Lady Audley's Secret*, p. 377]), than one of Robert Audley's recognition of his own insanity and of the mad nature of his society, and of his subsequent informed choice to remain complicit in that madness and to become active in supporting it.

Throughout the novel, Braddon offers observations on the nature of insanity. Although she gives the reader current medical and scientific information about madness through the voice of Lady Audley, she reserves comments regarding the ubiquitous nature of madness to her own narrative voice, linking madness and violence specifically to calm, placid surfaces and idealized images:

We hear every day of murders committed in the country. Brutal and treacherous murders; slow, protracted agonies from poisons administered by some kindred hand; sudden and violent deaths by cruel blows, inflicted with a stake cut from some spreading oak, whose very shadow promised – peace. In the county of which I write, I have been shown a meadow in which, on a quiet summer Sunday evening, a young farmer had murdered the girl who loved and trusted him; and yet even now, with the stain of that foul deed upon it, the aspect of the spot is – peace. No crime has ever been committed in the worst rookeries about Seven Dials that has not been also done in the face of that sweet rustic calm which still, in spite of all, we look on with a tender, half-mournful yearning, and associate with – peace. (p. 54)

Here is clearly one characteristic of sensation literature – the location of crime and intrigue in the idealized domestic setting. The explosion of distinctions between the "degenerate" urban and "idyllic" rural land-scape, however, and explicit association of evil with male violence against women are not as often remarked, yet Braddon repeatedly refers to them, as when Phoebe explains that she must marry Luke because she is afraid that he will kill her otherwise (p. 107).

When Robert Audley begins to have hallucinations, immediately after incarcerating Lady Audley, Braddon speaks directly again: "Do not laugh at poor Robert... There is nothing so delicate, so fragile, as that invisible balance upon which the mind is always trembling. Mad today and sane tomorrow... Who has not been, or is not to be, mad in some lonely hour of life? Who is quite safe from the trembling of the balance?" (p. 404). At the very point at which the madness is contained, the Lady locked away forever (in "France", amusingly enough, surgi-cally excised from the "clean and proper" body of England), Braddon speaks directly to shatter that containment, reminding us that not only is madness ubiquitous, but that the very man who judges Lady Audley is himself mad, placing him and the reader and the Lady in the same category, "trembling on the balance."

As Robert Audley journeys toward knowledge, and suspects that the aunt with whom he has fallen in love is a murderess, like Hamlet he comes both to denounce women and to associate them with evil:

The Eastern potentate who declared that women were at the bottom of all mischief should have gone a little further and seen why it is so. It is because women are *never lazy*. They are Semiramides, and Cleopatras, and Joan of Arcs, Queen Elizabeths, and Catherine the Seconds, and they riot in battle, and murder, and clamour, and desperation... To call them the weaker sex is to utter a hideous mockery... I hate women. (p. 207)

The more he misses George, and is attracted to George's lookalike sister Clara, the more he rails against women in general. One irony in his growing animosity toward women is that it is his own femininity that he is rejecting, and must reject, in order to take on the active masculine role as judge of Lady Audley, head of household, husband, etc. To become a fit husband, he must come to associate femininity in an active state with evil, since women are to be passive and let men act out social ambitions. Thus, it is through Clara Talboys' strength that Robert pursues Lady Audley; her strength is precisely that she can drive a man to do what she wants to do while she remains ostensibly passive under the rule of a dictatorial father. For Robert, women are evil when they have mascu-line ambitions and take on masculine roles; paradoxically, it is precisely because he does not have these characteristics that he finds them hateful. Yet the women who really do evil in *Lady Audley's Secret* – Lady Audley and Phoebe – do not do so out of a desire for leadership, but out of a desire to avoid the pain inflicted by an active masculine element (Lieutenant Maldon, Luke) and to seek passive comfort in the socially and financially secure role of wife. Thus, contrary to Robert's perception, Lady Audley's story shows that women are most evil when they conform to social expectations – a lesson which Robert must deny if he is to take his place as an active male member of the ruling class. By the end of the novel, he has successfully done both.

Thus, the novel simultaneously presents and validates two contradictory points of view, in two complementary storylines: the coming of age and social integration of Robert Audley, a traditional high-culture theme, and the decline and fall of the scheming adventuress, a popular culture melodrama. This second plot exceeds the bounds of the usual "adventuress" narrative in that the lady speaks for herself, and in that she does not present herself wholly as a villainess. Together, these two narratives create a dramatic tension born of the ideological contradictions in their mutually exclusive portrayals of feminine evil, a third rhetorical space in which the coherence of the oppositions which drive either of the first two narratives unravel into incoherence, the madness which is finally located and at least superficially contained in the imprisoned bodies of the Maldon women.

Critics have often noted the detective plot in *Lady Audley's Secret*, setting up the opposition between Robert and the Lady as detective and arch-criminal. There are, however, important distinctions between Robert and the traditional detective. The detective is usually an outsider, who represents an objective principle of justice and is unwavering in his quest. Perhaps because of this quality, he is usually a static character, who does not change or learn in the process of his pursuit, and to the extent that he does, such growth is subordinated to the reader's interest in the unfolding of the mystery which is the object of his detection. He uses his will and his reason to pursue his cause. In *Lady Audley's Secret*, however, the reader knows almost from the beginning the general solution to the mystery, if not the details, and Robert Audley changes and grows considerably in the course of the novel; in fact, Robert's growth is one of its primary foci. He is motivated by a personal interest and often questions both the means and the ends of his detecting. Finally, his detection is based on chance and what he calls "Providence" and what Braddon frankly labels monomania.

If we ignore the Lady Audley storyline momentarily, and consider only the Robert Audley storyline, the pattern of the coming-of-age story appears clear. Braddon uses the traditional model of *The Odyssey*, first referring to Odysseus explicitly to set the stage, and then interpreting the story loosely to fit her needs, combining Telemachus' character with Odysseus' journey. A young male character on the brink of manhood has not yet accepted adult responsibilities. He is called a barrister, yet has never submitted a brief. He prefers the company of his male schoolfriends to women, and regards marriage with consternation. He is content to "play" and let others manage the serious business of life. Into this Edenic peace comes conflict. The boy must take adult responsibilities, must act and make decisions. The hero's descent into hell is represented, as it often is in modern literature, by a crisis of values, an episode of madness. At the story's end he has withstood the temptations of the mermaid, come through the dark night of the soul, rescued the patriarch of his family, and returned home to take his own place as husband, father, and powerful leader of the community (distinguished by his successful prosecution of a breach of promise case – a typical bit of Braddon irony). In short, Robert Audley is a Telemachus of recognizable form, if diminutive proportions, faithful himself to the social order and ready to punish those who stray from the code.

Braddon makes the Odyssey comparison early in the story. George Talboys' first description of his wife to Robert describes her playing a guitar and singing: "She's for all the world like one of those what's-its-names, who got poor old Ulysses in trouble" (p. 35). Throughout the novel, Lady Audley is associated with the ocean, and we are informed that George first met her at the end of a pier (p. 247). It is perhaps not coincidental that she pushes him into a well (a pocket-version of the ocean which he crosses to find her), which he survives largely because there is no water in it. Robert dreams of Audley Court "threatened by the rapid rising of a boisterous sea ... the sleeper saw a pale, starry face looking out of the silvery foam, and knew that it was my lady, transformed into a mermaid, beckoning his uncle to destruction" (p. 246). Although mermaids are not unique to *The Odyssey*, the initial comparison recalls their function specifically as impediments to the hero's journey. (For more on literary and artistic manifestations of the mermaid in Victorian and *fin-de-siècle* culture, see Bram Dijkstra's *Idols of Perversity*.)

However, Robert Audley's story does not stand alone; it runs alongside the story of the "syren" he must overcome. Braddon's radical departure from tradition is not in presenting the evil mermaid, but in giving her a voice which does not only sing sweet lies for men but tells them unpleasant truths. Lady Audley's secret is that evil does not originate in the mermaids or the Clytemnestras, but in the system of representation which makes mermaids and Clytemnestras out of the Melanthos who are pretty enough to attract male attention and unfortunate enough to have no other source of security. (It is worth noting that Braddon's rereading of *The Odyssey* occurs in the context of other Victorian rereadings, most notably Tennyson's 1842 poem. While most readers note Tennyson's construction of Ulysses as imperial hero, it is often forgotten that this Ulysses is Dante's, not Homer's, and is speaking in the moment of his damnation, that is, specifically, the moment of his betrayal of divinely ordained domestic responsibility in favor of the heroic role.)

When women like Lucy Audley are not singing and amusing men, however, they speak truths that destroy the idyllic representations of rural feminine beauty and domestic tranquillity as surely as Braddon's murder in a quiet meadow does. When Lady Audley is exposed, she speaks of her childhood:

'I was not happy, for the woman who had charge of me was a disagreeable woman ... who was irregularly paid; and who vented her rage upon me when my father was behindhand in remitting her money ... at a very early age I found out what it was to be poor' ... He [Sir Michael] sat silent ... he ... had believed ... as he had believed in the Gospel ... a very brief story of an early orphanage, and a long quiet, colourless youth spent in the conventual seclusion of an English boarding school. (*Lady Audley's Secret*, p. 349)

Her story is most horrifying because it violates a previous narrative which is consonant with the ideal of the unsullied woman. Lady Audley goes on to discuss her fear of poverty and understanding of "what every schoolgirl knows" but none discusses – that her future will depend on a good marriage. The institution of marriage is exposed as founded on the helplessness and fear of women, rather than on love. In another scene, Phoebe is frank with Lady Audley about her own motivations for marrying: "I daren't refuse to marry him. ... When he was a boy he was always violent and revengeful. I saw him once take up that very knife in a quarrel with his mother. I tell you, my lady, I must marry him" (p. 107). Throughout the novel, women express a clear understanding of the relations of power which underlie cultural representations while male characters prefer the "pretty stories" themselves. The contrast is neatly set up in the second chapter of the novel, "On Board the Argus." George and a "pale governess" are discussing their reasons for returning to England, and the governess explains that she has worked for fifteen years in Australia to save up enough money for her marriage to her English fiancé, who has not done well financially. She fears, however, that he may have died, or that his feelings might have changed, or even that he may marry her only for her savings. George is horrified, because, although he had abandoned his wife and never written her, these possibilities had never occurred to him. With great pride, he explains to the governess that he has worked for three and a half years to make his fortune, and finally struck gold. "How brave you were!" she responds (p. 22). Although Braddon presents the governess as sincere in her admiration, surely the reader must sense a rich irony in the disparity between the woman's fifteen years of toil and realistic assessment of the possibility of change in her fiancé, whom she recognizes as a subjectivity distinct from her own, and George's blithely unconscious self-aggrand-izement and conflation of his wife's subjectivity with his two dimen-sional image of her. The male's "coming of age" therefore, is based on his ability not only to assume the masculine role of hero in the epic narrative that patriarchy approves, but to enforce the subordination of other voices and other subjectivities to their supporting roles in that same narrative. If Melantho's had been the narrative voice of *The Odyssey*, how differently might the story have been told!

It is, of course, sexual attraction which brings the two storylines together; first, Sir Michael's attraction to Lucy and later his nephew's. Characteristically, sexual passion is defined as a "fever," and in Lady Audley's case, great care is taken to distinguish this diseased attraction from a more ordinary, healthy love:

What had been his (Michael Audley's) love for his first wife but a poor, pitiful, smouldering spark, too dull to be extinguished, too feeble to burn? But *this* was love – this fever, this longing, this restless, uncertain, miserable hesitation; this sick hatred of his white beard; this frenzied wish to be young again... Sir Michael Audley had fallen ill of the terrible fever called love. (p. 7)

Lucy, source and object of this affliction, lives as the governess to the local surgeon's children. In the governess position many oppositions meet: family and not-family, lady and working woman, mother-figure and domestic servant. In Lucy's case, the undomesticated woman is naturalized within a domestic setting; thus, her true nature is disguised and she is enabled to make contact with "good society" like Sir Michael.

The source of disease is disguised within the surgeon's home, the very hearth of health. This disease is infectious; Sir Michael

> wondered why Robert failed to take the fever from the first breath of contagion that blew towards him. He forgot that there are men who go their ways unscathed amidst legions of lovely and generous women, to succumb at last before some harsh-featured virago, who knows the secret of that only philter which can intoxicate him and bewitch him ... He forgot that love, which is a madness, and a scourge, and a fever, and a delusion, and a snare, is also a mystery, and very imperfectly understood by everyone except the individual sufferer who writhes under its tortures ... who lies awake at night until he loathes his comfortable pillow and tumbles his sheets into two twisted rags of linen in his agonies, as if he were a prisoner and wanted to wind them into impromptu ropes ... He ignored all those infinitesimal differences in nature which make the wholesome food of one man the deadly poison of another. (p. 332)

In this interesting series of images, we move from the disease metaphor, to a food-consumption image (the philter, the "wholesome food") to a more specifically sexual image of nocturnal crisis. Material is taken into the body, initiating an illness that cannot be healed without releasing it from the body, in this case a desire for sexual fulfillment that can only be "healed" by ejaculation into the body of the Other. Despite Sir Michael's bemusement, however, Robert has indeed been "infected."

The progress of this infection is a most curious one. Robert Audley, indolent and comfort-loving, presented as something of an exquisite, is first presented as largely unmoved by women, especially his pretty cousin, Alicia, who annoys him with her exuberant energy and strong affections. Robert affects foppish "turn-down collars," surrounds himself in his rooms with flowers, songbirds, and stray dogs, and rides the fringes of the hunt to avoid being in at the death. This portrait borders on what Freud would later call "inversion," and is certainly at the very least laced with feminine characteristics. In fact, the person Robert Audley resembles most is not any of his blood relatives, but his relative by marriage, Lady Audley, vain, comfort-loving, lazy, and an avid reader of French novels, as is Robert. The first person for whom we see Robert Audley having real feelings is a male, his old Eton schoolmate, George Talboys. When George discovers that his wife is dead, Robert takes him into his home and nurses him, and they become constant companions. Although Robert twice claims that he is falling in love with his aunt, and compares himself to the hero of a French novel in so doing, all his concern is for George:

If anyone had ventured to tell Mr. Robert Audley that he could possibly feel a strong attachment to any creature breathing, that cynical gentleman would have elevated his eyebrows... Yet here he was, flurried and anxious, bewildering his brain by all manner of conjectures about his missing friend, and, false to every attribute of his nature, walking fast.

"I haven't walked fast since I was at Eton," he murmured. (p. 82)

Robert marvels on the strength of his emotions – "To think that it is possible to care so much for a fellow!" (p. 89) and determines to go to "the very end of the world" if he must, to find him. It seems evident that Robert does not so much love Lady Audley as he *is like* Lady Audley – even the object of his "affection" was once the object of Lady Audley's similar care as her first husband.

Braddon is clearly on dangerous ground here; she can allow Robert, as a "good" character, to pursue neither his aunt nor his childhood pal. Oddly, however, instead of taking the ready-made alternative and matching him to his cousin, as foreshadowed throughout the text, she introduces another character in the second volume: Clara Talboys, George's lookalike sister. This woman acts as a substitute for George, as Robert muses, "It's comfortable, but it seems so d – d lonely tonight. If poor George were sitting opposite to me, or – or even George's sister – she's very like him – existence might be a little more endurable" (p. 208).

Ultimately, Robert will marry this acceptable substitute, and George, found again, will live with the couple. In all ways, Robert replaces Lady Audley – as George's companion, and as the ostensibly normal center of a normal family group whose mind has yet "trembled on the balance" between sanity and insanity. In fact, Braddon takes great pains to show the similarity of Lady and Robert Audley's natures and tendencies; it is the circumstances, not the individuals, which are different. Robert, a privileged male brought up with a great deal of freedom and luxury, is tolerated as a likeable eccentric, and never faces any circumstances which would make him liable to unacceptable behavior. Lady Audley, on the other hand, has little freedom and faces great hardship, and, had the crisis of George's unexpected return never occurred, would probably, as she says to Sir Michael, have been "a good woman for the rest of my life" (p. 354). She does exactly as she is supposed to do, marry well, and for this she is abandoned, penniless, with a young child. She attempts to work to support her family, and her drunken father gambles her earnings away. Desperate, she leaves the child with her father, runs away to earn her living independently under a different name, and sends money back to support her child. These might be read as the actions of a

hero, not a villain. (It is, in fact, quite parallel to George's abandonment
of family in the "heroic quest" for success.) Believing herself widowed,
she marries again without disclosing her true identity, which is her first
crime, and one which is at least explicable within the mores of middle
class society, if not entirely morally justifiable. It is not until her new
identity is threatened that she becomes a true villain, and resorts to
attempted murder. Between the law as represented in the person of
Robert Audley and the chaotic madness of Lady Audley lies only a
difference of circumstance; their natures are the same.

Braddon's purpose in drawing the characters so identically becomes
clear in light of her references to the role of the artist. Several times,
Braddon refers to the Pre-Raphaelites and their paintings in characterizing Lady Audley's appearance; the most pointed of these is her
description of the full-length portrait by which George first recognizes
her. The portrait is a perfect likeness, and yet seems very unlike the Lady
in its hard, cruel, almost demonic expression. Alicia suggests that,
"sometimes a painter is in a manner inspired, and is able to see, through
a normal expression of the face, another expression that is equally a part
of it, though not to be perceived by common eyes. *We* have never seen
my Lady look as she does in that picture; but I think she *could* look so"
(p. 72). Robert responds with a plea not to be so "German ... I'm not
metaphysical; don't unsettle me" (p. 72). The upsetting metaphysical
truth here is that the artist is indeed exposing a hidden reality; under-
neath the "normal" face of society and its laws is another visage, one
normally hidden from the gaze of people like the Audleys, but one that
the poverty-stricken and the dispossessed know only too well. In Lucy
Audley/Helen Maldon, the two faces really do coexist; in Robert
Audley, the potential lies just below the surface, unrealized because of
his masculine and class entitlements to security and luxury.

It is this coexistence that cannot be tolerated. If one reads *Lady
Audley's Secret* as a coming-of-age novel the hero of which is Robert
Audley, one may clearly see that Robert's task is to transfer his affections
from unsuitable objects and turn that attraction, which is really an
attraction to the unacceptable elements in his own personality, to denial.
The attraction that once led Robert to violate the privacy of Lady
Audley's locked rooms, burglarizing her suite in order to gaze upon her
portrait and personal effects leads him to continue violating the privacy
of her past in order to expose her "secret." It is significant that this
obsessive pursuit generates symptomatic behavior of such a nature that
the other lawyers in Robert's environment speculate that he is in love

(p. 211). It is the forced "penetration" of Lady Audley's identity, prefig-
ured in the invasion of her rooms and bonnet box, which will signify
mastery over the feminine elements in Robert's own nature. Perhaps
even more significantly, at the terminus of this penetrating journey lies
not a woman, but a man. In marrying George's substitute, Robert is
able to acceptably release the fever that has contaminated his body,
restoring his own health and the health of the social body. Fortunately
for Robert's fragile mental health, he is not confronted with the final
horror of pursuing George down into the well, the womblike opening
half-hidden on the Audley estate into which the mermaid has propelled
her tiresome first husband. George has, in fact, birthed himself, ably
midwived by Luke, who brings home this "gentleman as was wet
through to the skin, and was covered with ... slime ... [who was] like a
child in my hands, and helpless as any baby" (pp. 419–424). Robert and
Clara, newly married, spend their honeymoon recovering his body, very
much alive, from abroad.

Lady Audley's secret, of course, is not her prior marriage, alcoholic
father, hidden child, or even her series of attempted murders; it is her
madness that she so carefully conceals. However, many critics have
questioned this "insanity," seeing in it merely a convenient device for
explaining away perfectly rational behavior unacceptable in a female
protagonist.[2] Braddon's ironic references to the madness that lives in all
of us certainly undercut the definition of Lucy as mad. As early as
Chapter One, she stresses the socially constructed nature of "mad"
behavior and shows Lucy's decision to wed Michael Audley as very sane
behavior: "It was a tacitly understood thing in the surgeon's family that
whenever Sir Michael proposed, the governess would quietly accept
him; and, indeed, the simple Dawsons would have thought it something
more than madness in a penniless girl to reject such an offer" (*Lady
Audley's Secret*, p. 9). From the perspective of the lower middle class,
marriage is a largely financial arrangement into which love enters as a
happy afterthought. Sir Michael, on the other hand, is "disappointed...
as if he carried a corpse in his bosom" when Lucy tells him plainly both
that she does not love him and that she "cannot be disinterested" in the
financial aspects of his proposal. Nonetheless, he demonstrates a remarkable flexibility; having said a few moments before Lucy's an-
nouncement that he thinks it is the greatest possible "sin" for a woman
to marry a man she does not love, he states immediately afterward that
he sees no reason, so long as she loves no one else, "why we should not
make a very happy couple. Is it a bargain, Lucy?" (p. 11). Later, how-

ever, Braddon speculates that he had never really trusted her since that moment. Where Michael Audley fails is in his inability to enforce the representation of the pure woman as marrying for affection, and as ignorant and unconcerned with crassly material issues like wealth. The problem here is not so much that Lucy does think the way she does; it is that he allows her to think this way, knowingly collaborating in her violation of socially approved representations of bridehood by using a term like "bargain" to refer to their marriage. He endangers himself by using language that recasts his own role as a character in her narrative, rather than insisting on preserving the integrity of her representation within his narrative. The epic narrative rights itself by re-representing Lucy as the deceptive and dangerous siren – the only representation which can contain a woman like Lucy when she steps out of her role as the adoring wife.

However, when the Lady speaks, instead of preserving a well-bred silence, we see a woman who has tried to be principled – working as a governess, sending money for her son, attempting to be honest with Sir Michael about her motives for marrying him. She feels guilt, and wonders if she is *"really* wicked," or merely thoughtless (p. 297). Braddon writes, not of a "mermaid" who is innately wicked, but of a person raised to have certain ambitions without the means of satisfying them, a person who has been driven to desperation by adversity and the betrayal of comparatively powerful males who failed to meet their obligations to her. In short, Braddon gives Lady Audley what no siren has ever had: a history, out of which a complex character with complex motivations may be constructed by the reader – if she or he chooses to do so.

"My secrets are every body's secrets" says Lucy bitterly (p. 300). Although she is referring to her own lack of privacy, another meaning is suggested as well – Lady Audley's Secret is patriarchy's dirty little secret, and Robert's epic narrative depends on how well he can keep this secret once he has discovered it. His "sanity," the coherence of his epic identity, depends on how well he can resist the urge to read Lady Audley on her own terms, as a character in her own story, one who has a history, who has tried to play by the rules and implicitly critiques those rules merely both by articulating them so baldly (and thus calling attention to their arbitrary and artificial nature) and by citing their failure to work. He must read her only as a mermaid, a representation who has no existence separate from her relation to the epic text. To the extent that he fails to do this, he is mad. He regains his sanity by locking her away and her secret with her, protecting the Audley identity from scandal and the epic narrative from the intrusion of the voice of the Other. Victorian critics, presented with a choice of narratives, which is also a choice of tasks, chose Robert's and cried out against the possibility of choosing the other, which would entail formulating a critique of a social narrative which creates Lady Audleys and then refuses to grant them recognition.

Like the relationship between Lucy's body and that of Sir Michael, the intersection of the two narratives is defined by disease. It is the "fever" of sexual passion that brings the patriarch and the Lady together; wherever difference exists between the two interacting stories that cannot be hidden, there is the disease of madness. As Jacques Sarano tells us (see chapter 2, above), disease defines our bodies as both part of the self and alienated from it through the experience of pain. Robert Audley discovers himself as a member of the patriarchal social body through the pain of contact with one alienated from it. If a healthy body is a body all of whose component parts are telling the same story, without dissonance, then the healthy body is a body largely unconscious of that story as a story – it seems a truth that requires no telling. The healthy body is unconscious of its components because it experiences itself as a unity. That unity is violated when one component of the body tells a different story from the whole. (Cancer, for example, is a kind of counter-narrative to the narrative of the healthy body.) On the social level, Lady Audley's story must be absorbed into the overall narrative of the healthy social body, if unity is to be maintained. If her story cannot be "absorbed" or healed in this manner, then it must be excised or expelled from the body in order to maintain its unity and health. Robert becomes the sanitary policeman whose task it is to escort the seductive vector of disease to the appropriate lock hospital, risking infection by the contact (and in fact becoming infected with a mild case of madness), excising the Lady neatly from the afflicted area. Sir Michael does his part by refusing to speak of "that person" again, or to know what has been done with her (p. 399), refusing the possibility of any further contamination by her separate story. Every effort is made to restore the unity of the body, the integrity of the epic narrative, to reduce Lady Audley to a representation having no subjectivity, no story of her own. But in any surgery, there is bound to be a scar, a mute testimonial to the vulnerability of the body and the possibility of other stories, just as the epic ending of *Lady Audley's Secret* does not and cannot negate the subversive insistence of the Lady's voice.

## THE DOCTOR'S WIFE[3]

In 1864, Mary Elizabeth Braddon attempted a decided break with the sensation genre, and decided to write, as she called it, "a novel of character." Always an admirer of the French realists, Braddon was "very much struck" by the premise of *Madame Bovary* (then less than a decade old), and set out to adapt the idea to her own purposes. Many consider the result, *The Doctor's Wife*, to be one of Braddon's finest novels, even if it is derivative of Flaubert's. Braddon's letters to Edward Bulwer Lytton repeatedly refer to her desire to write something "better" than her other bestsellers. Of *The Doctor's Wife* in particular, she writes: "[I am] especially anxious about this novel; as it seems to me a kind of turning point in my life, on the issue of which it must depend whether I sink or swim... I am always divided between a noble desire to attain something like excellence – and a very ignoble wish to earn plenty of money.[4] Braddon clearly accepts the distinction here between money-making, "popular" novels and the more privileged realist novel that is aligned with non-commercial motives. In line with her intention to create a realist novel, she attempts to reposition the novel internally; knowing that critics will place the novel in the sensation category by default, she includes many internal references to anticipate and forestall possible undesirable readings. Kate Flint has noted that Braddon tends to be understandably critical of the tendency to blame novels for the irresponsibilities of their readers;[5] though this is generally true, the attitudes expressed in Braddon's writing are more complex and vary more over time than such a categorical statement would imply. (Flint also uncritically categorizes *The Doctor's Wife* as a sensation novel.) Since the novel hinges on a love interest, Braddon anathematizes popular love stories, blaming her heroine's "addiction" to them for her lack of maturity and susceptibility to adulterous romance, signaling that, although she is a woman writing about love, this is not a love story *per se*. The heroine does not, in fact, read sensation – but she does read Byron. More significantly, her key supporting character is himself a sensation novelist in penny numbers who provides a constant and very droll commentary on the way in which sensation is constructed and defined, providing also, in the process, a defense of sensation itself by throwing the blame for the corruption attributed to sensation on the love story instead. This character, Sigismund Smith (he has changed his first name, which used to be Sam, for professional reasons), provides a key thread of contrast between the characteristics of the sensational and the "real life" story in which he plays a minor role. Braddon found this *alter ego* so invaluable that she continued his career in another novel (*The Lady's Mile*), again in a supporting role – something she never did with any of her hugely popular heroines. Early in the novel, Sigismund articulates the dilemma of the penny-a-liner:

If a man can't have a niche in the Walhalla, isn't it something to have his name in big letters on the play-bills on the boulevard?... Do you think I wouldn't rather be the author of "The Vicar of Wakefield" than of "Colonel Montefiasco?" I *could* write "The Vicar of Wakefield" too, but ... I should do the Vicar in the detective pre-Raphaelite style ... There wouldn't be much in it, you know; but the story would be pervaded by Moses's body lying murdered in a ditch half a mile from the vicarage, and Burchell's ubiquitous eye. I dare say some people would cry out upon it, and declare that it was wicked and immoral, and that the young man who could write about a murder would be ready to commit the deed at the earliest convenient opportunity. But I don't suppose the clergy would take to murdering their sons by reason of my fiction, in which the rules of poetical justice would be firmly adhered to, and Nemesis, in the shape of Burchell, perpetually before the reader. (*The Doctor's Wife*, pp. 43–44)

The dangerous lure of sensationalism is not, then, in the tendency of readers to imitate the actions they read about; the danger is simply in its addictive quality:

I like writing for them [the penny public]. There's only one objection to the style – it's apt to give an author a tendency towards bodies ... the penny public require (*sic*) excitement ... and in order to get the excitement up to a strong point, you're obliged to have recourse to bodies. Say your hero murders his father, and buries him in the coal cellar in No.1. What's the consequence? There's an undercurrent of the body in the coal-cellar running through every chapter, like the subject in a fugue or a symphony ... And when you've once had recourse to the stimulant of bodies, you're like a man who's accustomed to strong liquors, and to whose vitiated palate simple drinks seem flat and wishy-washy. I think there ought to be a literary temperance pledge by which the votaries of the ghastly and melodramatic school might bind themselves to the renunciation of the bowl and dagger, the midnight rendezvous, the secret grave dug by lanternlight under a black grove of cypress, the white robed figure gliding in the grey gloaming athwart a lonely churchyard, and all the alcoholic elements of fiction. But, you see, George, it isn't so easy to turn teetotaller ... and I scarcely know that it is so very wise to make the experiment. Are not reformed drunkards the dullest and most miserable of mankind?... I would rather ... hear my audience screaming with laughter ... than write a dull five act tragedy, in the unities of which Aristotle himself could find no flaw, but from whose performance panic stricken spectators should slink away or ere the

second act came to its dreary close ... the father and prince of melodrama ...
was never a great man; he was only popular. (pp. 42–43)

There is both defiance and capitulation in these lines: Smith offers a
spirited defense of his craft while yet accepting the distinction between
the great and the popular; he seems to accept the critics' charge that
sensationalism is like liquor, and yet equates its absence with the absence of pleasure and the substitution of a sterile critical pedantry for art.
Yet Braddon assures the reader of *The Doctor's Wife*, "This is *not* a
sensation novel. I write here what I know to be the truth" (p. 309).
Braddon does want to write Goldsmith's *Vicar* (or Flaubert's *Bovary*), and
sternly denies herself recourse to bodies, ghostly figures, or even Ghastly
Secrets – until the ending, which she depreciated as "rushed."

Here also is the common equation between sensation and alcohol
addiction, and more importantly, the equation of both with "bodies."
Bodies are what sensation has in common with the love story. In the
first, a corpse is offered to the reader, whereas in the second it is the
sexualized body of the heroine, but in both it is the hidden, the secret
quality of the body, its tendency to transform, whether through decay or
sexual excitement – to get out of control and to betray or embarrass. In
each case the body does indeed run like an "undercurrent" throughout
the story, and the question is indeed one of accessibility. Will the corpse
be found? Will the woman be seduced? Anxiety over the permeability of
the body creates a center stage for the body itself as the chief protagonist, and sexuality, addiction, disease, and decay are the chief expression
of that "grotesque" permeability.

Yet sensation fiction's dead bodies, we are shown, are relatively
harmless compared to the live bodies found in love stories and novels of
high life. The narrator continually repeats that Isabel Sleaford, the
heroine of *The Doctor's Wife*, reads novels constantly, imagines herself the
heroine in a novel, and is unfitted for real life because of this. She is first
introduced to both the reader and her future husband reading in a
garden, and when she rises to make acquaintance, she holds the book
open so that she may return to it as rapidly as possible. She is described
as "addicted," and addiction, like any other passion, represents the
dependency of the body on something outside itself, and thus its connectedness to the Other, its non-closure. Within the world of *The Doctor's
Wife*, novels are extensions of Isabel's body – or her body is an extension
of the body of popular fiction and its disruptive intrusion into realist
"high" culture. Symbolically, Isabel is rarely in the "real world" of *The*

*Doctor's Wife*, but often in the fictional world of other narratives, which is the only framework that she is able to use to interpret her experiences in the "real world," and so she forms a sort of conduit between the fictive world of the popular and the "real" or "realist" world she "lives" in. Through her, the realist world and the privileged fictive form are invaded by elements of the popular – the squire falls in love with the country wife, a murderer and his victim are incidentally brought together, etc. If the popular is the "lower strata" of the body of culture, something to be acknowledged only with amused embarrassment, then Isabel Sleaford represents the carnivalesque collision of romantic idealism with its sordid underpinning – a banal sexual transgression.

Sigismund says of Isabel that, "She reads too many novels... No wise man or woman was ever the worse for reading novels. Novels are only dangerous for those poor foolish girls who read nothing else, and think that their lives are to be paraphrases of their favourite books" (p. 27). Not only does popular fiction make such girls potential victims of seduction by the aristocracy, it also makes them more directly revolutionary. Part of the problem stems from the edict that the middle-class domestic heroine must be passive, yet passivity and melodrama are not always complementary. Braddon's narrative voice explains:

She was so eager to be *something*... I think Isabel Sleaford was just in that frame of mind in which a respectable, and otherwise harmless, young person aims a bullet at some virtuous sovereign, in a paroxysm of insensate yearning for distinction. Miss Sleaford wanted to be famous. She wanted the drama of her life to begin, and the hero to appear ... [but] Beauty must wait, and wait patiently, for her fate.

Isabel does not become a regicide; however, what she does do is marry George, a good-hearted but prosaic young doctor whom she does not love. The murder of a king and the foreshadowed sexual betrayal of the domestic patriarch are thus equated. Isabel's openness to the fictive, her willingness to collapse the borders between the real and the fictive, are a betrayal of the real – the social order, the family, the empire itself. Braddon says of George that he "had those homely, healthy good looks which the novelist or poet in search of a hero would recoil from in actual horror" (p. 6); he is a "model youth of Graybridge," the backbone of middle-class England, a foundation for an empire which is the opposite and natural enemy of the fictive elements that Isabel seditiously introduces into his home.

The effects of Isabel's passion are manifested in the two male protagonists in terms of disease. Roland Lansdell refers to his passion for Isabel as a "fever" and compares it to delirium tremens as well (p. 204). Isabel is thus both a contagion and a drug. Isabel herself is an addict, and Braddon frequently compares her novels to opium: "[They are] Dangerously beautiful ... sweetmeats with opium inside the sugar [says Smith, and when he asks if they make her happy, Isabel responds] 'No, they make me unhappy; but' – she hesitated a little and then blushed as she said – 'I like that sort of unhappiness. It's better than eating and drinking and sleeping and being happy that way'" (p. 22). The blush, the unhappiness, the indifference for the material needs of the body – all are classic fictional signs of passionate love. She later loves Lansdell as a romantic ideal, as an element of popular fiction, and is confused and horrified when he suggests that she become his mistress. What Isabel really loves are her fictions; the novels are the true object of desire and source of contagion, and through them, the men in Isabel's life become infected – in Lansdell's case, by sexual desire for her which will eventually lead him to take steps which will cause his death. In fact, Isabel is particularly fictive herself; not only is she constantly compared to the heroine of a novel, but Lansdell's jealous cousin warns her that Roland's fancy for her is nothing more than the craving for "a new sensation" (p. 225). Since Roland has come into her life, Isabel sees that her life is indeed like a novel and that it has been "altogether like one long fever since Roland Lansdell's advent" (p. 229). In Isabel's unsuspecting husband, the disease manifests itself as a literal fever. As Lansdell is consumed by a "feverish" love for Isabel, his tenants experience a minor epidemic of typhus; George attends the families, and himself succumbs to typhus. The two men die within twenty-four hours of each other.

As in many of the other novels discussed here, the principal character inhabits a borderland. Isabel Gilbert lives between the popular and the realist novel for the reader, and for the other characters, between the fictive and the real. Coming from an indeterminate background, raised as a lower-middle-class woman yet really the daughter of a petty con-artist, she breaches class boundaries both by marrying into the solidly respectable middle-class and by her liaison with her aristocratic would-be seducer. Isabel is iconically aligned with boundary transgression as well. George first proposes to Isabel on a bridge, and she later frequently meets Lansdell at another bridge; on this second bridge he will ask her to run away with him. All of this takes place within the domain of the town of Graybridge itself. Isabel is a creature of crossings, of misty indeterminate midway points. If the vampire is only limited by the inability to cross running water, Isabel seems only to exist in that transitional space, in which all her major decisions are made and actions taken. With her pale face, black hair and huge yellow-black eyes, Isabel's resemblance to the type of the Victorian vampire is not accidental – both are transitional creatures, not wholly alive, and both possess sexual attractions that spell doom to the unwary.

As in Broughton's *Not Wisely But Too Well*, Braddon's novel manifests as a storyline the critics' indictments of popular fiction. Through it, a middle-class woman is unfitted for domesticity, and rendered ripe for a seduction which will be the ruin not only of her own home, but of the aristocracy which is infiltrated by the sexually active woman of a lower class. Her desire – which is really the transformation of the fictive desire which drives the popular book market – is murderous and destroys the relatively virtuous men in her life. As in *Not Wisely*, the adulterous passion is manifested as a fever which destroys the men who love her and, following the established pattern of Greek tragedy, extends to affect the lower classes of the surrounding area, representing the failure of the moral stewardship of the upper classes. By turning critical concerns about the novel into a novel itself, Braddon both naturalizes and neutralizes their commentary: "You are precisely right – novels are terribly dangerous," she says, and uses the novel as a cautionary tale to prove that point, thus collapsing the distinction between the "moral" critical discourse and the "immoral" fictive one – a preemptive strike in every sense.

Ironically, although Braddon denies that *The Doctor's Wife* is a sensation novel, it is in large measure Sigismund Smith the sensation novelist who creates a context for the story. He introduces Isabel and George; it is through him that they continue their courtship and that Isabel finds the employment with the family friend of Roland Lansdell, the man whom she will come to love. Smith is presented as a minor character who provides comic relief and incisive commentary from an outside point of view, yet he has an integral function as the very nexus of action, out of which the entire story is generated. In that sense, Smith acts out Braddon's intention to write a non-sensation novel while protectively retaining his own identity as a sensationalist; perhaps by placing Smith in the text, Braddon was exerting control over her public persona as a sensationalist, and placing herself as an author above and outside of that fictive identity. Smith becomes one of many layers of buffers between Braddon as a well-known sensation author and *The Doctor's Wife* as a realist novel which yet situates its "real world" among multiple referents of the landscape of popular fiction. The novel defines itself by references to the thing that it is supposedly not, in fact is created out of webs of those referents, perhaps precisely because the concept of a privileged realist fiction can only exist positioned opposite the popular, mirrored rather than absorbed by its multiple reflective surfaces. The novel uses the fictive to repudiate fiction, references to the popular to repudiate the popular, the theme of passion to repudiate passion – in short, it is a text built entirely on the denial of its textuality. In response, *The Spectator* granted Braddon its first favorable review of her work.

Thus, in *The Doctor's Wife*, we see a number of familiar tropes: reading as a kind of foreplay; reading as a drug; novels as seducers who undermine the middle-class family through the wife; and the sexuality of female readers as diseased. The use of these themes implies an agreement with critics' denunciations of the sensation novel, yet does not so much oppose the concerns of Braddon's own sensation novels as it transforms them. The dangerous sensuality of the female is still the driving force of the narrative, although the heroine of *The Doctor's Wife* is traditionally passive rather than sensationally active – and ironically, it is in her passivity that the danger lies. This mocking bow to the conventions is later highlighted by Smith's (now Smythe – as a three-volume novelist, he has upgraded his name yet again) cynical comments about the differences between middle-class and lower-class fiction in *The Lady's Mile*; his three-volume bestseller is *The Mystery of Mowbray Manor*, a "legitimate three-volume romance, with all the interest concentrated on one body."[6] The difference, Braddon suggests, between the penny public and Mudie's public is simply a matter of quantity, of how many bodies it takes to sate their appetites. It is the same mocking intelligence that transforms a sensation heroine from an active but basically virtuous girl who makes an unfortunate early marriage (Aurora) to a passive, idealistic "heroine" (Isabel) whose near adultery wreaks havoc on the community; the acceptable Victorian three-volume heroine is by far the more dangerous of the two.

# CHAPTER 4

# Rhoda Broughton: anything but love

Rhoda Broughton (1840–1920) produced her twenty-seven novels between the years 1867 and 1920. Her work sold widely and well, and was translated into German, French, Italian, Dutch, Spanish, Danish and Swedish. (For details on editions, see Marilyn Wood's very welcome 1993 literary biography of Broughton.)[1] Initially categorized as a sensation novelist when her first, extremely popular novels came out in the 1860s, she was later classified as a writer of love stories, long after love had ceased to be even arguably the primary theme of her novels. Broughton's focus was always principally on the exposition of character, usually of a woman protagonist. Resolutely a middle-class novelist, Broughton's later novels are social satires with a fairly light, humorous touch. Her technique recalls Jane Austen in that her range of representation is usually narrow, her focus precise – on the manners, fads, and prejudices of the middle classes and in her witty and engaging dialogue. Her attention to the particular difficulties of middle-class women makes available a broader critique of gender and, less frequently, class, but does not insist upon it. Her touch, especially in the later novels is consistently light, her satire Horatian rather than Juvenalian. Plot, in Broughton's novels, has little significance compared to its relative primacy in M. E. Braddon's work; it exists primarily as a unifying structure to hold together a succession of crises, often internal, wherein the protagonist gains insight and maturity. Even in the most comic novels, surprisingly, Broughton rarely offers a conventional happy ending, recalling Shaw's wry observation that when one has learned something, one always feels one has lost something.

Despite the fact that Broughton's novels are only nominally about love and that in the later novels, love often fades from the novel entirely, Broughton's marketing niche was always identified as the love story, a designation which Broughton never seemed concerned about challenging. Within the security of that designation, Broughton's primary vul-

nerability was to critics' accusations of depictions of too frank sexuality –
a reputation which probably earned, rather than cost her sales, and
about which she was increasingly careful and adept after a few missteps
in the earliest novels. (The most frequently retailed Broughton anecdote
is one in which her father forbids her to read the anonymously published
*Cometh Up As A Flower* (1867), not realizing that she is the author.) The
designation of love story focused critics' watchfulness on the representation of passion and left Broughton free to make social commentary
relatively unassailed, if also unregarded by her critics; what her readership may have thought of it remains elusive. Unlike Braddon, whose
very self-conscious manipulation of audience, generic placement, and
critical reception is evident throughout her career, or Ouida, who
explicitly if ineffectually stated her theories of authorship and her
intended audience, Broughton generally accepts and works quietly
within the space which the marketplace has reserved for her. In a
remarkable late novel, however, she does take on authorship and the
publishing world as the target of her satire, showing cynically that the
young author who is unable to separate her notion of artistry from her
understanding of the novel as a dangerous commodity is bound to fail.

The female body is a central trope for Broughton, and the "love
story" genre facilitates both the central placement of that trope and a
rather less complicated reading of it than her work, read "against the
grain," offers. In her earlier stories of passionate love, the body of the
central character is the site of self-construction, self-betrayal – its openness or closure generates the action of the story. In *Not Wisely But Too
Well* (1867), the openness of the body corresponds to its dangerousness;
the protagonist's lack of self-control – which is evidenced and perhaps
caused by her taste for dangerous narratives – constitutes her as a vector
for disease which destroys and subverts all she comes into contact with.[2]
(A similar structure appears in *Cometh Up*, in which the commodification
of the protagonist's body contains her dangerous sexuality in marriage,
turning it inward to destroy her own flesh – she dies, appropriately, of
consumption.)[3] In *A Beginner*, the novel which the protagonist writes
becomes the woman's body entering the realm of exchange – although
"innocent" and "virginal" in its purposes, to the extent it succeeds in the
market, it becomes dangerous, contagious, and seductive.[4] Disease, as
the sign of the body's alienation, is a consistent metaphor. Broughton's
early protagonists are consumed and destroyed by fever; in the later
novel, it is the book which metonymically stands for the protagon-

ist–author which is ritually burned, allowing the character, purified, to reenter private (domestic) life, while Broughton, the author behind the author, escapes to write again. It is this macabre reenactment of the destruction of the female body at the heart of these novels which provides both their market appeal as a spectacle of containment and a poignant critique of the costs of Broughton's financially advantageous placement in the market as a witty and acceptably *risquée* woman author of minor love tales.

### NOT WISELY BUT TOO WELL

*Not Wisely But Too Well* was Broughton's first novel, a bestseller that earned her a great deal of attention in the critical press, much of it disapproving. Published in 1867, it was almost immediately eclipsed by *Cometh Up As A Flower*, Broughton's blockbuster second novel which was published in the same year. However, it commands attention, not only as an extremely popular novel, but as a good example of a new author's effort to position her work in the marketplace. The novel traces the progress of a young middle-class woman who falls in love with a man unsuitable both by position (he is an aristocrat) and by nature (he is morally bankrupt). In an ironic twist on the bigamy theme in sensation novels, wherein the heroine usually has a not quite dead first husband lurking on the grounds of the second husband's estate, Kate, the heroine of *Not Wisely But Too Well*, is almost persuaded to run away with this man before he confesses that he already has a first wife in London. Kate refuses to see him again, and subsequent volumes elaborate her life without him, focusing on her struggle to be a good Christian. Years later, they meet again by chance; again she is almost persuaded to run off with him, and again she resists temptation. More time passes, as Kate struggles to lead a "good and useful" life in the absence of her great love. At her sister's wedding ball, Kate sees her hero for the last time, when he is fatally injured in an accident near the site of the party. He dies in Kate's arms, and, after a brief period of mourning, she becomes a Sister of Mercy. At that point, the narrator succinctly summarizes the few years of her work with the Sisters, and her death. Ironically, in a novel about love, we are only allotted a few pages of love scenes after the first volume; in fact, the lovers only *meet* about once per volume after their initial courting. The story's focus, if measured by the sheer amount of text devoted to it, is, as the narrator insists in the first chapter of the

book, how a human soul "ennobled" by love is purified through suffering. Kate grows from thoughtless self-gratification to a life of religious
self-sacrifice. Yet the critics unerringly pegged the novel as a story of
"passion," and most reviews focused either on the charms of the heroine
(if positive) or the indecent warmth of the few love scenes (if negative).

Kate's sexual passion is figured forth as disease, and, as she works to
cure herself, she actually spreads contagion wherever she goes. Her
body, constantly described in minute erotic detail by a narrator with a
confessed attraction to her, becomes the primary focus of interest in the
story as, supposedly in order to gain control of her illicit desires, she
places herself in situations and locations where she is increasingly out of
control; in order to become pure, she seeks corruption. Kate's body is
literally uncontainable, and becomes a "bodying forth" of disease,
foreign invasion, and class blending; like Isabel Sleaford, she becomes a
creature constituted of transitions and transgressions.

Broughton attempts to control the interpretation of her text through
the authorial/narrative voice which tells Kate's story. The narrator is
self-identified as an upper-class male (the novel was published
anonymously). This voice frequently intrudes into the narrative in order
to dictate the way in which scenes should be constructed by the reader.
Not only does he, as mentioned above, summarize the theme of the
book in the first chapter, but he breaks in at every point that Kate's
behavior is such that it might be criticized. In the key love scene in the
first volume, the narrator intrudes to clarify the proper attitude toward
Kate's behavior:

> Let no one think I am defending this girl, or holding her sentiments up as the
> pattern of what a young woman's should be; nor let anyone, however incapable
> of separating the historian's own ideas from those of the people whose history
> he is telling, imagine that I am describing Dare [the object of Kate's affections]
> as being in anywise a hero or fine fellow. I think him as great and unmitigated a
> scoundrel as any strictest censor of morals... To describe bad actions is not, as
> I would meekly submit to indignant virtue, to be an accomplice in them;
> otherwise he who relates a murder is equal in iniquity to him who commits it,
> and the police reporters are deeper dyed in guilt than any other members of the
> community. (*Not Wisely But Too Well*, p. 184)

Journalistic representation is morally irreproachable, but imaginative
love stories are not. Kate first appears to us in the act of contemplating a
love story she has just finished reading, and its effect on her bodes no
good: "Her brain was passively recipient of the idea they [the words]
conveyed, and her deep eyes looked out over the water [she is at the

seaside], full of a girl's speculations" (p. 21). Kate's passivity is emphasized, both in the sense of her uncritical acceptance and her submissiveness, which will be stressed again later in her ill-fated romance; here, the
love story is itself the seducer. She reflects that love is "an odd sort of
pleasant dangerous drunkenness ... [with] dreadful hot and cold fits
that one is subject to in typhus fever and in love" (p. 22), and although
she congratulates herself for having escaped it so far, the reader knows
(courtesy of the narrator) that she is to fall in love, and that love is here
aligned with the seductions of love novels, drunkenness and disease.

Broughton consistently uses the rhetoric of disease and contagion to
underline her treatment of sexuality throughout the novel, and Kate's
tastes in reading reflect the degree of her exposure to contagion. When
Dare first decides to pursue Kate, "an ill light flashed over his face ... a
light bred of earthly exhalations – a will-'o-the-wisp, potent to lead
astray ... Kate came up ... and her face caught a reflection of the
will-'o-the-wisp light" (p. 91). Following her exposure to this miasma, we
see her at home, rejecting Lamb's *Essays* for Byron's *Francesca di Rimini*,
since Lamb's "delicate flavour" was "too healthy and wholesome to
tempt a diseased palate" (pp. 109–110). Passion is a contagion that
invades the body and corrupts the mind. As the critics identify the
sensation novel as a substance that stimulates the appetite it feeds, we
see the peculiarity of a diseased appetite for illicit passion that feeds its
own illness. The first crisis of this particular infection is precipitated by
the news that Dare is married. Kate refuses to run off with him, and
immediately succumbs to a brain fever.

Although Kate recovers from this particular attack, the fever is not
eliminated from the text but transformed from an individual to a
community concern, escaping its containment within the individual to
prey on society at large. The next time we see Kate, a year and a half
later, she is rather unwillingly taking on the duties of "district visitor" in
an area which is starting to be troubled by a seasonal fever (probably
typhus, often called the "autumn fever"). A curate friend advises her to
heal her griefs by visiting the sick, which will dwarf her troubles by
comparison, but dares not speak too long on the topic of religion, "for
he is dreadfully afraid of giving her an overdose of that which to him is
most palatable food, but which to her sickly palate tastes like unsavoury
physic" (p. 231), rather implying that Kate is among the sick who might
require visiting. Disease is endemic within Kate and is complemented
by epidemic, specifically in the lower-class community. Although this
disease does not touch the middle-class neighborhood in which Kate

resides, Kate goes to the diseased areas as a kind of missionary, and her family fears that she will bring the fever back to them from her visits. Throughout the rest of the novel, Kate will represent the link between the middle class and the lower classes; interestingly, it is the lower classes whose condition will consistently mirror Kate's, linking Kate's "sensations" with those of the more bestial, dirty, and licentious lower classes. There are also indications that Kate may have become permeable to external conditions – subject to a lower-class vulnerability.

There are two dangers for Kate in her district visiting, and her upper-middle-class cousins name them both. Kate laughingly says that she is "going to make a tour of all the diseases in Queenstown tomorrow" and her cousins remonstrate: "You'll only be catching some of those horrid nasty diseases that those kind of people are always having... You'll be getting something nasty said to you ... it is not right at all for such a pretty girl as you to be walking about" (p. 251). Again, sex and disease are discursively related; a middle class woman who goes among the suburban poor is liable to two kinds of assault, two kinds of penetration, and both are classed ("those kinds of people" have those kinds of "nasty" diseases, and say those kinds of "nasty," overtly sexual things). Nonetheless, this kind of exposure seems to be a counter-inoculation for Kate's illness; the next time we see her reading, she has decided on a life of "self-abnegation" (although she still likes to flirt), has been reading with real enjoyment essays and biographies of great men, and has decided to repudiate romances. Her first acts of charity are to bring "good books" (tracts) to the poor.

However, poverty and "foul air" are not so easy to overcome with reading material, and in discouragement, Kate sets down her basket of tracts and thinks longingly of the new story in *Macmillan's*. She continues to be tempted away from her duties by the pleasures of reading (although reading "better books" than before – Cowper, Shakespeare, etc.), and her voluntary vulnerability is appropriately punished when she is accosted by an uncouth "bargee" who frightens her with a remark which he might have addressed to a prostitute. We are told that Kate's "unreasonable" fear (just why it is so unreasonable is never clear) of men of the "lower orders" dates back to being accosted by a drunken sailor while alone on a country road "a year or two ago." The narrator stresses constantly that her fear is foolish and ridiculous; the impression is given that middle-class women are simply not in real danger from men of this class, yet clearly, Kate has been given good cause to fear that she will be approached. Significantly, the first incident is placed in the same time period as her affair with Dare, when she was indeed walking alone on country roads (to and from assignations) as young women of good family should not be; there is a subtle hint that these encounters may be Kate's fault, since she should not have to fear them. Chaste women, so the logic goes, do not inspire that kind of interest. Perhaps Kate's awakened sexuality even draws such men as customarily patronized the diseased prostitutes whom the Contagious Diseases Acts legislated against in port towns (sailors with the British navy). When fleeing the scene of the incident (at which she drops her basket of tracts, leaving the bargee with symbolic if not actual victory) she literally runs into her curate, who immediately feels that he has been made "drunk" by the physical contact and realizes he is in love with her, which he fears as "Satan's snare." In attempting to forget her passion through charitable activity, Kate "carries" the sexual fever wherever she goes, and the battle against this fever is transferred to her spiritual "doctor," the curate.

Ironically, the more Kate tries to do "good," the more dangerous she is, since every contact is an opportunity for contagion. Her conscious will has no control over her body. Kate, who does not realize how the curate feels, is upset by his avoidance of her, yet determined to continue to pursue spiritual peace:

She had a ... new taste in letter writing, and that ... was a sort of desire for self-justification and self-assertion. Though he had deserted her and reneged the situation of spiritual guide and teacher to her, she would show him that she still kept persistently in the laborious path that he had chalked out for her; for these destructive [destructive because they feed his passion for her] little billets hardly came under the head of billets-doux. They were business notes ... James groaned in spirit sometimes at the riotous, ungovernable way his heart would leap up when he caught sight of one of these little compositions ... It would have been a droll sight enough, if anyone had been by to watch the gingerly way in which he held them between his finger and thumb, as if cholera, typhus and small-pox lurked in every fold of them ... [he read them and] invariably tossed them into the fire. (pp. 70–71)

Kate's disease is such that even with the purest intentions, she is dangerous, and doubly so when she turns writer herself. Writing, here, becomes an extension of the woman's physical body, sexually exciting and capable of infecting through touch. Like her body, her text is not under her control; although she wills it to mean something innocuous, it always carries the fever of her sexuality, which can only be purified by fire.

This infection comes to another crisis when Kate runs into Dare at the Crystal Palace, and her desire for him returns with all its old force. Kate determines to run off with him, and it is the curate who discovers her secret, and follows her on to the train to dissuade her, at which time the narrator compares the two men's passions for Kate: "Dare's mad, wild-beast passion was as a stinking stagnant pond to a leaping, pellucid, mountain brook" (p. 155). Kate's perverted tastes, in other words, are sending her back to the heart of urban London and disease and away from the country and health.

Once again she is saved from "the abyss"; again the crisis is manifested physically as that most convenient of all Victorian afflictions, "a brain fever." When she recovers, she commits herself without reservation to a life of charitable visiting and religious austerity. Once again, with her apparent recovery, illness breaks out in the community. Fall returns, and with it, the fever, particularly to the riverfront slums that Kate visits: "Fed by the fog, and the river mist, and the warm drizzle, the fever shot up like a tropical plant, from an infant into a full grown giant. Scorching, livid faced, it stalked and ramped stealthily among the reeking crowded courts and alleys" (p. 178). Kate's "wholesome" sister expostulates with her, trying to convince her to leave off visiting the contagious area. Finally Kate's family leaves the area entirely for the duration of the epidemic, leaving Kate to her own devices. Kate feels safe from the fever because she has "just tumbled out of one fever [the brain fever caused by her decision to leave Dare], and it is not very likely" she would catch another immediately following (p. 180), indicating that the passion for Dare and brain fever have inoculated her against the contagion – another hint that the fevers are similar in kind. Soon after, she becomes a hospital head nurse in the fever ward set up to handle the huge volume of patients. The curate succumbs to the epidemic; Kate survives. After Dare's death, Kate ends her life and the novel as a Sister of Mercy "among the smoky reeking alleys and courts of filthy, suffering, heart-rending London" (p. 288).

Although they are apparently set in contrast, both Kate's love for Dare and her charity for the community seem equally sinister. In each of the latter two volumes, there is a plague, which structurally mirrors the function of the courtship in the first volume; in each, Kate meets Dare again and struggles with her own passion. In fact, it is precisely when Kate in some measure overcomes the passion in herself, the fever in her own body, that the plague strikes the community. Kate, immune from contagion herself, nurses her district through the plague, which always strikes immediately following a resurgence in her visiting. Although the text overtly presents this as merely coincident, it happens with astonishing regularity. And it is Dare's death that supposedly "frees" Kate from her passion, yet she immediately returns to the filthy urban areas with which he is metaphorically linked; indeed, her inclination for such work is set against her "wholesome" sister, who has a healthy if uncharitable dread of "those people." Kate's need to conquer passionate fever leads her to a religious transformation which yet feeds on fever, and perhaps even breeds it, as the love for her which "well hidden, was killing" the curate "by inches" (p. 154), finally achieves his death by driving him to work until he weakens and succumbs to the fever that he and Kate are working together to succour. Kate is a species of typhoid Mary, a vector for contagion who is herself immune to deadly fevers so long as her passion for Dare is endemic within her. For this very reason, she is attractive to the men around her. Kate is "bewitching" and "irresistible" because she is permanently hectic with sexual arousal. Each of the three volumes ends with a crisis in the fever which is manifested physically in Kate, the last manifestation being her death.

Kate occupies an equivocal and highly charged space. At the beginning of the novel, we see her at the seaside and in the woods; after her encounter with Dare, who represents urban London, she moves to the suburbs, a kind of liminal area between the countryside and the city. Within that space, she moves between the upper-middle-class and upper-class dwellings of her cousins and friends and the slums for which she is district visitor; she carries texts in one direction and, her friends fear, contagion in the other. She is in love with an upper-class man yet is accosted by men of the lower classes. Additionally, she is courted by men of her own class, making her the object of a desire that threatens to breach all class barriers. (It is interesting to note that Dare's wife is a lower-class woman, which establishes Kate as one of a series of "inferior" and inappropriate choices.) Kate hovers on the border between proper, sexually chaste middle-class womanhood and unrestrained passionate transgression, between health and disease, good and evil. Both morally and physically, she inhabits a borderland, and represents an unduly permeable quality of that borderland. Kate is literally like the riverfront land in that the fever is endemic and recurring within her; she does not go to it so much as she goes with it. Broughton uses the theme of fever as both a structuring agent within the text, marking time and structural transitions between volumes and phases of Kate's life, and as a way of underscoring Kate's crossings of the multiple borders set up in the novel. Even the Sisterhood which she finally joins occupies a troubled position between Low and High Church concerns, a "band of holy devoted women whom Evangelical clergymen condemn as acolytes and handmaidens of the Scarlet Woman," a position in which the religious chastity of an all-female community is aligned both with heresy and the illicit sexuality of the prostitute. Even the "cure" which Kate chooses is located in a discursive "war zone," a troubled area between religious factions – and of course, even in the cure, Kate follows the fever. It is to be noted that Kate in no way reverses her geographical progress within the first two volumes, but continues it – from the seaside, to the riverside suburbs, to the commercial heart of the Thames, and the source of its heaviest pollution, in London – from health to disease, from country to city. This directly contravenes the overt moral message of Kate's spiritual reclamation, suggesting that some borders may not be crossed with impunity, some fevers can never really be cured, but only placed in remission. Ironically, it was precisely Kate's moral turnaround that angered some critics, who felt that it was impossible for one who had behaved as she did to ever be reclaimed. Margaret Oliphant writes sarcastically of the piety

which generally associates itself with this species of immorality; for sensual literature and the carnal mind have a kind of piety quite to themselves, when disappointment and incapacity come upon them. The fire which burned so bright dies out into the most inconceivably grey of ashes; and the sweetest submission, the tenderest purity, take the place of all those daring headstrong fancies, all that self-will and self-indulgence. The intense goodness follows the intense sensuousness as by a natural law.[5]

The critic has seized on one of the central and perhaps most unsavory messages in this novel; Kate is, in fact, not reclaimed, since both sex and religion are equated as feverish obsessions. Kate's healthy sister, who flirts strictly with middle-class men and ends by marrying her cousin (remaining not only within class boundaries but within her own family) refuses contact with the lower class and finds her sister's charitable visiting repulsive and frightening. Both sexuality and religion become illicit and unhealthy when they threaten to breach class boundaries, and it is perhaps this quality more than the alignment with Popery that makes the Scarlet Woman allusion appropriate. That Kate's passions are obsessive, Broughton's male narrator makes clear:

A woman's soul is such a small room that it has only space for one idea at a time; consequently, if a passion, a desire, an impulse lays hold of her, it possesses her with infinitely more force and concentration than it would a man in like case. Women have decidedly less of the brute ... than men, but *en revanche*, they have also infinitely less of the god. (*Not Wisely But Too Well*, p. 76)

And after her second brain fever: "It was evident that this exaggerated strictness, sprung from a morbid remorse, could not last. It was only the rebound from her former recklessness. Anyone could see that this girl was in a state of transition, though transition to what remained to be proved" (p. 167). Yet despite this judgment, Kate's only subsequent change is her move to the sisterhood. Her story even gets away from its narrator; Kate is not temporarily in transition, for she has been in a constant state of transition throughout the novel, although in a manner perfectly consistent throughout all her actions. The change of direction that the critic attacks and the narrator defends is entirely superficial; Kate changes the object of her obsession, but never its direction, as she burrows inward, from the healthy Welsh coast of Britain to its fevered urban heart.

This, then, is less a love story *per se* than a story of a woman who has a passion for boundaries, borderlands. She is drawn to the edges of the "abyss" of sexual indiscretion, she moves among the margins of the suburbs, of society, of the river, of life itself. She spends her time with the dying whenever possible. Even on her best behavior, she exists in the realm of the extreme, the excessive, the "transitional." Because she is excited by the marginal, she is dangerously open to its influence and this is manifested by both her sexual vulnerability and her susceptibility to brain fever – the latter being a polite substitute for the former.

The sexual permeability of the middle-class female body is analogous to the vulnerability of British soil to that foreign invader, the "tropical" fever. If the "moist warmth" of the land mirrors the female body in its periodicity, fever that "shoots up" and "ramps" in the narrow alleys, penetrating first the working-class and then the middle-class neighborhoods, represents both an (endemic) pregnancy and an (epidemic) male tumescence. The discursive opposition of epidemic and endemic recalls the discourses of rape (foreign invasion) and miscegenation. (As discussed in chapter 1, cholera was thought to be endemic to India. Its epidemic manifestations in Britain were feared as evidence that it was "invading" British subsoil and in the process of becoming endemic there.) Broughton's representation of the lovers' first kiss, which takes place in a greenhouse, is instructive: "Dare set his teeth hard ... keeping shut the sluice gates of the great flood that was surging, boiling, raging within him ... the flowers rustled their leaves, and waved their bright heads sympathetically. They had seen something of that kind before, when they lived in the tropics" (pp. 166–167). Broughton's description of the setting lays heavy emphasis on the "warm damp atmosphere," and Kate answers Dare's questions "mistily"; in short, although the conservatory is beautiful and sweet-smelling and the riverside slums are ugly and foul-smelling, the settings mirror each other. Male desire rises like the river over the land in the warm season; the tropical plants that thrive in such conditions are passion and disease. The free expression of sexual arousal is presented as endemic to the tropics, or to colonial savages; when Kate is with Dare, she is a "docile... Circassian slave on the market at Constantinople" and if she exposes her skin to the sun, as she threatens to do, she will become "a dear little negro" (pp. 157–158). The domestic female body is alienated when it is receptive to illicit sexual passion; it betrays the unity of the empire, and through its doubleness, becomes Other than itself. If the passionate woman is constituted as a threat to the imperial subject, it is to her own subjectivity first that she is dangerous. The title of the novel is telling; Kate loves "not wisely but too well" and Kate is the outsider, the "dear little negro." Yet it is Dare who is violent, who amorously threatens to cut Kate's throat if she ever kisses another man. Dare is the soldier, yet it is Kate who plays passionate and honest Othello to the "supersubtle" upper-class Dare. Although Kate is passive and "submissive," it is through that very submissiveness, passivity, "openness" that good society is disrupted, just as the Moor's sexual intrusion into good Venetian society could only be permitted to end in tragedy. The troubled imbrication of the "feminine" and the colonial Other with the threat of a very unfeminine violence is clearly apparent. Although born a middle-class British woman, inappropriate sexual desire transforms Kate into a foreign invader in the healthy body of Victorian society who unmans the imperial male.

This alienation is traceable to its origin in the love novel which Kate reads on the beach at the beginning of *Not Wisely But Too Well*, the original seducer of which Dare is the secondhand beneficiary. As noted above, Kate's progression toward "goodness" is emphasized by her movement toward more "respectable" reading material. On the other hand, reading the story of doomed lovers (Byron's *Francesca*) is replaced by living it, in the same way that the metaphorical "fever" of love is replaced by physical fever. Broughton's book positions itself in opposition to love novels and apparently confirms the superiority of religious self-sacrifice over passion, yet just as Kate escapes one obsession for another, *Not Wisely But Too Well* becomes what it denounces. The critics condemned the novel for precisely the same reasons that the novel itself condemned love stories – rendering it precisely as attractive as the sins which it supposedly sought to prevent.

Just as the fever threatens to spread through Kate from the lower-class areas outward, the story itself seems to be an unstable element, threatening to break out of its appointed boundaries and "spill over" into other territories. The persona of the narrator is the reader's link with a story and a woman who preexisted the novel itself, and he himself exists in an intermediate space between the reader and Kate. The omniscient narrator traditionally shares a privileged space with the reader, a space in which power is absolute and the play of voyeuristic desire is fairly unlimited. In "speaking for" the author, as the omniscient narrator generally is perceived as doing, the narrator shares a status of "reality" with the reader in the world of the novel. However, such a narrator rarely establishes him- or herself as a central character in the story s/he "tells." Confusingly, Broughton's narrator establishes himself as an upper-class individual who knew Kate well and was in love with Kate himself – which lends a curious intimacy to the lingering physical descriptions of Kate that he regales his readers with – yet he never appears within the story as a character. In fact, he acts the part of an omniscient narrator, describing thoughts and feelings of several characters, and scenes in which no observer could credibly have a role. While the narrator contains Kate's story by distancing it in time, digressing and moralizing, the reader still sees her always through the eyes of a man in love with her, whose part in the narrative remains forever hidden; thus, in some sense, the reader participates in a story yet to be written – that of the narrator and his own history with Kate. In that sense Kate's story is not fully "contained" in the story the narrator tells, for the narrator himself becomes a "bridge" to a part of Kate's story that is not contained therein.

The comfortable containment of the narrative is also breached by the frequent references to the reader–text relationship. Not only are readers often reminded, both by the narrator and by references to Kate's improving taste in reading (they are pointedly reminded that, if this is a love story, then "good" reading is not defined as the sort of reading they are doing), that we are reading a story, and not a very reputable story at that (not a biography or philosophical treatise), but readers are periodically distracted by invitations to speculate on the role of their interlocutor, a role which remains unresolved. The novel simply stops with the end of the narrative of Kate's life, and, despite the long introduction with which it begins, and within which the narrator identifies himself and explains his motives for writing, refuses to complete the narrative frame that the novelist has begun and extended by periodic digressions. The result is a strange and deliberate lack of closure in the reading experience, even though the story itself ends in the approved manner, with marriage or death for the primary characters.

In other words, because the reader sees through the narrator's eyes, and because the narrator's relationship with Kate is both amorous in its intent and ill-defined in its actuality, Kate's sexuality is offered to the reader in a double gesture, one within the story (we watch her flirt with Dare, or flee the bargee) and one within the intermediate text (the narrator has a relationship with Kate outside the story and his descriptions of her charms are conditioned by that hidden subtext). The reader is not entirely free to suspend disbelief and act as a voyeur of events that do not concern her or him directly, for s/he is constantly reminded both that this is a story, and that there is another "outer" story with which s/he has an incomplete and partially understood relationship. If the reader exists in "reality" and Kate and Dare exist in the "story," then, at least during the act of reading, the intermediate story, or the "frame" in which narrator and reader interface is granted a status between reality and story; it is the realm in which the reader becomes a character him- or herself. The failure in the expected and customary closure in that frame leaves the story "open" and does not allow the reader to disengage her- or himself from the "space" in the story which s/he occupies with certainty of how the reader's *own* story within the story ends. The reader ends the novel without a clear sense of his or her own relationship to Kate in the context of the intermediate story; the comfortable invisibility of the voyeur who enjoys the story without being a part of it is exchanged for the uneasy liminality of a reader who both participates directly in the story at some level and who is yet never allowed to forget that it is a fiction, and that s/he participates in the machinery that creates it. A striking example of this movement occurs when Dare lies dying after his accident, and the narrator digresses on the subject of sensationalism:

Strange, is it not, that the rabid love for horrors should be an instinct, so deeply planted in the vulgar mind, that it requires the education of a lifetime to outroot our love for "raw head and bloody bones"? A murder, of course, is the source whence the keenest enjoyment is to be derived – a wife murder with a good deal of poker, and of hair torn out; but still there is a fair amount of pleasant excitement to be extracted from a good accident, always presupposing plenty of mangling and broken bones. (pp. 273–4)

This is a direct commentary on the excitement of the crowd which has heard of Dare's accident, yet in its connection to both journalistic and novelistic sensationalism, it both distances the reader from the ensuing scene (it is only a text, like a newspaper or sensation novel) and dictates an attitude ("educated" readers do not relish such "horrors" – though they apparently manage to read them anyway). It also serves both to suggest a generic position for the text within the marketplace (this is not a sensational scene, but a tragic one) and to cynically remind readers of their role as consumers (readers enjoy sensationalism, but stigmatize it as uneducated). Here, the reader is obliged to construct the stories of the novel, not merely as fictive experiences, but as commodities in a market actively shaped by his or her own demands, and not demands determined by the purest motives.

Kate's refusal to be contained within a particular level of textual "reality" simply parallels her general "grotesque" openness. As a desiring body, she remains forever open, continuous with her surroundings. Her unhealthy appetites draw her to disease, and, true to her nature, she quickly becomes one with that contamination, infecting any who, desiring her, become themselves guilty of an injudicious openness – including the reader. Ostensibly, this is a novel about achieving closure – mastery over desire and the subordination of the desiring flesh to a religious principle which denies the body. Yet the dualism engendered in Kate by her unconsummated desire for Dare disrupts closure and breaches apparently impassable boundaries. Despite Broughton's avowal that the novel tells a story of purification, the story of contamination on which the trope of purification depends and by which it is subsumed allowed her 1860s readers to locate *Not Wisely But Too Well* within the genre of sensation.

A BEGINNER

If every novel, as a commodity, reflects the market conditions in which it is produced, then every novel, to some extent, has as a subject those market conditions. As ideology, these concerns must remain submerged until an ideological shift makes them visible. In 1894, the year in which the libraries declared the demise of the three-decker, and thus, tacitly, their own enfeeblement, Broughton produced her own "novel of the literary marketplace" – a book in which the incidental romantic interest is thoroughly subordinated to a dissection of the market in which such commodities flourished.

Broughton opens her novel *A Beginner* (1894) with the quote "A young girl knows enough when she knows the names of all the great men, ancient and modern, when she does not confound Hannibal with Caesar, nor take Thrasimene for a general, nor Pharsalia for a Roman lady" (*A Beginner*, p. 1). Here she demarcates the acceptable intellectual limits of a woman's writing within a story of a young woman who attempts to violate those boundaries. That this ironic little tale is meant to reflect on her own experiences as an author is clearly indicated to the audience. First of all, the title would seem to be in response to the infamous Oliphant review in *Blackwood's* (1867) which lambasted the young Broughton's first bestseller (*Cometh Up As A Flower*), and which dissected the moral anatomy of her female character's emotions:

Nelly Lestrange has no particular objections to meeting her soldier out of doors whenever he pleases to propose it. He takes her in his arms after he has seen her about three times, and she still has no objection ... She wonders if her lover and she, when they meet in heaven, will be "sexless, passionless essences" and says God forbid! She speaks, when a loveless marriage dawns upon her, of giving her shrinking body to the disagreeable bridegroom ... And here, let us pause to make a necessary discrimination ... If two young people fall heartily and honestly in love with each other ... and one is forced to marry somebody else, it is not unnatural, it is not revolting, that the true love unextinguished should blaze wildly up ... This is wrong, sinful, ruinous, but it is not disgusting; whereas those speeches about shrinking bodies and sexless essences are disgusting in the fullest sense of the word. Would that the new novelist, the young beginner in the realm of fiction, could but understand this![6]

The "beginner" in Broughton's novel, Emma Jocelyn, has just anonymously published her first three-volume novel, *Miching Mallecho*. The title is an obscure reference to Shakespeare, for choosing which as titles early in her career Broughton herself was also heartily teased (*Cometh Up As A Flower, Not Wisely But Too Well*): "There is no mistaking the hand that has already spoiled for us two or three sacred bits of our literature by filching them to serve as the catch-titles of her ignoble tales."[7] But most telling of all is the steady criticism of the novel's "impurity," (for which Broughton herself was often criticized) which finally corrupts the author's cousin, leading her into an adulterous affair, and which finally breaks Emma of writing anything at all.

Broughton's deft handling of the tale both pleases her readers' conservatism (Emma gives up writing and her romantic infatuation for author and critic Edgar Hatcheson, and settles down to a thoroughly "sensible" domestic life) and makes a number of telling points about both the literary marketplace and gender relations therein. The quote (above) which begins the novel is ambiguous. Is Broughton giving it this privi-leged place as a truth which the novel will illustrate, as Emma's eventual decision to give up writing would suggest? Or does she place it there to show the limits placed on women authors striving to compete intellec-tually with males? Emma is chided by her reviewer for having the "colossal presumption to use the tremendous subject of heredity as a lever by which to move her paltry puppets" (*A Beginner*, p. 173), and for the recondite choice of title, both of which indicate her desire to move beyond the realm of the merely entertaining and into the more intellec-tual territory of the social problem or *tendenz* novel. How thoroughly Broughton herself managed to disassociate herself from such accusa-tions of intellectualism can be seen in the final words of an extremely favorable *Temple Bar* review: "She is neither a great artist nor a profound philosopher; but she is a good story-teller, a brave lover, a true woman and a smart writer; and, being all these, she can well afford to dispense with the rest."[8] *A Beginner* shows us a young, inexperienced "New Woman" writer, perhaps with potential, perhaps not, who steps outside the appropriate subject boundaries for her gender and class and is made to suffer for it, losing her admirer, gaining the disapproval of friends and family members and the approval of the foolish, causing marital strife, and finally, giving up writing entirely to restore order. On the other hand, the man she loses is one whom class differences prevented her from seeing as a possible mate anyway, the man she marries is not one she apparently feels passionately about, and the very existence of *A Beginner* as the product of a successful and continuing woman author who has weathered some of the very criticisms directed at Emma in the novel decries the appropriateness of Emma's decision. Hence, this is also readable as the story of a graceful capitulation to social pressures, rather than a story of a confused young woman finding her true domestic vocation.

In the first chapter, the novice receives her first bound volumes, in their "neat and rather coquettish" covers, under "virginal white" wrap-ping. Immediately, we become aware of the double bind: the coquettish book is female, must please and invite while retaining its purity, yet the author thinks to herself,

"Miching Mallecho." "Yes, surely a good title. It excites curiosity, and tells nothing, and 'By a Beginner.' That must certainly disarm hostility. No critic could be harsh to one who owned herself a beginner. I say 'her,' but I have my hopes that the reviewers may be at fault in that respect, that they may take me for a man. There are one or two passages that –" She turns the pages fondly, seeking for some of those "purple bits" of virile dealing with the passions, and handling the problems of life, which are to turn the hounds of criticism off the track. (*A Beginner*, pp. 7–8)

It is these purple bits, of course, which will get her into trouble later, particularly with Edgar Hatcheson, the author of *Warp and Woof*, a little volume of essays which she has admired immoderately. In the second chapter, Emma meets Edgar for the first time, and finds herself speaking solely about his literary accomplishments, since her idol mentions that he has little respect for women who write.

The reception of the book and the generic category the book is "read within" will depend on the perceived gender of its author and intended readership. Emma intends her novel as a *tendenz* novel on the subject of hereditary vice, detailed through the exploration of a love relationship. Her cousin, Lesbia, reads it for the love story:

[Emma argues] "There are subjects one *must* face – that are a part of our century"...

[Lesbia responds] "That is like one of the moralizing bits in the book, which I skipped at the first reading to get on with the story ... do not imagine that I am finding fault with it for being so-so – impassioned! If I have a love story I own I like it *boiling*!"...

[Emma] "How frightfully you have misunderstood me!... What I tried most earnestly to bring into strong relief – I can't think how you can have missed it – was the absolute need for greater self control"...

[Lesbia] "I have no doubt that was in all the stiff bits which I skipped ... but after all, why should you mind? One does not go to a novel to learn one's moral duties, but to forget one's own tiresome jog-trot existence." (pp. 112–113)

This tension between the two genres will repeat itself throughout *A Beginner*; the reviewers who like *Miching Mallecho* will read it as a social-problem novel and assume a male author; the negative review assumes a woman author attempting a romance novel who overreaches herself.

Broughton pits the male working-class author who is attempting to climb socially and intellectually through the privileged literary form – the essay – against the upper-middle-class woman who writes the devalued form – the novel – for purposes of self-expression. Although this sets up the traditional duality of the hard driven intellectual male against the frivolous female, Broughton constantly undermines this dichotomy by invoking the realities of the marketplace and class and gender prejudices; "Emma smiles to herself at the discrepancy between this statement and the version that had been given her by the young writer himself ... of the cause and scope of his literary labours, from which it was evident that 'Warp and Woof,' if it had seated its writer among the immortals, had also ignobly boiled the pot!" (p. 56).

The novel itself both ridicules and validates the powerful reviewing system. *Miching Mallecho* is shown, through its effects and through the judgment of "reliable" characters, to be a morally questionable novel, possibly deserving of the rather vicious review it receives from the almighty *Porch*, a major London literary journal, to which "the sheeplike race of circulating-library readers look in order to make up their minds for them" (p. 131). Yet, Broughton also shows the capriciousness of the system in her absurd character Miss Grimston, a failed novelist and feminist who has "confined herself to tomahawking others" in reviews since her own disastrous literary debut. Indeed, the perceived gender of the anonymous critic is crucial to indexing the accuracy of the criticism:

"You say *he*" says Lesbia ... "but how do you know that it is a man? How do you know that it is not a woman? It reads to me much more like the work of a spiteful woman!"

"Do you think so?" asks Emma, raising her head from its abased position on her arms, and with a ray of revived hope in voice and eye. (p. 177)

(*The Porch*'s review bears a striking resemblance to *Blackwood's* hatcheting of the young Broughton.) Of course, we will later discover that the unknown critic is not only male, he is none other than Edgar Hatcheson, the object of Emma's literary admiration. In fact, we are told that Miss Grimston is not allowed to publish in *The Porch*, even though her uncle is the editor. Presumably, she reviews for the less prestigious local papers. Women are clearly active in the literary marketplace; just as clearly, they are excluded from power within the critical edifice which controls that marketplace.

It is Hatcheson, the future editor of *The Porch*, who provides a portrait of the ideal woman in his mother; widowed and with five children to support, she must work at something suitable. Hatcheson explains to Emma:

"If I could tell you how my mother pinched and slaved, and what a plucky uphill fight she made of it! What odd out-of-the-way methods of making money she hit upon! Once she mended pens for Government offices, and for six months we waded knee deep in old goose-quills!" ...

"Is it not from her, then, that you inherit your – your bent? Does she herself never write?"

"Never; she does not belong to the species ... My mother knew, at all events, that she was doing something useful and harmless." (p. 192)

Emma is reminded that her own novel is turning out to be other than harmless and is properly rebuked for placing her work, even anonymously, before the public eye. A "good" woman, we infer, is one who works only to support her children, and then does the kind of work that supports and complements male power – mending the pens so that others may write, without ever wishing to write herself. Broughton may well have intended an ironic reference to Mrs. Oliphant, the purported author of the *Blackwood's* article cited above, who explained her own writing as an attempt to support her children in her widowed and helpless state, yet still chose writing instead of some less public vocation. Mrs. Oliphant could be a pitiless reviewer of other women's novels, particularly if she thought them wanting in womanly "reticence." *A Beginner* carries much the same message as many of Mrs Oliphant's reviews, yet the very act of its publication undermines its message about the inappropriateness of the writer's career for women, even as Mrs. Oliphant's presence in the market did.

The critic insists that the purpose of criticism is moral judgment and prescription. Yet, as Broughton constantly reminds the reader, the practical function of this criticism was purely market-based. The review of the major journals will make or break the new writer, since it is there that the circulating library patron will seek a recommendation. Therefore, much of *A Beginner* is concerned with the progress of *Miching Mallecho* through the reviewing system, first in the local papers, which are favorable, then in the all important London journals. Broughton parodies the language of such criticism beautifully; the *Pudbury Post* review mixes food and illness metaphors with abandon: "It is written with a verve and sparkle most refreshing to the mental palate, and yet with an unflinching grappling of the more painful problems of the age, a fearless cauterization of the wounds of poor humanity" (p. 126). Finally, however, the book receives the coveted notice of the powerful London literary journals, represented by *The Porch*, whose negative review sounds remarkably like *Blackwood's* 1867 vivisection of Broughton. Interestingly, when the book is reviewed well, it is a "cauterization" of wounds, yet after *The Porch*'s review, Emma wonders if it is not merely a treatment of a "scabrous subject" with "noxious effect." Emma's intent is therapeutic, but as a woman author, her actions may serve only to disseminate moral disease. Only the male author can gaze upon or represent immorality without being tainted thereby. Emma refers to *The Porch*'s review as a "philippic," wondering if indeed her book is too "warm." But Lesbia, representative of the average circulating library patron, enjoys the book for precisely those "warm" moments, and refers to the review as a "Billingsgate" (p. 178), shifting the moral grounds of the novel's criticism to the arena of the marketplace wherein one fish vendor devalues another's wares. Thus are the two competing models of literary value set against each other: the noble (male) orator with a moral message of national importance, and the fishwife vending her vulgar merchandise.

Lesbia's opinions are significant here precisely because she is represented as the typical consumer – a somewhat insulting portrait of the reader in the text: "If only Lesbia's opinion were better worth having; but, after all, she may be taken as a fair representative of the average public; and, in some notable instances, the verdict of the average public has proved in the long run a more veracious one than that of the adepts" (p. 107). Broughton, of course, is one of those notable instances; as the *Temple Bar* states, "Miss Broughton is one of the novelists who owe all their success to themselves and the public, and nothing or comparatively nothing, to the press."[9] And the reader she is writing to, that is, the one who is presumably reading this assessment of Lesbia, would be precisely that public to whom Broughton is indebted for her success. However, since Lesbia is clearly characterized as charmingly silly and absurd, the reader also is invited not to identify with Lesbia, but to see herself as superior in kind to *Miching Mallecho*'s readers and to see *A Beginner* as superior in kind to the novel whose fortunes it chronicles. Thus, the meta-narrative both incorporates the reader into the text itself and displaces that text in the act of doing so: Broughton is Emma and not-Emma; the reader is Lesbia and not-Lesbia; *A Beginner* is text and not-text, that is, meta- or even con-text. This equivocation with the subject of the text put the *Athenaeum*'s reviewer out of patience:

"A Beginner" is devoid of anything approaching a plot. Were it not for the lightness, vivacity and sense of movement inherent in Miss Broughton's touch, it would hardly be even what is called "a story without a plot"... We are told little about the volume (Miching Mallecho) except that it is concerned with "passion." Yet it is the principal feature of "A Beginner."[10]

Indeed, there is a kind of tantalizing frustration in reading so much about a book that cannot, itself, be accessed; *Miching Mallecho* lives up to its early description as "coquettish." We are given tidbits of information about it in conversations, are privy to various reviewers' opinions, and are even witness to its destruction, but are never afforded so much as an excerpt from the book itself. Emma is, in fact, offered to us as the substitute of the book, regardless of her valiant struggle to disassociate her own experiences from those described in her novel. Again, the indelicacy of the novel reflects directly on the flesh of the female author/mother (Emma is referred to several times as the book's parent); as Emma's readers say "What beats me is, where have you got your experience – such very startling experience – ... from?" (*A Beginner*, p. 109). Again, the woman is supposed to merely re-present personal experience; the realm of the imagination belongs to "Shakespeare and Fielding" (p. 109). Appropriate subject matter for women authors, then, is domesticity. When Emma seeks advice from her publisher, he tells her that, after *The Porch*'s review, the book has "ceased to move." In an attempt to comfort her, he advises her to pursue safer topics:

It is always difficult to foretell what the public will like. The only perfectly safe line is the domestic. Now, there is a slight work which we have just brought out... "Hame! Hame! Hame!" As you may see by the title, it is on purely domestic lines, the reviewers have been almost unanimous in its praise, and we can't print it fast enough. (pp. 252–253)

Emma has, however, gone outside the domestic sphere for her subject matter, and the "infant" (p. 166) betrays the traces of the mother–author's illegitimate textual activity. Such activity is a gender and class betrayal. Significantly, the county papers that favorably notice the book assume a male author whose class is not called into question, yet *The Porch* attacks on both fronts:

We can predicate with absolute certainty four things concerning the author of "Miching Mallecho": that she is young, female, foolish, and innocent of any personal acquaintance with the lofty society to which, with such generosity, she introduces us ... among the milliners and 'prentices who will pasture on this masterpiece, one or two may be found silly enough to take it seriously, [so] we utter our protest against this vicious trash ... let her give us her views of the nobility and gentry, as seen through the "airy" railings, but let her beware of again putting out her feeble hand to clutch Jove's thunderbolt. (p. 174)

Not only does the critic attack the writer as a woman who has chosen a gender-inappropriate topic, he labels her lower class, writing to a lower-class audience, whom she may corrupt. This is an amusing reflection of the *Blackwood's* statement that "Miss Braddon and Miss Thomas [Broughton] ... might not be aware of how young women of good blood and good training feel."[11] In both the fictional and the actual case, however, the targets of these aspersions were of the classes of whom they wrote. This irony is sharpened in *A Beginner* by Broughton's revelation that the critic is, in fact, Hatcheson, who is working class. In fact, class is a key issue, both in the marketing of *Miching Mallecho* and in the relationship between Emma and Edgar. Edgar is an inappropriate companion for the upper class Emma, so when Emma's aunt notices Emma's admiration of his work, she is horrified that this admiration may extend to his person: "It is illiberal and an anachronism on the part of Mrs. Chantry, but to hear her adopted child *entonner* this hymn of praise on behalf of a young male Hatcheson gives her almost as great a shock as it would do to see her walking arm in arm with the footman" (*A Beginner*, p. 121). For Emma, however, "the man is swallowed up in the Mind. Could even Mrs. Cave point the finger of scorn at her for treading the stubble [taking an unescorted walk] in company with an Intelligence? Not that she formulates to herself this delicate difference; but it is unconsciously yet reassuringly present to her" (p. 95). As an author, class does not "mark" Hatcheson as it does Emma. As a woman, however, Emma is marked primarily by gender and class in everything she does; consequently, her writing is judged by those criteria first. Sexual activity is rigidly policed by class concerns, and as a woman, Emma is defined by her sexuality in all of her activities – her every action represents the penetrability or impenetrability of the upper classes, whereas Edgar's class only becomes important in relation to his sexual interaction with upper-class women. Again, while Edgar's text is a product of his intellect, which is not class-bound, Emma's text is representative of her body, which is subject to the class which dictates its uses and assigns it its value. Broughton uses the class issue to problematize the personal relationship between Emma and Edgar in the reader's mind. Emma is infatuated with Edgar Hatcheson's writing, and her image of him as a "great" writer, but his lower-class status make him an impossible love object in himself. Yet Broughton encourages the reader to flirt with the possibility that Emma will betray her class in a choice of mate, just as she did in writing her novel, while Emma is sublimely unaware that Edgar may be interpreting her hero worship as something rather more personal. When she is made aware of the possibility of this interpretation, she is more horrified than pleased, yet intrigued by the prospect of such a sacrifice to the intellect. When Edgar visits her to give her his new volume, which he has dedicated to her, he announces that, by virtue of his accession to the editorship of *The Porch* and a small inheritance, he may now propose to her. At this point, she opens the volume, sees the reprinted review of her work, learns that he is the "slasher" of *Miching Mallecho*, and tells him that she can never speak to him again. Criticism delineates the boundaries of class- and gender-appropriate behavior, ending all possibility of transgression, intellectual or otherwise, in the novel.

It is through such details that the whole justification of the judgment of the critics upon *Miching Mallecho* and the appropriateness of Emma's decision to give up writing are called into question. The "clues" the reader is given about the book and the workings of the publishing industry are sufficiently ambiguous to suggest that the book may very well be worthwhile. Yet the genre of *A Beginner* and its reflection of the formula which the Broughton reader expected demanded that Emma repudiate authorship in favor of domesticity. As events in the novel bring pressure to bear on Emma to do so, the desire of the reader for the "appropriate" ending becomes a part of that pressure; we, too, are willing to sacrifice *Miching Mallecho* and its author to the traditional narrative and the narratives of tradition. Like good circulating library readers, we are willing to accord *The Porch* the authority to evaluate what we will read, even though we know that such an authority may well be spurious.

Thus, in Broughton's book, the critics – represented by Hatcheson and Grimston respectively – really do make the readers' decisions by placing both the book and the author out of reach – even though Lesbia, the reader's representative, thought it "the most beautiful love story" ever written. By holding the text out of the reader's reach and focusing on the con-text of publication, Broughton implicates the reader in a complicity with the values that keep Emma out of the market. She constructs *A Beginner* in such a way that it ultimately, if somewhat problematically, validates those values, and invites the reader to do the same. At the end of the novel, most copies of *Miching Mallecho* are recovered and made into a bonfire. Broughton insists that in the act of reading, we deprive ourselves of the text, that we burn *Miching Mallecho* even as we desire it, that we destroy the thing we love even as we enjoy its pleasures. In short, we must recognize ourselves as participants rather than as mere voyeurs of an existing spectacle.

These substitutions – of one text for another, of character for author – are extensions of the fundamental structure of the popular romance, which depends on the tension between repetition and substitution. As the *Temple Bar* points out, "As her [Broughton's] stories are always essentially love stories, and nothing else, it would be impossible to write them without hitches, more or less severe, to make the plot and carry on the play."[12] To the extent that this is true of Broughton's work, we may say then that their appeal depends on the repetition of a theme (two people fall in love) and the variation or substitution of the specific characters, the particular obstacles to their happiness, and the backdrop against which the spectacle is seen. However, this in turn creates a condition in which the repetition of theme – supposed to be the main attraction of the text for the reader – must in some sense "disappear" in the reading process, that, in fact, the ubiquitous love theme becomes the background for what is specific to the text, although supposedly subordinate, which is the substitution. In this way, each novel becomes a part of a larger text of "formula" novels in the same genre, and the reading of the individual novel is conditioned by that intertext, within which the love-interest both overshadows all other concerns and disappears beneath them. Broughton takes such very good advantage of this contradiction that often the love-interest is in fact conspicuously absent from her "love stories." Frequently the object of the woman's affections is physically absent for most of the story, and he is generally the shallowest of cardboard constructions. Sometimes a secondary character for whom the heroine evidences no particular attraction will become the *deus ex machina*, and in later novels, the love theme may be given entirely to secondary characters, whom the protagonist advises. In this sense, the genre with which Broughton is identified conditions the critics' reading of her works; even romances are rarely *about* love "and nothing else" and Broughton's stories, particularly the later ones, are quite frequently about everything *but* love – which is treated as a sort of given, necessary but, in itself, uninteresting. In the same way that the interpretation of *Miching Mallecho* as a romance trivializes the explosive social content of the book, while rendering it all the more dangerous, the definition of Broughton as a writer of romances directs attention away from *A Beginner*'s critique of the literary marketplace. Broughton's use of the love-interest in *A Beginner* is paradigmatic. After the reader's equivocal flirtation with Edgar as the love-interest in the novel – a flirtation in which Emma does not, for the most part, participate – Emma is unceremoniously given to "Old George," a fatherly adviser, in marriage; this is an event of such little interest that it is not even part of the text, but is summarized in the epilogue. Truly, the real focus of this "romance" is not the tender passion, but a much hardier and more dangerous one – the passion for writing, for transgression, for "mischief" indeed, as "Miching Mallecho" is supposed to mean. The ultimate failure of *Miching Mallecho*, and even the reader's possible approval of that failure, do not eradicate the desire for transgression that motivates the reader to peruse the rogue progress of Emma and her book, and their eventual neutralization.

As mentioned above, *A Beginner* ends with a bonfire. With the exception of five public library copies, all extant copies of Emma's novel are retrieved and burned. The action is a ritual cleansing: "There is only one final act of expiation to perform, and without perceptible wincing the high-priestess advances to the edge of the fire, and tosses the original MC. – the beloved, the much-treasured, the sole – into the heart of the furnace!" (*A Beginner*, p. 391). This self-immolation takes place at Easter. The regeneration of the authoress occurs through an *auto-da-fé*, she is reborn at the closing of the book, and the epilogue assures us that she has married and is "not very fond of literary society" (p. 394). Emma's rebirth into domesticity is literally a death of the author; with the burning of *Miching Mallecho*, *A Beginner* ends, and Emma is beyond the text and therefore, closed and impermeable. The fire is therapeutic; Emma is cured of the mania for self-expression. (On the other hand, five public library copies linger; apparently, the text is never completely under the author's control.) The reassertion of order, through the patriarchal and patronizing discourse of the critic, and through the domestication of Emma by marriage to her *"vielle pater"* after her purification by fire deprive the reader of the possibility of transgressive passion as *Miching Mallecho* burns. The narrator's (and Emma's) ambivalence toward Edgar make this palatable to some degree, yet present a problem in interpretation. Hatcheson's attractiveness rests in his intellectual power, his intelligence which has allowed him to rise from the lower classes to the editorship of *The Porch*. Yet he is judged to be a mere follower, a traditionalist who is politically backward, "the shoe upon the coach-wheel" of progress. This judgment is offered by Miss Grimston, herself an absurd character who has "unsexed" herself by speaking, as a politically active feminist, of inappropriate topics like women's rights and Malthusianism. Miss Grimston is, of course, suspected of writing the negative review of *Miching Mallecho* and is shown, through Emma's jaundiced eye, as quite objectionable and foolish. · Yet Emma's novel also is accused of gender-inappropriate speech and the review was actually written by Hatcheson. If the maligned Miss Grimston is reinterpreted as a positive character in the light of the information disclosed at the end of the novel, then Edgar may indeed be a reactionary conservative representing a reactionary critical institution whose opinion is unreliable, as his prejudice against all women authors, in a novel written by a successful woman author, would seem to suggest. In this case, the judicial homicide of Emma's career is to be mourned, even as she is congratulated for escaping a liaison with Hatcheson. If his opinion of her novel is correct, however, it validates his intelligence and hence, his suitability as a love-interest, in which case Emma's marriage to George would be a failure of the romantic plot. Thus, regardless of which interpretation the reader favors, the story cannot be said to have a thoroughly "happy ending," wedding or no. While the traditional format of the love story ending in a marriage trivializes the story of Emma-the-writer, the fact that Broughton begins her novel with the "birth" of the novel and ends with its "death" by fire, and that the novel is burned for crimes of (representing) passion, suggest that *A Beginner* is more a story of destruction than creation, more of hate than love. In this way, the story mirrors the traditional mechanism of the formula romance (the love theme is submerged beneath the exigencies of plot, *Miching Mallecho* recedes into the text of *A Beginner*) without duplicating it (love is not, at any time, the primary concern of this text.) The object of pursuit, of passion, is shown to be a commodity whose availability is determined by a market constrained by gender, class, and genre expectations (is *Miching Mallecho* a social-problem novel or a love story, masculine or feminine?) and the reader is implicated in the enforcement of those constraints in the act of reading/consuming itself.

# CHAPTER 5

# Ouida: romantic exchange

Ouida (1839-1908), although a tireless self-creator, and consummate performer of her identity as an artist, had the least comfortable relationship with the literary establishment with which she worked of the three authors we are concerned with. Expatriated, she may have found it easier than most to sustain an image, both publicly and privately, which was under constant assault in the literary press. By adopting a specifically Romantic identity as an artist, which she claimed nullified her femininity, she sidestepped a good many of the issues surrounding the woman's popular novel – she was neither writing what was merely "popular" nor was she, in her writing, feminine, she would argue. She was, of course, marketed precisely in the manner she repudiated, but as an artist who had nothing to do with commerce, it was perhaps convenient for her not to be aware of that.

Ouida produced over thirty novels, many volumes of short stories, essays, drama, and other occasional work. In the 1870s, at the peak of her popularity, Ouida wrote roughly a novel a year with some other work, and thus generated an income of approximately £5,000 per annum.[1] She devoted her voice, especially in the later novels, to social causes. Her target was the abuse of power, of any sort, and she had an especially keen sense of the abuses of the power accorded by wealth; she also fetishized both that power and the commodities it can procure. Her books are as likely to feature male protagonists as females, yet, once again at the center of the text is always the body of the woman.

Ouida's early novels, mischievous stepchildren of the silver-fork genre, are much more adoring of the "high life" and those who live it than the later novels. The later novels often take a sharply critical stance toward the wealthy and powerful, and may have as a protagonist a peasant, or penniless artist, or even a dog (as in *Puck*). The Italian novels often eschew the aristocracy altogether in favor of village life, wherein the powerful villains are petty bureaucrats and mercenary merchants.

The common thread in this widely differing set of topics and settings is the focus on power and on the commodification of the body, especially the female body, a theme it has in common with much Victorian melodrama. This focus duplicates the actual relation of capital to the female body in Victorian culture, which is both to enshrine it as prototypical commodity and to displace the lived, material body – a gesture which encompasses both uses of the female body under capitalism: that is, as either a sexualized body which derives its value from its capacity for exchange (the prostitute) or as a body which, as Jeff Nunokawa has argued, achieves its value in the moment in which it is withdrawn from exchange and becomes "safe capital" as someone's wife.[2] By enshrining the commodity at the center of its narrative, the novel of high life exploits the spectacle of the commodification of the woman's body. By retaining that focus in her later novels which were not of high life, Ouida makes clear that commodification of the woman's body is simply concomitant to the exercise of power under capitalism, regardless of the presence of actual commodities or "gewgaws" which figured so prominently in her early work.

Most interesting is Ouida's concept of gendered power. Both her men and women must negotiate with the demands of power in the realm of exchange, which pressures them to become commodities themselves. Men, and bad women, can "safely" enter this process of circulation – women by yielding to it and directing their own commodification, and men by a dangerous and careful negotiation of identity and the exercise of their ability to control other commodities. Ouida's ice-princess female characters designated as love objects for the men manage to stay outside this realm whether through aristocratic birth or through their identities as artists. More interesting and active (and poor) "good" women, however, rarely escape unscathed. Against their will, they must enter the realm of exchange, into which they are inexorably drawn, thus losing their identities as subjects, a process figured as the opening of their bodies by sex, violence, and illness. Only through self-sacrifice (usually in the service of helping the male protagonist enter that same realm without loss of subjectivity), can they paradoxically "save" themselves, destroying their bodies to cancel out their shameful openness. Ouida repeatedly draws parallels between femininity and colonial identity, and her tragic women tend to be hybrids: Cigarette, the French–North African of uncertain parentage and Folle-Farine, bastard daughter of a French woman and a gypsy father are only two examples. In *Under Two Flags*, in particular, the multiple plots dramatize her marked ambivalence toward colonial/imperial practices, which Ouida sees as brutal, unjust, and genocidal, yet necessary, racially and scientifically justifiable and noble, often all at the same time. Within her own text Ouida demonstrates some of the passionate uncertainty gripping Victorians in their attitude toward the colonial and imperial project.

## UNDER TWO FLAGS[3]

*Under Two Flags*, published in 1867, was Ouida's fourth novel to gain a wide popularity, but the first to really attain sales figures that caused her name to be mentioned in the same breath as those of M. E. Braddon and Mrs. Henry Wood. (It went into sixty-three editions in England alone.[4]) Ouida's extravagant descriptions of people and places she had never seen left her open to sniping by critics for whom realism and correct grammar were prerequisites for fine writing. Her many readers apparently preferred gorgeous, if somewhat confusing, fantasy. Monica Stirling calls *Under Two Flags* a "rapidly moving, highly coloured, frequently preposterous, and frequently touching novel."[5] An anonymous *Athenaeum* critic winds up a sarcastic review of the novel by admitting that "Ouida has certainly the gift of speech; and though her speech is not standard silver, it is capital electro-plate, and her nonsense has a spirit and dash about it which keep the reader from finding flaws or asking questions."[6]

*Under Two Flags* follows the career of a young aristocrat, Bertie Cecil, living a life of fabulous luxury on the edge of bankruptcy in England. Through a series of catastrophes, he finds himself in trouble with the law and dishonoured among his peers; he is actually innocent of any wrongdoing, but cannot clear himself without disgracing both a married woman with whom he is having an affair, and his beloved younger brother. He flees Europe, where he is thought dead, and joins the French foreign legion under an assumed name. He serves in Africa for many years as a valiant soldier, under grueling conditions, perhaps the worst of which is the enmity of his commander, Chateauroy. Ouida also introduces here one of her most interesting characters, and one for which she is best remembered – the character of Cigarette, a *vivandière* of the French army. The nameless daughter of a camp follower and an unknown father, she grows up in the midst of the army, treated first as a sort of mascot and later as an honorary soldier. Adored by her male comrades, Cigarette has her choice of lovers, but becomes intrigued by Cecil, who is not only unresponsive, but completely unaware of her infatuation with him. Instead, he falls in love with Venetia, a woman "of his Order," whom, of course, he cannot approach. Through a complex series of events, it becomes possible for him honorably to reclaim his lost identity and court the woman he loves, but he is nearly prevented from so doing by a firing squad. Cigarette saves him by stepping in to take the bullets herself, thereby simultaneously saving his life and allowing him to realize her true worth and the greatness of his loss (while gracefully eliminating her status as a plot complication and inappropriate love object).

*Under Two Flags* combines the high society romance with the adventure story, the common theme being that both Belgravian boudoir and African desert are exotic and rather lawless places. In stark contrast to most popular English novels, adultery is represented as the norm in the upper classes, keeping wealthy men very busy attending both their aristocratic mistresses and their fashionable courtesans. Why this was tolerated in Ouida's novels is unclear; it may have had something to do with her residence in France and the perception that her novels were really simply French novels written in English. The English reading public certainly tolerated more open sexuality in French novels than they did in English ones, seeking out French novels for precisely this quality. Many critics pointed out this distinction with pride, while a few commented with annoyance on the "absurd limitations" placed on English writers, but the awareness that such a difference existed was apparently general. Ouida frequently commented humorously on such restrictions herself; in *Puck*, a playwright discusses the difficulties in adapting a French play for the British stage:

They never stand any nonsense with the seventh commandment, remember. You must change the illicit love into a decorous bigamy. Indeed, you might try trigamy. They wouldn't at all mind three husbands ... The English conscience is so intensely mercantile, that it has no notion of a passion that does not result in the cheating of somebody ... Bigamy is fraud; and the fraud commends it to the public of these very commercial Isles.[7]

Obviously, however, Ouida managed to avoid the use of this formula. When she later writes, "At risk of arousing the censure of readers, I confess that I would leave to society a very large liberty in the matter of its morality or immorality, if it would only justify its existence by any originality, any true light and loveliness,"[8] she is being disingenuous; she knows exactly how much censure she could expect – as well as how that censure might increase her readership.

It is also possible that part of the appeal was similar to that of the exposé and the newspaper accounts of the divorce court; like many novelists of her day, particularly sensation novelists, Ouida sought and found inspiration in the newspapers; in fact, an article on *vivandières* of the French army, complete with detailed sketches, in *The Illustrated London Times*, may have been the spark that lighted Cigarette.[9] Critics wrote of their concern that lower-class readers would take Ouida's depictions as the gospel truth about the aristocracy, and George Gissing has a character in *The Odd Women* warn a jealous working-class husband to read Ouida's accounts of the European lifestyle before he takes his wife on the Continent. Ouida's readership, however, was largely middle class: as Vincent E. H. Murray notes with great disapprobation, "The price at which they are published renders them inaccessible to those whom it is customary to call 'the people,' and it is clear that... [Ouida] does not address herself to them. These books are issued by one of the first houses in the trade; they are written for and read by society."[10] Whether this largely middle class readership would have had such faith in Ouida's veracity is unknown, but certainly the demand existed, for Charles Mudie forgave scenes in Ouida's books which he would never have tolerated in, say, George Moore. It may well be that Ouida's matter-of-fact presentation of the *demi-monde* and of adulterous wives was tolerable because she did not try to gain sympathy for them as essentially virtuous but erring natures, as Wood or Mrs. Gaskell do for their controversial heroines. In what Margaret Oliphant calls "very fine and very nasty books," the reader may regard the fallen, but generally beautiful, charming, amusing, and fairly happy woman with guilty fascination, without ever being called upon to challenge her or his own beliefs about the fallen woman's spiritual or moral condition. Perhaps also the fact that the main characters of Ouida's early novels are all males, and that the erring woman is not central, as she is in Wood's, Gaskell's, and many other sensation novels may play a part in readers' acceptance of these characters. Ouida tended to be denigrating in her comments about women, being, even in the 1890s, opposed to suffrage and anything that smacked of feminism, and she is unsparingly negative in her evaluation of most of her female characters' moral qualities. Yet she grants these women a remarkable power and energy in manipulating and controlling their environment, and a capacity for doing damage that may have been a potent attractant for female readers who felt that their own control of their lives was at best tenuous. In an essay decrying female suffrage, Ouida warns of the dangers of unleashing women in the political arena, since, "There is in every woman, even in the best woman, a sleeping potentiality for crime, a curious possibility of fiendish evil. Even her maternal love is dangerously near an insane ferocity."[11] As unflattering as this "view" is, it at least does not portray woman as weak.

Like *Lady Audley's Secret, Under Two Flags* chronicles the growth of a young man from immaturity and irresponsibility to maturity. Like Robert Audley, Bertie Cecil is frivolous and lazy, even effeminate at the start of the story; like Robert Audley, Bertie Cecil is ready to assume his rightful place in the social order, as an English peer and family patriarch, at the end. And, as in *Lady Audley's Secret*, the logic of the story demands that a woman be sacrificed in order that this may be so. Robert Audley takes the place of Helen/Lucy, both in the affections of her first husband and ultimately in Audley Hall. Cigarette, shielding Cecil from the firing squad, is executed in his place. Cigarette is Cecil's logical complement; just as he is "feminine" in many of his characteristics, so she is masculine. However, Cecil never loses his masculine identity or privilege, while Cigarette, the author repeatedly tells us, is both "unsexed" and "doomed" by her sex.

When Cecil is first introduced to us, we find him in the midst of a costly and spectacular disarray reminiscent of Lady Audley's sitting room:

A Guardsman at home is always, if anything, more luxuriously accommodated than a young duchess ... the hangings of the room were silken and rose-colored, and a delicious confusion prevailed through it pell-mell, box-spurs, hunting-stirrups, cartridge-cases, curb-chains, muzzle-loaders, hunting-flasks and white gauntlets being mixed up with Paris novels, pink notes, point-lace ties ... [the nickname] "Beauty," gained at Eton, was in no way undeserved; when the smoke cleared ... it showed a face of as much delicacy and brilliancy as a woman's ... his features were exceedingly fair – fair as the fairest girl's. (*Under Two Flags*, pp. 6–7)

The constant reference to Beauty's "woman's face" and feminine accoutrements have raised eyebrows among later readers; as Stirling dryly remarks, "Fortunate Hon. Bertie, able to indulge in scent, turquoise-studded dressing-cases, French pictures, point-lace ties, and startling eyelashes without anybody misunderstanding him!",[12] but it is fairly clear that Ouida presents these "feminine" characteristics as positive, or at least neutral; these are the signs of Cecil's aristocratic lineage, and are not inherently negative since they are balanced by a "masculine" self-control and sense of honor, although they may betray negative, though dormant, tendencies. His younger brother Berkeley, however, is characterized as "very girlish in his face and ways" with a "girlish weakness in his temperament" and it is made clear that in Berkeley's case, these are negative traits, without the requisite balance of masculine self-control. After an exciting and life-threatening steeplechase, Bertie Cecil's manner is described:

Bertie looked as serenely and listlessly nonchalant as of old, while he nodded to the Seraph with a gentle smile... Outsiders would sooner have thought him defeated than triumphant... No one could have dreamt that he was thinking in his heart of hearts how passionately he loved the gallant beast that had been victor with him, and that if he had followed out the momentary impulse in him he could have put his arms round the noble-bowed neck and kissed the horse like a woman! (*Under Two Flags*, p. 45)

Berkeley, on the other hand, has no such control. Cecil finds him gambling away money he does not have: "Little Berk's pretty face was very flushed; his lips were set tight, his eyes were glittering... He was playing with a terrible eagerness" (p. 85). Unfortunately, Berkeley suffers from "the absence ... of that delicate, intangible, indescribable, sensitive nerve which men call Honor" (p. 94) and which we might call the Phallus, with which pretty features are an asset to one's masculinity and without which they are an emasculating liability. Cigarette, however, has a strong sense of honor, but is none the better for it, since in gaining it, she has become "unsexed." Cigarette, overhearing Cecil's pitying judgment of her, poses the question thus: "Unsexed? Pouf! If you have a woman's face, may I not have a man's soul? It is only a fair exchange" (p. 230). Her question, however, is answered in the negative, both in repeated narratorial asides, and in the plot equation that exacts her death as the surcharge of the "fair exchange" of the two characters. Ouida is specific about the disadvantages of Cigarette's sex, as she is about its charms:

"What a gallant boy is spoiled in that little amazon!" he thought ... she had not much interest for him ... save that he saw she was pretty ... But he was sorry a child so bright and so brave should be turned into three parts a trooper as she was, should have been tossed up on the scum and filth of the lowest barrack life, and should be doomed in a few years' time to become the yellow, battered, foul-mouthed, vulture-eyed camp follower that premature old age would surely render the darling of the tricolor, the pythoness of the As-de-Pique. Cigarette was making scorn of her doom of Sex, dancing it down, burning it out in tobacco fumes ... but strive to kill it how she would, her sex would have its revenge one day and play Nemesis to her... [And] when the bloom should leave her brown cheeks ... the womanhood she had defied would assert itself, and avenge itself, and be hideous in the sight of men who now loved the tinkling of those little spurred feet ... Cecil thought that a gallant boy was spoiled in this eighteen-year-old brunette of a campaigner; he might have gone further and said that a hero was lost. (p. 294)

A hero, however, is not lost but gained in Cigarette's death; by fixing her identity forever in the twin preservatives of youth and death, her martyrdom gives her the mystique that the living Cigarette can never have, with her sexually active behavior evocative both of desire and disease, of fertility and mortality. The "scum and filth," which refers both to the human beings with whom Cigarette interacts and to the filthy living conditions, also functions as a fairly direct reference to the bodily fluids and products of disease that make up a part of that filth. Ouida ties together images of the "yellow" (diseased), "vulture-eyed" (death and disease consuming) camp follower (sexually promiscuous woman), who is "foul mouthed" (consuming and spewing filth) with Cigarette's attractiveness, i.e., her sexual availability. Ouida makes much of Cigarette's soiled mouth, "which was now like a bud from a damask rose branch, though even now it steeped itself in wine, and sullied itself with oaths, and had never been touched from its infancy with any kiss that was innocent" (p. 293), and refers to Cigarette as floating on the "sewer waters" of "vice" (p. 294). Cigarette's mouth is referred to whenever Ouida invokes Cigarette's sexuality, standing for all the openings of the body and Cigarette's femaleness. Ouida's description of Cigarette's heroics are constantly undermined by references to the grotesque body that is both the body of war-torn Franco-Africa (the torn bodies of soldiers, the disease-ridden bodies of hospital patients, the raped bodies of Arab women) and that is the female, and therefore by its nature grotesque, body of Cigarette, defined by its openings and its permeability. Only in death, its breast pierced by hundreds of bullets, is the permeability of the upper body sufficient to balance Cigarette's femaleness, to achieve sufficient closure and masculinization of the grotesque lower body that she may be identified as a hero, "the color ... passing fast from her lips and a mortal pallor settling there in the stead of that rich bright hue, once warm as the scarlet heart of the pomegranite" (p. 592).

The "Two Flags" in *Under Two Flags* refers to the flags of England and France, but it might very well stand for all the dualities in Cecil's nature and experiences – the extremes of wealth and poverty, luxury and hardship, domestic Britain and exotic Africa, masculinity and femininity. The entire novel becomes a mechanism to define Cecil's mature masculine identity, by pitting him against characters and situations that body forth ambiguities in his own nature, and force him to commit himself to appropriate objects of desire (his identity, his homeland, his future wife); after years of reacting (feminine), he finds his identity as a masculine, desiring subject. It is his exile that "saves" him:

On the surface it seemed as though never was there a life more utterly thrown away than the life of ... a man of good blood, high rank, and talented gifts, had he ever chosen to make anything of them, buried in the ranks of the Franco-African army ... Yet it might be doubted if ... any other ... would equally have given steel and strength to his indolence and languor as this did. In his old world, he would have lounged listlessly through fashionable seasons, and in an atmosphere that encouraged his profound negligence of everything and his natural nil-admirari listlessness would have glided from refinement to effeminacy. (p. 266)

If the feminine grotesque is defined by openness and hedonism, masculinity is defined by closure and control. Control, however, is nothing without desire to master and contain. The story, then, of Cecil's coming to manhood is one not only of control being tested, but of becoming able to desire both intensely and appropriately. Bertie Cecil the aristocrat desires nothing intensely because his needs are met, which is to say that he is never confronted with the permeability and the neediness of the body. He runs the risk of becoming lax and effeminate (open) because he has never faced the need to maintain closure. It is only when that openness becomes both a risk and a desire that control is truly invoked and mastery tested.

Homosocial bonding both constitutes the occasion for and the threat to that self-mastery, as it does in *Lady Audley's Secret*. Like Robert Audley, Cecil undertakes his quest at least partly out of love for his closest male friend, the Seraph, in whose eyes Cecil believes his honor has been tarnished. Also like Robert Audley, Cecil marries the sister of his closest male friend, who can hardly compete with her brother in moving Cecil's most intense emotions. When, several years after Cecil's flight from England, the Seraph turns up unexpectedly in Africa, Cecil is "powerless" (p. 439): "[Cigarette saw] the startled amaze, the longing love, the agony of recognition, in his eyes! ... '[I fear] my own weakness.'... He felt that if he looked again on the face of the man he loved, he might be broken into self-pity, and unloose his silence, and shatter all the work of so many years" (pp. 437–440). He runs from the sight of the Seraph's face "as men flee pestilence" (p. 490), and does it so successfully that it is only when he faces the firing squad that the Seraph finally sees and recognizes him, and "a great shuddering cry broke from them both . . . Cecil's eyes filled with slow, blinding tears; tears sweet as a woman's in her joy, bitter as a man's in his agony . . . he knew that this love, at least, had cleaved to him through all shame and against all evil" (pp. 585–586). However, in each of these scenes Cecil is powerless to aid himself, or to act at all. The description of Cecil's emotional danger is both feminine and sexual ("broken" and "unloosed"); it is the language of the open and opened body. Somehow, these openings must be closed or at least mediated or cleansed; otherwise, direct contact with the Seraph through them may lead to "pestilence."

In each instance, Cigarette is the agent who saves him, first by getting him orders to leave the camp, and finally by throwing herself in front of the firing squad while the Seraph struggles helplessly in the grip of the soldiers. The Seraph is the occasion for Cecil's Odyssey to gain self-control; however, Cecil cannot effect a reunion with his friend without threatening that very control, i.e. masculine identity. Through the death of Cigarette (the sexual woman) and marriage to Venetia (the non-sexual and therefore non-threatening woman of "race"), Cecil can be reunited with the Seraph while his own masculinity is safeguarded; i.e., he does not act on his desire to be with the Seraph, or his desire to escape the firing squad, but is able to become husband, brother, and patriarch, and to assume his title and position as an English peer and active, masculine member of the power structure.

Feminine openings are dangerous and liable to contamination, yet they are the only means through which passages or boundary crossings may be effected. Cecil goes to Africa to learn desire and need (awareness of the body's openings) and therefore how to control that desire (how to close the body's openings). In his ultimate moment of desire, in the moment he sees the Seraph's face, he must not take steps to fulfill that desire, for that would show a lack of self-control or ability to maintain closure; it is Cigarette who serves as a conduit between the men, so that Cecil's desire may be gratified without Cecil releasing ("unloosing") his self-control, his closure. Cecil reenters fellowship with the living through the opening of Cigarette's body by the bullets, and the fellowship of the Seraph through the opening of Venetia's body in the marital relation; Ouida emphasizes several times that Venetia, although previously married, is a "pure" virgin, and learns her "passion from him [Cecil] alone" (p. 596). In contrast to Cecil's early affairs with promiscuous married women or courtesans, his relationships with women in Africa stress female purity and monogamy. Cigarette holds little appeal for him, partially because she is "unsexed," but also because, in his newfound fastidiousness, he cannot contemplate her without evoking the specter of her middle age as a diseased prostitute. This is a scruple which never was at issue in his earlier liaisons with London courtesans. This may partly be an economic difference; a London courtesan might well retire on her earnings at a decorous age, whereas a camp follower would be less likely to do so. But as Cigarette is not a prostitute, but a wine-seller who has had a number of lovers, Cecil's concern may also be linked to the very perception of Africa (or India, or any other colonial holding) as a country "whose sun was as flame and whose breath was as pestilence" (p. 596).

*Under Two Flags* is thus devoted to defining the appropriate aristocratic masculine English character, and all Cecil's travails are means for refining and testing that character. As an aristocrat, Cecil is born with the raw materials, e.g., a fine physique, instinctive self-control, and that "sensitive nerve," but in England, surrounded by luxury and "Paris novels," he runs the risk of degenerating – that is, of developing exclusively the feminine aspects of his nature. The (in this case, French) colonial setting, with its exposure to disease and deprivation, seems to be necessary to "tighten" the English character:

> He had suffered, braved, resented, fought, loved, hated, endured, and even enjoyed, here in Africa, with a force and vividness that he had never dreamed possible in his cold, passionless, insouciant world of other days. He had known what the hunger of famine, what the torment of fever, what the agony of forbidden pride, what the wild delight of combat were ... he had known all these, the desert passions, and while they left him much the same in character, they changed him vitally. (p. 267)

The English character, then, is defined through the experience of its opposite. Cecil becomes worthy of his heritage after experiencing the lack of privilege of a common soldier, worthy of "the glad, cool, green, dew-freshened earth that was so sweet and so full of peace, after the scorched and blood-stained plains" (p. 596), worthy of health after the "torment of fever." His transition from passive recipient of stimuli to active agent is set forth also in literary metaphor. A French officer praises him: "[Y]our sword writes in a brave man's fashion – writes what France loves to read. But before you wore your sword here? Tell us of that. It was a romance – wasn't it?" Cecil responds, "If it were, I have folded down the page, monsieur" (p. 257). Just as the manly world of battle is contrasted against the feminine domain of love, the masculine genre of the war novel or adventure story is pitted against the feminine genre of the "romance," the novel of high life in which it is embedded.

Ultimately, however, that masculine genre is both contained and domesticated within its feminine counterpart. The first half of the novel is in fact the novel of high life, and the reader's commitment to the novel is based on that generic choice. The adventure story within the overall novel – Cecil's twelve years in Africa – tests and proves Cecil's worthiness to return to England as the protagonist of the romance of high life, and so end the story in marriage, the classic feminine-genre ending. "It was worth banishment to return ... It was worth the trials I bore to learn the love that I have known," Cecil explains to Venetia in his last lines in the book (p. 596). Just as Africa only acts as a sort of finishing school for Cecil's manhood, the adventure novel functions to prepare Cecil for his role as bridegroom–hero of the romance of high life. His return to England signifies that the transition is complete.

As is so often the case in sensation novels, class identity and class conflict are the signs of boundaries and their permeability. Usually, boundary transgression takes place at the plot level through inter-class romance, as in *Lady Audley's Secret*; here, however, it takes place also at the level of genre, and a gender role reversal must take place in order for the romance to begin again. Since a loss of class identity on Cecil's part is the occasion for the beginning of the adventure story, he must regain it to resume the romance. However, his loss of caste places him in an inferior position to his love-interest, Venetia; he is therefore placed in the feminine role relative to her. Whereas a difference in class may be passable (although still dangerous) if the woman is inferior, and therefore merely more feminine, more powerless, and therefore potentially more appealing, it is impassable if the man is inferior, at least in a heterosexual or heterosocial relationship. Interestingly, within homosocial relationships, class differences are acceptable for men, as in the friendship of Cecil and his valet, Rake, whereas close homosocial bonding between women of different classes, even in the patronage relationship, are often represented as threatening, as is Phoebe Marks' closeness to Lady Audley. Perhaps women, being "open," are more liable to class contamination than men are. Even Cigarette avoids the company of other women. Ouida, in a later essay, is specific about the deleterious effects of physical closeness between women, as she is supportive of the homosocial and even homosexual bond between men: "When a girl has a common bedchamber and a common bathroom

with other girls, she loses the delicate bloom of her modesty. Exposure to
a crowd of women is just as nasty as exposure to a crowd of men."[13] If
women do lose this modesty, men are likely to be inclined not to risk
contamination in their company:

The New Woman declares that man cannot do without woman. It is a doubtful
postulate. In the finest intellectual and artistic era of the world women were not
necessary to either the pleasures or the passions of men. It is possible that if
women make themselves as unlovely and offensive as they appear likely to
become, the preferences of the Platonic Age may become acknowledged and
dominant, and women may be relegated entirely to the lowest plane as a mere
drudge and child-bearer.[14]

*Under Two Flags* is full of cautionary tales in which men are emas-
culated in socially inappropriate sexual relationships, such as Leon
Ramon, a young painter of genius who is deprived of his ability to paint
when he is "dropped" by the aristocrat who hires him to paint her
portrait and enjoys an affair with him during the period of the sittings.
He fails to recognize that he is not her equal socially, and that it is
therefore impossible for him to have a sexual relationship with her that
is not based on dishonor, i.e., male powerlessness. Her treatment of him
as a prostitute feminizes him; his failure to recognize the true basis of the
relationship and refuse it results in his destruction. Jonathan Loesberg
has argued that the sensation novel's obsession with secret identities
stems from the anxiety over loss of class identity; here, with a masculine
protagonist, it becomes possible to understand how directly class and
gender identity are equatable, at least for the male reader – loss of class
identity is, quite simply, castration.

Class conflict is the one of the main sources of anxiety for Ouida's
critics, who are concerned that her portrayal of the upper classes might
cause them to sink in the estimation of Ouida's (presumably lower-class)
readers. Certainly class conflict is a theme which might well be expected
to be of central importance in a story which follows its main character
from the houses of royalty to the barracks of common soldiers and
which chronicles the excesses of wealth in such minute and profuse
detail. Often it appears as envy of the upper classes by the lower, out of
which no good can come. Cecil's initial ruin is wrought by a bookmaker
whose hatred of him is based as much on Cecil's aristocracy as on actual
conflict between the two characters, and his life in Africa is made
particularly miserable by a commanding officer, Chateauroy, whose
title of Marquis is a recent acquisition and whose sensitivity about his

peasant ancestry causes him to resent Cecil's unadmitted but evident aristocracy bitterly. The most dangerous liaisons between classes come through female sexual desire; Cigarette's love for Cecil leads her to contemplate the murder of Venetia as she recalls an anecdote of the Revolution in which a peasant woman jilted by her aristocratic lover takes her gory vengeance on the severed head of his noble wife. In a fury, Cigarette confronts Venetia with spirited and rather convincing speeches about the injustice of class inequality, but finds herself subdued by the intangible power of Venetia's nobility. Although Venetia fails to completely convince Cigarette, she seems to be speaking for Ouida's point of view:

"As far as in us lies, we strive to remedy its [poverty's] evil; the uttermost effort can do but little, but that little is only lessened – fearfully lessened – whenever Class is arrayed against Class by that blind antagonism which animates yourself."

   Cigarette's intelligence was too rapid not to grasp the truths conveyed by these words; but she was in no mood to acknowledge them. (*Under Two Flags*, p. 526)

The real occasion for Cigarette's resentment of Venetia is jealousy over Cecil, and thus the reader is made to see the dangers of love crossing over class boundaries. About prostitution, however, Ouida is less concerned; Cecil's mistress, "the Zu-Zu," rides with the hunt along with the married noblewoman with whom he is having an affair; the ladies manage their hostility by simply not acknowledging each other's presence, and the Zu-Zu seems to be in no hurry to upset the social order. Critics were concerned that the glorification of unlikely romances between lower-class girls and aristocratic men would lead young servant girls into disastrous relationships in which they would be seduced and abandoned. Ouida certainly did not waste ink on the pathos of the courtesan's plight:

The Zu-Zu was perfectly happy; and as for the pathetic pictures that novelists and moralists draw, of vice sighing amid turtles and truffles for childish innocence in the cottage at home where honey-suckles blossomed and brown brooks made melody . . . the Zu-Zu would have vaulted herself on the box-seat of a drag, and told you "to stow all that trash;" (*sic*) her childish recollections were of a stifling lean-to with the odor of pig-sty and straw yard, pork for a feast once a week, starvation all the other six days, kicks, slaps, wrangling, and a general atmosphere of beer and wash-tubs; she hated her past, and loved her cigar on the drag. The Zu-Zu is fact; the moralists' pictures are moonshine. (p. 62)

The danger lies, not in the economic exploitation of lower-class women's sexuality, but in romantic involvement between the classes. Of the plight of the waif seduced and abandoned to the streets, Ouida is contemptuous; in a later essay she writes, "In nine cases out of ten the first to corrupt the youth is the woman. In nine cases out of ten also she becomes corrupt herself because she likes it."[15] In *Held in Bondage*, one of Ouida's earliest works, "the Trefusis," a lower-class woman who expects marriage of her aristocratic lover, avenges herself by tricking him into marrying her under a false upper class identity. Ouida makes it clear that this is a heinous act on the part of a scheming and unscrupulous woman, while her aristocratic male lover is to be pitied.[16] Women who abuse the power they gain through sex are "Faustines," Satanic figures. (They are also some of Ouida's liveliest characters.) It is particularly important that the intangible and therefore literally price-less qualities of nobility not be allowed to escape the boundaries of the upper classes through reproduction, either through incautious marriages or marriages of monetary convenience. In one essay, Ouida complains

All the unpurchasable, unteachable, indescribable qualities and instincts which we imply when we say he or she has "race" in him, are growing more and more rare through the continual alliance of old families with new wealth. We understand the necessity of keeping the blood of our racing and coursing animals pure, but we let their human owners sully their stock with indifference.[17]

This (in)valuable blood is sullied through the sexual act in which it, as sperm, is passed through the lower openings of the female body; thus, it is through sex and the grotesque (too open) female body that the "unpurchasable" crosses into the realm of the merely commercial. Again, the female body, specifically the vagina, is the dangerous liaison between realms that are, ideologically, mutually exclusive. Thus, since all female characters embody this openness, this potential for transgression, the type and degree of openness and its appropriate uses for the male must be established, and clear distinctions made in order that no contamination take place during the male's transition through, or contact with, female openness.

In order for the adventure novel to take place, Cecil must journey to Africa. In order for the romance to resume, he must return to England. However, since he must not initiate such a return, it is necessary for the domestic romance to "come and get him." Enter Venetia, touring the barracks of the army of France (!), who stops to ask the price of an ivory chess set which Cecil has carved, as many of the soldiers extend their incomes through the sales of various curios and handmade items. He refuses to sell, but, forgetting his station, he offers them to her as a gift – a gentleman's privilege, but an insult coming from one of his social position to one of hers. She refuses, and this starts the long series of transactions which will eventually expose his identity and lead to the climactic confrontation with the firing squad. The conflict revolves around his class identity, upon which hinges her right to purchase versus his right to give; her class position places her in the masculine role wherein, although she may give or buy, she may not receive without reciprocity.[18] As a lower-class male, he is feminized in his relations with her, and this is what must not happen if he is to be the hero of the romance. His simple refusal to sell the chessmen does not protect him, however; incensed by Cecil's behavior, Chateauroy commands that he give the chess set to Venetia, and before his commanding officer, Cecil is helpless to refuse. The situation is analogous to prostitution, with the commander as the pimp: "Victor, Madame la Princesse honors you with the desire to see your toys again. Spread them out" (*Under Two Flags*, p. 299). Venetia refuses to "rob" him, and Cecil again asks her to keep them, leaving before Venetia can respond with another offer of compensation. In this way, his masculine identity as "giver" rather than feminine "vendor" or "recipient" is kept intact. They meet again by chance; again she insists on paying Cecil for the chessmen, again he refuses. The scene is acceptably resolved when she spends the money she would have given him on charity for his men in the hospital. Later, in an attempt to goad Cecil, Chateauroy gives him money, intimating that it is from Venetia in payment for the chess set. Cecil goes to Venetia in indignation, the lie is exposed, and he gives Venetia the money to return to Chateauroy.

It is imperative, both for Venetia and Cecil, that neither accept the feminine role at this time. For Cecil, it would mean emasculation and disqualification for his future role in the romance. This role reversal in gift-giving is a persistent theme in Ouida's novels. In *Folle-Farine*, a male character sums up the doctrine succinctly: "Gifts of gold from man to man are bitter, and *sap the strength* of the receiver, but of a woman to the man they are – to the man, shameful."[19] For Venetia, it would be a breach of chastity which would likewise disqualify her from her future role as the hero's love-interest. For her to be femininely receptive (open) to a lower-class male would be to risk contamination; she must achieve closure by exchanging money for the chess set, "closing" the transaction. Later, after his correct social class is known, she is able to thank him for a favor (he finds a lost piece of jewelry and returns it) without offering recompense, simply saying "I am greatly indebted to you" (*Under Two Flags*, p. 484). Immediately following this declaration, his true identity as her brother's close friend is revealed, and he discovers her identity as well.

Interesting and clearly unresolved conflicts regarding class and gender emerge in this series of exchanges. Although Ouida's avowed belief is that such customs and divisions are appropriate and necessary, the prerogatives of conqueror over conquered, upper class over lower, and male over female are repeatedly presented as rapes; in fact, Chateauroy is explicitly presented as a rapist in an earlier scene, wherein he abducts an Arab princess and plans to rape her and then give her over to the "general enjoyment" of his men. His attempt to make Cecil complicit in this rape, by sending him to the princess's husband with a message detailing his plans, is analogous to his attempt to make Venetia complicit in his humiliation/rape of Cecil, and underscores the ways in which the relationship of the upper class to the lower is similar to the relationship of the imperial colonist to the indigenous population. Further, the placement of Cecil, the sympathetic protagonist, in humiliating situations engages the reader's resentment against not only the abuse of power by Chateauroy, but the "appropriate" level of coldness and distance employed by Venetia. Clearly the reader's knowledge that Cecil is, in fact, of Venetia's class is intended to mitigate our sense of the injustice of class inequities; however, the feeling remains that there is a cruelty here, not only in the deliberate malice of Chateauroy, but in the system itself:

He had been used to the impassable demarkations [*sic*] of caste, he did not dispute them more now that he was without than he had done when within their magic pale ... [he stood] with a certain serene dignity that could not be degraded because others chose to treat him as the station he filled gave them fit right to do. (p. 300)

Yet Cecil does dispute those "impassable demarkations," as his resistance against selling the chessmen reveals. Cigarette is also an eloquent spokesperson against both gender and class inequality; indeed, however often to the contrary the narrative voice pontificates, the characters' "lived experience" seems directly to critique the naturalness of gender and class distinctions.

Another challenge to the dominant order is mounted through the depiction of the colonial struggle. Ouida is adamant, even in the novel's glorification of the French army, that the Arabs have "the right of" the struggle. She presents the indigenous population of Africa as fighting a gallant but inevitably losing battle against superior military strength, which is used to rape, rob, and murder the native population. This sentiment seems at variance with the book's consistent message that the imperial character demands the challenge of maintaining or extending colonial domination, a message that is also prevalent in critics' anxious warnings that sensation novels weaken the imperial English character by focusing readers' intellectual attention on narrow domestic concerns and encouraging physical passivity. Cecil folds down the page of his French romance and leaves his boudoir for the African battlefield where he wades "ankle-deep in blood" (p. 267); apparently the lives of "hundreds" of innocent Africans are a small price to pay for the tonic effects of this healthy exercise on a future English peer. Despite one Ouida fan's statement that the reason she liked Ouida's books was that the distinction between good and evil was always perfectly clear,[20] it seems that the distinctions between "the fine and the wicked," despite the insistent moralizing of the narrative voice, are in fact almost entirely unclear.

The reader's attempt to make moral judgments is both engaged and frustrated constantly throughout the novel. Ouida's disregard of conventional sexual morality (or perhaps too open acceptance of the double standard) combine with her praise of her male characters to invite the reader to suspend moral judgment – to take the tale on its own terms. On the other hand, the constant narrative asides evaluating the character and quality of various characters and actions invoke the reader's acceptance of a fairly detailed ethical system. These asides are worded so as to imply that the reader of "race" or at least some refinement will immediately understand this system, while a reader who lacks these qualities has little hope of grasping it; the "snob intimidation factor" may work to secure this acceptance. The conversion to the novel's ethical system, or at least suspension of the conventional ethics during the reading is indeed subversive. Although Ouida herself tends to claim the Romantics, particularly Shelley, with the ethic of free love, as her tradition, she is in fact more closely aligned with the Regency, with its witty exploitation of a double standard, both in gender and class mores, which it does little to overturn. Ouida's offer of sexual freedom without censure only extends to men, and a very few women "of genius."

The woman reader is offered, as always, two distinct choices in female characters to identify with; the fallen and the chaste. The difference is that here the fallen woman's is a role with many attendant pleasures and with few serious penalties. However, the average reader may be comforted; it is the chaste and passive woman to whom the spoils of marriage are actually awarded. Perhaps the most exciting opportunity novels like *Under Two Flags* can offer the woman reader, however, is the opportunity to identify with the male protagonist – a rare item in the "woman's novel" of the time – and thus to enjoy sexual, geographical, and aggressive freedoms without fear of reprisal. For the female reader, the embedded adventure novel offers an opportunity to escape the confines of the romance into a purely masculine fantasy, a fantasy therefore free from the need for moral self-monitoring, since, as a male, Cecil is doing nothing inappropriate. Thus, the elaborate negotiations between Cecil, Cigarette, and Venetia are not merely necessary to the plot, but helpful to the reader in providing ways to renegotiate an identity appropriate to the return to the romance. Just as Cecil's "woman's face" and feminine love of luxury provides a point of identification for female readers initially, it becomes necessary to ease the female reader out of the role of the now thoroughly masculinized Cecil at the end. Cigarette becomes this transitional vehicle for the now "unsexed" reader-in-the-text; she is Cecil's equal in power and aggressiveness, but female. Like the adventuress, she is charming, she is adored; unlike the adventuress, she is a hero, she is purified in death. Cigarette provides a vehicle for the reemergence of the romance while allowing what Judith Fetterly calls the "resisting reader" a voice with which to protest the narrator's gender- and class-role double standard. Although madly in love with Cecil, she is also allowed to hate him for his continual rejection of her, and to contemplate the murder and literal de-facement (the fantasy of the destruction of the woman's decapitated head and, specifically, facial features) of the cold, passive, chaste Venetia. In her masochistic self-sacrifice, she achieves his love, the humbling of Venetia (who will ever after compare her own love for Cecil to Cigarette's and find it "little worthy of the fate it finds" [*Under Two Flags*, p. 596]), and the final role reversal in the novel – by giving Cecil a gift he can never repay, Cigarette assumes the masculine role with Cecil, gaining an ultimate ascendancy over and penetration of him that Venetia may never be allowed to have. If what we might call the "assenting reader" (i.e., the reading subject who accepts conventional literary gender roles) is left to identify with Venetia in the happily ever after of the standard marriage plot, the resisting reader has the last word in the guerrilla gender-warfare that flourishes in the border areas between the two genres of *Under Two Flags*; the last line of the novel returns to Africa for a simple assertion of identity,

> "one name on which the Arab sun streamed as with a martyr's glory:
> 'CIGARETTE,
> Enfant de L'Armée, Soldat de la France.'"

The woman reader can have her rebellion and eat her wedding cake too. What she may find more difficult is the reconciliation of her investment in both Cigarette and Venetia.

### FOLLE-FARINE

Norman Douglas said of Ouida that "she was not an artist, but just as surely, she was a genius."[21] Whatever one thinks of these terms, they seem to reflect a truth about Ouida's appeal; it is slippery, mysterious, and contradictory. Her prose style was often considered excessive and flamboyant in the nineteenth century, and surely seems more so to the tastes of today. Her situations strain to the uttermost the credulity of a suspended disbelief nurtured on realism. However, there is an enduring charm in Ouida for tastes conditioned to intricacies, like an Elizabethan garden carefully planned and then allowed to run riot. If the Ouida of *Under Two Flags* is the author whose plotting skill W. M. Thackeray openly envied, the Ouida of *Folle-Farine* is the author whose aesthetic sense and cutting irony were admired by George Meredith, Max Beerbohm, and G. S. Street.

Ouida bases the novel in part on Goethe's *Faust*, with its pot-pourri of genres and references; however, whereas *Faust* splits melodrama and "high" drama along gender lines, between Gretchen and Faust, *Folle-Farine* pulls a single female character through both registers.[22] Both authors use their Mephistopheles to provide social commentary; of the two, Ouida's entirely human tempter is perhaps the more sinister. Melodrama and social satire are a rare and usually incompatible mixture, perhaps because melodrama is traditionally a popular feminine genre rooted in acceptance of traditional values and set in the realm of the personal, while social satire lies in the masculine domain of the political commentary, set in the public. Ouida's combination of the two in *Folle-Farine* (1871) jars, but intrigues also, finally shifting toward tragedy, away from the social and its relativist moral codes and toward the absolutist – from which realm the reader is carefully excluded. As in

*Under Two Flags,* Ouida is concerned with the capacity of the mechanisms of exchange to undermine and transform identity. As a very young, poor, and uneducated woman, Folle-Farine is defined by powerful, wealthy, more sophisticated persons in her environment, that is, directly by certain male characters and indirectly, by the reader. Folle-Farine eludes those ineluctable forces, however, through her non-identity; having no "self" to value, she escapes the forces in the novel (including the reader) which are confident in their ability to put a price on everything.

Ouida's eighth novel, *Folle-Farine* was the last one of her forty-seven books that was written on English soil.[23] Already, however, she had left England behind as the setting for her stories, and settled on France. In *Folle-Farine,* Ouida explores the exploitation of a noble nature made powerless by circumstance. Folle-Farine is a later incarnation of Cigarette, and indeed, this could, in some particulars, be Cigarette's story. Like Cigarette, Folle-Farine is nameless; she has only her nickname, which refers to the worthless dust produced in the milling of grain, that blows away on the wind. Like Cigarette, Folle-Farine is doomed by her sex to victimization; if she will not capitalize on her own sexuality as a prostitute, she will be deprived of her chastity anyway. Much like Cigarette, it is for love that Folle-Farine makes the ultimate sacrifice. She sells her body to Sartorian, a man she dreads, in order to save the life and advance the career of the man she loves, who does not return her love or comprehend her sacrifice. Once he is safe, she kills herself.

Her mother is a young French peasant who dies in childbirth, having been seduced by a gypsy. Her father leaves her to die, but she is taken under the protection of another member of the gypsy band, who takes her at the age of six to her maternal grandfather when her father announces his intention of selling her, first as a child-performer and later as a prostitute. She is "saved" from this fate, at least initially, by her grandfather, who sees her ability to labor unceasingly as an asset more valuable than her beauty. This grandfather, an intensely religious but cruel and bigoted person, hates the shame she represents, and treats her with cruelty so appalling that one critic who labeled the book a work of genius still felt that the explicit brutality was sufficient to spoil it.[24] Early on, therefore, we see Folle-Farine constructed both as a potentially valuable commodity and as a currently valueless human being.

As Folle-Farine is systematically stripped of her power and dignity, the novel poses the question: at what point will woman "fall" and be damned? Conventionally, that point should be at the moment of sexual penetration, and indeed the drawn-out seduction plot prepares us for that outcome. In fact, in this fully packed three-volume novel, Folle-Farine again and again is placed in situations which are metaphorical penetrations, while Ouida appears to reserve actual sexual violation for the novel's "climax." However, Ouida challenges this convention by allowing Folle-Farine to maintain her integrity at a level "above" physical closure, even after the bartering away of her virginity. She constructs Folle-Farine as the counterhero of a spiritual anti-quest modelled on Goethe's *Faust*, framed in references to the "Walpurgis-nacht" intermezzo where Faust dances as Margarethe awaits execution. (The Faust/Margarethe story seemed to have an irresistible appeal to the popular writers of the day. Ouida herself had done it at least once before in "Two Little Wooden Shoes: A Sketch," although it was not until the early 1890s that both Rhoda Broughton and M. E. Braddon came out with their versions, *Dear Faustina* and *Gerard*, respectively.[25]) Whereas the male Faust sells his soul freely for personal gain, Folle-Farine sells hers with great resistance, for the sake of a man's gain. Whereas Faust seeks growth and additional power, Folle-Farine seeks only to hold her ground against the erosion of power. Folle-Farine is Faust's nature in Gretchen's circumstances, and whereas Faust must invoke his Mephistopheles, Folle-Farine finds herself relentlessly pursued by hers.

Folle-Farine's gender dooms her from the beginning. She has no choice but to either become corrupt or a victim. In volume one, she is beaten, hated, and kept in utter ignorance by her grandfather and the townspeople who do not understand her dark "Eastern beauty" and think she is the daughter of the devil. Like Cecil contemplating Cigarette, Folle-Farine's only friend Marcellin, also outcast because of his populist role during the French Revolution, considers her inevitable fate:

It was a pity to make you a woman... You might be a man worth something; but a woman! – a thing that has no medium; no haven between heaven and hell; no option save to sit by the hearth to watch the pot boil and suckle the children, or to go out into the streets to mock at men and to murder them. Which will you do in the future?

Since she does not understand the question, Marcellin answers it himself:

"I spoke idly... slaves cannot have a future... Many will love you, doubtless – as the wasp loves the peach that he kisses with his sting, and leaves rotten to drop from the stem!"

She was silent again, revolving his meaning; it lay beyond her, both in the peril which it embodied from others, and the beauty in herself which it implied. (*Folle-Farine*, vol. 1, pp. 172–173)

In her innocence, Folle-Farine draws hope from others' ironic promises that the devil will help her, as he always helps women. She believes the devil is her father and hopes that she will inherit his kingdom. It is not until she becomes aware of her sexuality that she understands what is being told her; when she "enters her father's kingdom," both her hopes and her sanity will be stripped from her.

Like the other novels examined here, the dynamic of the plot revolves around the opening and closing of Folle-Farine's body, or more precisely, her struggle to maintain closure against the struggle of surrounding forces to open/seduce her. The reader is in the position of voyeur throughout volume one, which traces Folle-Farine's childhood and early adolescence. Ouida offers detailed descriptions of Folle-Farine's physical beauty (often only partially dressed), the abuse she sustains (whippings, etc.), and the marks it leaves upon her body. Folle-Farine's lack of self-consciousness or even a self-concept absolves her of complicity in this exposure. Natalie Schroeder notes that Folle-Farine gains power by masochistically submitting to men, which is indeed the case. Schroeder also notes that this submission is erotically rendered; characteristic of sensation fiction, woman bids for power sexually: "Ouida's description of the naked female's submitting to her grandfather's sadistic violence becomes a veiled metaphor for incestuous violation, and it echoes flagellation scenes in Victorian pornographic literature... I do not think it is straining the point to note the metaphorical significance of the adder-like rope that bites the pubescent girl and causes her to bleed."[26] Schroeder is correct in her assessment of the eroticism of the scene, an eroticism which implicates the reader. However, it is precisely Folle-Farine's ignorance of her sexuality which is her strength. When she strips for these beatings, she is "insensible of humiliation because unconscious of sin," and thus she is a closed system, untouched even though the rope penetrates her body.

Interestingly, it is the contact of other women which first makes her vulnerable to shame. After a Fall of "feverish" drought comes a famine winter, which leads to more viciousness on the part of the peasants. Several women seize fifteen-year-old Folle-Farine and, employing a sixteenth-century method of investigation, pierce her breast to see if she will bleed (if she does not, she is a witch.) The scene is strikingly like a rape:

[A] dozen eager hands seized a closer grip upon her, pulled her clothes from her chest, and, holding her down on the mud floor, searched with ravenous eyes for the signet marks of hell ... the nail drew blood ... The muscles and nerves of her body quivered with a mighty pang, her chest heaved with the torture of indignity, her heart fluttered like a wounded bird – not at the physical pain, but at the shame of these women's gaze, the loathsome contact of their reckless touch. The iron pierced deeper, but they could not make her speak. (*Folle-Farine*, vol. i, pp. 244–246)

When Folle-Farine sees "the blood trickle ... she understood what had happened to her; and her face grew savage and dark, and her eyes fierce and lustful ... It was the shame of defeat and outrage that stung her like a whip of asps" (vol. i, p. 251). By the time she gets home, she is "hot with fever" (vol. i, p. 254), indicating that she has indeed been penetrated and contaminated. Folle-Farine has thus in some measure been "opened" by her contact with the women, her "perfect health" disturbed with fever. Folle-Farine's illness following this attack is extended, and she recovers only to find that Marcellin is dead. This preliminary awakening to sexuality and mortality ends the first volume of the novel. Folle-Farine's shame derives directly from her awareness of having been the object of the gaze of the women, which is passionate in its hatred. The reader's gaze, passionate in its pity but as "ravenous" for sensation as the women are for the "signet marks of hell," remains behind the gaze of the women; unperceived and untouched, we watch characters watch Folle-Farine, a process which will continue until the reader's gaze eventually merges with that of the powerful characters whose own gaze defines Folle-Farine. Her contact with the women increases her sensual awareness (opens her) to the extent that it becomes possible for her to conceive an erotic attraction (infection), and the second volume begins shortly after with the introduction of Arslan, the starving artist to whom Folle-Farine will give her unrequited love.

With Arslan, Folle-Farine begins an equivocal patronage relationship much like that of Cigarette and Cecil, beginning the identification of erotic with capital exchange. Just as Cigarette repeatedly saves Cecil's life and does him favors without his knowledge, Folle-Farine saves Arslan with anonymous gifts of food and fuel when she finds him dying of starvation and cold in the granary which he is using as a home and studio. Thus begins the first compromise of Folle-Farine's integrity, for she steals the food and fuel from her grandfather to help Arslan that she would have died before taking for herself. (She repays this debt eventually.) At this time, she makes a bargain with the portrait of Thanatos, drawn on the wall in chalk, which she believes is a real person: "'One life alone can ransom another' . . . the force of an irresistible fate seemed upon her; that sacrifice which is at once the delirium and divinity of her sex, had entered into her . . . 'Let him live!' she murmured . . . 'Let me die as the Dust dies – what matter?'" (vol. II, p. 40). The Faustian bargain is struck, and immediately Folle-Farine begins to pay the price when she learns she must steal food, must acknowledge the base neediness and openness of the body as she never had before in her own starvation. Ouida's choice of language makes clear that the weakness of character that leads to theft of food is a form of sexual transgression:

She had been so proud of her freedom from all those frailties . . . with the chaste, tameless arrogance of the women of her race . . . yet this cleanliness of hand and heart . . . which she had girded about her as a zone of purity more precious than gold – this, the sole treasure she had, she was about to surrender for the sake of a stranger. (vol. II, pp. 49–50)

Again the language is symbolic of defloration; again the result is shame and self-consciousness before the gaze of others. Whereas before, she had "passed through the crowds . . . not knowing why the youths looked after her with cruel eyes all aglow," now "a hot shame smote her, and the womanhood in her woke" (vol. II, pp. 65–66).

The danger of her indebtedness to her grandfather is complicated when Arslan, unaware that Folle-Farine is the anonymous food donor, offers her sketches in return for her sitting, attempting to assume the male–female patronage relationship and unconscious that his superiority is already undermined. Folle-Farine instinctively refuses, "a certain dullness and disappointment at her heart. She wanted, she wished, she knew not what. But not that he should offer her payment" (vol. II, p. 196). Men continually offer Folle-Farine gold throughout the novel, the plot of which revolves around the struggle to keep herself "pure" – i.e., not under the patronage of any man. Like Cigarette, although denied the power to maintain conventional purity, she becomes purified and assumes power within the patronage relationship through sacrifice, rendering up a gift to her lover that can never be returned or neutralized by any subsequent payment.

Ouida suggests that capitalism converts people into objects, commodities. She parallels Marx in her sense that the value of the commodity is located in its look or on its surface; the person Folle-Farine has no value, while the spectacle Folle-Farine has a great deal. However, the eroticism of the novel is not in the commodity itself, but in the inexorable force of the conversion of the subject into the commodity, or the transformation of depth into surface. The commodity's surface appeals because there is the lingering possibility of penetrating to some depth, in short, that there is some surplus value of "sensation" beneath the icon. Folle-Farine ultimately escapes this flattening because she is hollow to begin with – that is, she has no depth, no subjectivity to be "flattened." The themes of the gaze and of the exchange converge as characters and reader exert pressure upon Folle-Farine to make her "buy" the idea that she is a commodity, to alienate herself from her body. But she escapes the trope of exchange by invoking the trope of sacrifice, whereupon her body no longer becomes a commodity to be sold by her, but an embodiment of the collective crimes of the community. Thus, she vacates her body and invests it with the desires of her pursuers. Therefore, when we penetrate her surface, we find not the continuing erotic challenge of alienated consciousness to be converted (or, as Sartorian puts it, corrupted,) but only our own corruption, which we hoped to "infect" Folle-Farine with. Instead of being able to penetrate Folle-Farine entirely, body and soul, and therefore take her into our bodies, making her one with us and neutralizing her as a threat, we find that her essence is elsewhere, that even though her body submits to the laws of exchange, she remains outside the system, forever Other, a threat and reminder that we are open, needy, in danger of infection, because the thing that would have confirmed our completion has escaped us. The melodrama demands that Folle-Farine maintain her physical purity. As long as Sartorian has power over her, the only solution is for him to be "won over" by her goodness – the *Pamela* ending. Since Ouida's seducer is more efficient than Richardson's, the reader expects that Folle-Farine will die before losing her purity or will fall. By challenging the laws of melodrama, which the reader accepts in order to "play the game" of the book, Folle-Farine "opts out" of the game, leaving the reader and the other characters standing on the crumbling foundation of their avowals that there are no other rules. Artistic genius, however, as represented by Arslan, is brought into the realm of exchange (it is Sartorian's money that subsidizes Arslan's production and success). Whether his art is therefore debased or whether, like Folle-Farine, it escapes debasement by means of its two dimensionality is a question that remains open.

In fact, his art is based precisely on this ability to turn depth (subject) into surface (object) through the gaze. In the early stage of Folle-Farine's relationship with Arslan, the nature of power is exemplified in the erotic gaze. Because of the new modesty which results from her awakening, she does not allow Arslan to see her at first, but brings him food anonymously and watches him unseen as he works, admiring him and his art equally. She is in the position of power as voyeur and patron, but does not exercise this advantage to act upon him or gain from him. This female gaze is sympathetic, as well as erotic, as "a passionate sorrow for a human sorrow [his Faustian frustration] possessed her ... She gazed at him, never weary of that cold, fair, golden beauty ... of those lithe and massive limbs" (vol. II, pp. 151–152). When their roles are reversed, and he finds her asleep in the granary where she has ventured once too often, his gaze immediately objectifies her:

As she had once looked on himself, so he now looked on her.
    But in him there arose little curiosity and still less pity ... his only desire was to use the strange charms in her for his art ... he had time to study and to trace out every curve and line of the half-developed loveliness before him with as little pity, with as cruel an exactitude, as that with which the vivisector tears asunder the living animal. (vol. II, p. 177)

The villainous Sartorian's gaze is described in much the same terms as Arslan's:

The old man watched her ... He ... made his passions docile ministers to his pleasure, and never allowed them any mastery over himself. He was studying ... her ... "All these in Paris," he was thinking. "Just as she is, with the same bare feet and limbs ... only to the linen tunic a hem of gold, and on the breast a flame of opals. Paris would say that even I had never in my many years done better." (vol. III, pp. 91–92)

His pleasure in her is specifically aesthetic, he objectifies her visually, as does Arslan. He thinks of her, not as a unified subjectivity, but as a fragmented catalog of goods ("All these"). As Arslan likes "to hurt, to please, to arouse, to study, to pourtray her [*sic*]," Sartorian also "could not resist the pleasure of an added cruelty, as the men of the torture-chambers of old strained once more the fair fettered form of a female captive, that they might see a little longer those bright limbs quiver, those bare nerves heave" (vol. III, p. 95).

    Ouida constantly stresses Folle-Farine's animal nature, her likeness to the birds and plants, and finally to the reed which the god killed to make the first flute. As a woman, without any secondary forms of power such as wealth or male protectors, she is reduced to her "natural" status as an object for the use of the male. She learns what she is through the male gaze, a gaze which analyzes and evaluates (commodifies), rather than sympathizes. This objectification teaches her, for the first time, that she is beautiful, as Arslan tells her so, and then shows her the sketch, hoping to get her to continue posing for him. Her reaction is equivocal: "He watched her, letting the vain passion he thus taught her creep with all its poison into her veins. . . . 'You are glad?' he asked her at length. 'I am frightened!'" (vol. II, pp. 189–190). As Schroeder points out, although this realization frees Folle-Farine from some of her grandfather's abuse (she refuses to let him beat the body that has become "sacred" because Arslan thinks it worth painting,) she early on has a sense of "what beauty and sensuality meant in the 1870s – utter subjugation."[27] It means she can be assigned a certain value as a desirable commodity and entered into exchange. Ouida is explicit in her sense of what Folle-Farine's self-consciousness means: "Like Persephone she had eaten of the fatal pomegranate seed, which, whether she would or no, would make her leave the innocence of youth . . . and draw her footsteps backward and downward to that hell which none, – once having entered it, – can ever more forsake." (*Folle-Farine*, vol. II, p. 198). She is losing the fight to maintain her closure.

Arslan is a male counterpart to Folle-Farine. He finds Folle-Farine's company congenial, because his origins are similar to hers. He is the bastard son of a peasant girl, abandoned to die in childbirth. However, he is raised by a loving grandfather, and his artistic genius takes him all over the world, to gain education and culture because of his freedom, as a male, to move independently. Except for his passion for art and fame, he is utterly cold, once stopping to draw a man dying in the street without offering to save the man's life because it simply did not occur to him. He is the male Faustian character, who has genius and vision, but is constrained by circumstance not to enjoy worldly acclaim, power, and wealth: "the gaoler was poverty, and they who lay bound were high hopes, great aspirations, impossible dreams, immeasurable ambitions" (vol. II, p. 233). He is also much like Goethe's Faust in his tendency to "use up" ordinary people. Folle-Farine also has aspirations, although she cannot put a name to them: "'I do not want love,' she said, suddenly, while her brain, half strong, half feeble, struggled to fit her thoughts to her words. 'I want, I want, to have power, as the priest has' . . . 'Power!' he echoed, as the devotee echoes the name of his god" (vol. II, p. 238). However, as Arslan mockingly lists the kinds of power available to her as a woman, she rejects them all in confusion, finally thinking that the only god worthy of worship is Death, with whom she made the contract to save Arslan (vol. II, p. 246). In a scene that recalls Marlowe's Faust's necromantic conjuring of Mephistopheles, Folle-

Farine watches and listens unseen as he dissects a dead woman to study her anatomy while delivering perorations on his frustrated ambition:

"Oh God," he, who believed in no God, muttered half-aloud, "Let me be without love, wealth, peace, health, gladness, all my life long ... give me only to be honoured in my works; give me only a name that men cannot, if they wish, let die." ... This hunger of the soul which unmanned and tortured him ... thrilled her with the instinct of his greatness ...

"Oh Immortals!" she implored ... "Do what you choose with me ... kill me ... let me be bruised, beaten, nameless, hated ... but grant me this one thing – to give him his desire!" (vol. II, p. 252)

The characters' actions and language mirror each other, except that he asks, not believing his plea will be taken seriously, for himself, and she asks, in perfect faith, for him. Ouida is clear that the male Faustian ambition is not worth having; the painting that Arslan would sell Folle-Farine's soul to bring to the world is a painting of a loathsome crowd adulating a "grinning, bloated, gibbering" Barrabas, and rejecting the genius-god (vol. II, p. 283). Folle-Farine gazes at the preliminary sketch and asks, with justifiable confusion, why he wants the adulation of such a world, and Arslan agrees: "He had drawn the picture in all its deadly irony ... only himself to desire and strive for the wine streams, and the painted harlotry, and the showers of gold, and the false gods, of a worldly success" (vol. II, p. 291). His cynicism extends to her, and he paints her in twin studies which introduce a new character who remains with Folle-Farine throughout the end of the novel:

In the first, he painted her in all the warm, dreaming, palpitating slumber of youth, asleep in a field of poppies ... amongst them, hiding and gibbering and glaring at her with elfin eyes, was the Red Mouse of the Brocken ... In the second ... there were the same limbs, but livid and lifeless, and twisted in the contortions of a last agony ... upon the stone there lay a surgeon's knife and a sculptor's scalpel; between her lips the Red Mouse sat, watching, mouthing, triumphant. (vol. II, pp. 297–298)

The introduction of the Red Mouse of the Brocken is another direct reference to Goethe's *Faust*. (Mephistopheles brings Faust to the magical Walpurgisnacht celebration on the Brocken to distract him from inquiring into the plight of Gretchen, the young woman Faust has seduced and abandoned to her fate – madness and execution. Faust dances and flirts with a young "fair woman" as Mephistopheles whiles away his time with another witch. Upon Faust's reappearance, Mephistopheles testily asks why he has left his partner "who sang so sweetly as you romped" and Faust responds that as she sang, a red mouse leaped out of her mouth. Mephistopheles chides him for his fastidiousness, and directly after, Faust sees an image which presages the death of Gretchen, but is willing to be distracted.) Faust is repulsed by the sexual advances of the woman when he learns she is corrupt inside, vermin infested, dead. Yet, as the apparition of Gretchen reminds us, death and corruption are the lot of the sexually active but powerless woman in nineteenth-century Europe. Ouida gives the Red Mouse a voice, and uses it to refer to spiritual corruption within the sexually awakened woman, but also to implicate the male desire which creates, and then rejects that corruption as a commodity. The gypsy who seduces Folle-Farine's mother explains his sexual desire for her as the need to destroy her purity: "She looked so white and so cold; and they all called her a saint. What could a man do but kill *that?*" (vol. III, p. 171). In this way, Ouida calls attention not only to the plight of Gretchen, but to Faust's culpability, referring to the seduction of the woman as murder.

This world revolves around capital, which Arslan needs, and upon overhearing this stated in one of his many soliloquies, Folle-Farine hits upon a plan to get it for him. Volume three opens with this plan; Folle-Farine will take some sequins she has to Prince Sartorian, an art fancier and collector she thinks will buy them. Once again, she risks vulnerability by complicating the existing economy between herself, Arslan, and her grandfather by introducing a new contributor. The moment Sartorian appears, his likeness to the Red Mouse is evident, "a small and feeble man, with keen and humorous eyes, and an elfin face, delicate in its form, malicious in its meaning" (vol. III, p. 28). Like Hades, this diminutive Mephistopheles offers his beautiful guest food; unlike Persephone, she is bright enough not to take it:

"I never took a crust out of charity."

"But when a man, old and ugly, asks a woman that is young and beautiful, on which side lie [sic] the charity then?" ... She was sharply hungered ... but he besought her in vain ...

[He asked] "How shall you bind me to keep bond with you, and rescue your Northern Regner from his cave of snakes, unless you break bread with me, and so compel my faith?" (vol. III, p. 39).

Eating is a directly physical penetration, often portrayed as analogous to and foreshadowing sexual penetration of the body (e.g., Thomas Hardy's Tess and her strawberries). Sartorian's religio-legal language recalls both the Faustian contract and various myths of female self-sacrifice. When Sartorian next tries to give her jewelry, offering the more subtle bondage of patronage (golden chains) instead of direct penetration, she responds "If I think your bread would soil my lips, is it likely I should think to touch your treasure with my hands and still have them clean?" (vol. III, p. 41). Even though we move from the openings of the body to its periphery, Folle-Farine recognizes the danger, and a moment later, asks him in startled recognition, "Are you the Red Mouse?" Folle-Farine has an intuitive understanding that to take anything from him that is not an even exchange is to render herself open to his influence; her refusal to eat is a refusal to let the mouse enter her lips. She is already more vulnerable than she knows; he has given her a great deal of money for the sequins that were financially worthless. Here again her ignorance is partial protection, just as Arslan's ignorance of her patronage saves his pride, and she is able to run away from the house unviolated.

Unfortunately, Folle-Farine's sense of the indignity of receiving gifts does not prepare her for the horror with which Arslan greets her offer of gold: "If I were mean enough to take the worth of a crust from you, I should no more be worthy of the very name of man. It is for the man to give to the woman... Have I seemed to you a creature so vile or weak that you could have a title to put such shame upon me?" (vol. III, p. 57). Understanding the light in which he would view the other gifts she has given him, she casts away the gold and wanders all night with "the sense of some great guilt" (vol. III, p. 63) and her grandfather guesses she has been at a "witches sabbath" (vol. III, p. 62), which, given her communication with Sartorian, is apt.

The stability of this economy is again undermined when Folle-Farine discovers that her grandfather has died leaving her nothing, and that she is homeless. Arslan drops by to say farewell, apologizes that he cannot love her, and compounds the injury by thrusting gold into the bosom of her dress as a parting gift. When she realizes what he has done, she wishes he had killed her instead: "The sight of the gold stung her like a snake. Gold! – such wage as men flung to the painted harlots... The horror of the humiliation filled her with loathing of herself" (vol. III, pp. 126–127). She is "violated" by Arslan's gift at the precise time that she is most economically vulnerable. Having no idea what to do next, she decides to follow him to Paris to return his gold and be near him. Once again, Folle-Farine is unwillingly placed in the inferior position in the patronage relationship; the gift of gold is a robbery of her power. In fact, this gold itself renders her vulnerable: she is found travelling with it and arrested as a thief. The gold is stolen from her, never to be recovered, and she is thrown into prison, where, in a striking scene, she loses her sanity. Already sick with fever, she lies in the prison cell at night when a dying, insane, drunken male tramp is thrown in with her: "She saw the looming, massive shadow of an immense form ... nature, instinct, youth, sex, sickness, exhaustion all conquered her, and broke her strength. She recoiled from the unbearable loathsomeness of such association; she sprang to the grated aperture ... and bruised her chest and arms against it ... shriek after shriek pealing from her lips" (vol. III, p. 165). No one comes, of course, (perhaps because, as Hardy writes, no one does,) and they are so close together that he clutches at her and strikes her in his delirium, singing and detailing "his lustful triumphs." Among these are references to Folle-Farine's mother. The narrative cuts off at this point; it resumes when the prison door opens, finding Folle-Farine mad and her father dead, "For Folle-Farine had entered at length into her father's kingdom" (vol. III, p. 171).

The references here are multiple. The father is a gypsy tramp; he is also the devil, with his "red eyes." If Folle-Farine is a reluctant witch at a "sabbath," she is also the sacrificial victim, once again described in terms of spectacle; although no one directly watches them, they are described as a gazelle and lion, caged together in a Roman circus entertainment. The gold, which for a man or a "corrupt" woman, would mean power, here acts as a literal curse to conjure up the persecution of the devil. The metaphor of incestuous rape runs through-out the scene, as does the reference to Gretchen's imprisonment and madness during the Walpurgisnacht (in the only house near the prison, a bridal dance is being given which drowns out Folle-Farine's screams). The price for the Faustian consumption of experiences is paid by the commodity itself, when that commodity resists its status. Given that her father had originally wished to sell her as a child-dancer and prostitute, her entry into her "father's kingdom" as sexual victim and sadistic "spectacle" is telling.

Like Persephone, the other rape victim to whom she refers continual-ly in her delirium, she has been given a tainted gift, which propels her into a role created for her by the desires of others. Also like Persephone, she remains in hell until the spring, when her reason returns. She is released to continue toward Paris, and when she collapses on the roadside, she awakens under her own picture, the first of the Red Mouse series, in Sartorian's house. The process of objectification which she has undergone is so nearly completed that she awakens unable to distinguish herself from the painting, or Sartorian from the painted Red Mouse. When she awakens again, she is screaming that the Red Mouse is claiming her soul from Thanatos.

It is her love for Arslan that saves her in these critical moments, because of the power of that love to make her self-less, that is, to destroy the self which is being drawn into the realm of exchange by the forces which operate to turn her into a commodity. When she is initially in Sartorian's house, she is saved from possible imprisonment and rape by the force of her self-sacrifice; when he points out that, with his help, Arslan will leave his poverty and forget all about her, she responds that her happiness doesn't matter. In his surprise, he is distracted sufficiently that she is able to run away from the house. Awakening in his house after her collapse, she feels threatened, but when she sees the picture "The Red Mouse had no power over her, because of her great love" (vol. III, p. 193). Even Sartorian recognizes his limitations. On one of the many occasions that she successfully resists "this voice of Mephistoph-eles – which tempted her but for the sheer pleasure of straining this strength to see if it would break ... of alluring this soul to see if it would fall" (vol. III, p. 96) she escapes him, leaving him musing, "The Red Mouse does not dwell in that soul as yet" (vol. III, p. 99).

To what extent it dwells in the reader's soul is another question. Throughout the novel, the reader has been in the position of voyeur, first when, as a child, Folle-Farine is presented to us stripped for beating, then when we see her through Arslan's clinical eyes, and finally through Sartorian's, as an object of sadistic and aesthetic appreciation. In this regard, the interest of the novel, like that of Richardson's *Pamela* or *Clarissa*, is driven by the anticipation of her violation; unlike Richard-son's rapist, Sartorian prolongs the foreplay deliberately: "he desired to tame and beguile her, and to see her slowly drawn into the subtle sweetness of the powers of gold; and to enjoy the yielding of each moral weakness one by one, as the southern boy slowly pulls limb from limb, wing from wing, of the cicala [*sic*]" (vol. III, p. 216). Yet it is the reader who, however intense her or his pity for Folle-Farine, draws the most pleasure from this erotic vivisection, and reads on, both dreading and anticipating the final violation of Folle-Farine's body and soul.

The reader is invited to participate in Sartorian's gamesmanship, while at no point does any human character in the novel cast doubt on what is presented as an inevitable outcome. It is, in fact, the Red Mouse who critiques the cynicism of the human community, when he speaks directly in his own person, rather than that of Sartorian. When the sun rises in the empty bedroom in which Folle-Farine was imprisoned, the Red Mouse in the painting holds a conversation with the sun in which he states that "Love is stronger than I." The sun asks if Eros is not always the Red Mouse's pander, and the Mouse replies "Anteros only." In a rare bit of outright feminism, Ouida blames men for the negative assessment of woman's nature; when the sun responds "And yet I have heard that it is your boast that into every female soul you enter at birth, and dwell there until death" the response of the Red Mouse is "That boast is not mine; it is man's" (vol. iii, p. 221). This apparent challenge to what looked like the inevitable conclusion functions both to bolster the reader's sense of suspense (perhaps Folle-Farine will escape Sartorian, perhaps Arslan will recognize her value and come to love her) and to foreshadow the actual ending; like Clarissa, she will not be spared, but like Faust, she will be saved in spite of all by the power of a love that is eternally and uniquely feminine in its absolute self-abnegation. In fact, Folle-Farine's self-abnegation is her identity; paradoxically, the Red Mouse cannot enter because her subjectivity is so entirely negated by the time her body is sexually violated that there is nothing there to penetrate. When Sartorian asks her, "You know that ... you are nameless and bastard because you are of a proscribed people, who are aliens alike in every land?" she simply responds, "I am Folle-Farine; yes" (vol. iii, p. 210), asserting her identity as a non-subject. She retains this identity as she retains her closure, even as Sartorian's mistress "her lips kept their silence to the last. They were so strong, they were so mute," that in dying "her eyes had a look of blindness; her lips were locked close together" until she approaches Thanatos, when her prayer is to die before she is "weak or mad" and opens her lips to speak, risking that Arslan might find out the debt he owes her.

The evocation of the capitalist economy as both a system and a place which is antagonistic to female purity runs throughout the novel. Folle-Farine is surrounded by men who understand that gold is power, and who see her as a commodity worth a certain amount of gold. Her struggle is to remain outside the realm of exchange. Ouida largely agrees with traditional Victorian middle-class beliefs: love, feminine chastity, "race," and art must remain outside of the commodity consumer market, "unpurchasable." Folle-Farine poses the question: how can a woman without race, without genius, and without power remain outside the public realm of exchange when she is constructed as a commodity by the only power that exists in her world: the power of capital? Arslan would happily sell himself, as his maleness gives him the right to do without censure; it is his art that keeps him outside the realm of the purchasable, and it is this genius for which Folle-Farine substitutes the market-price of her price-less chastity. When the child Arslan hears an itinerant preacher tell the story of Midas as a warning to the spirit of the times, Arslan challenges him with the statement that gold is a greater god than the preacher's: "Gold must be power always... And without power what is life?" The preacher knows, however, that Arslan "will not give his life for gold... For there is that within him greater than gold, which will not let him sell it if he would" (vol. II, p. 84). Yet even if he could, Arslan would not be contaminated by the sale of his life or art, although he would be if he accepted gifts without offering recompense. Since he is a male, the public realm of exchange is his rightful place, and his subjectivity remains intact while he sells that which belongs to him. A woman, however, does not own a commodity that she may sell; she is the commodity, and consequently cannot sell her services without bringing herself completely within the realm of exchange, where she is consequently degraded. As a woman, Folle-Farine should remain within the private, domestic realm, where exchange is based on the intangibles of emotion and blood relation; since she is denied that in her family, her only hope is to set up a kinship (marital) relation with Arslan through romantic love. This too is denied.

Both Arslan and Sartorian constantly offer her gifts, most frequently of gold, and it is to relieve herself of the taint of his gold that she follows Arslan to Paris, alternately described as "the hell of the Christians" and as a more pagan underworld into which Persephone is drawn, never to be fully ransomed back again. But most consistently of all, Paris is defined as the ultimate marketplace. Accosted by a brothel-keeper who extends an apparently kind hospitality, Folle-Farine insists that she must move on to Paris: "The old woman laughed roughly. 'Oh ho! the red apple must go to Paris. No other market grand enough! Is that it?'" (vol. III, p. 147). She is told that there are only two trades in Paris, "to buy souls and to sell them" (vol. III, p. 249). Paris as the place in which Sartorian envisions Folle-Farine's transformation into commodified spectacle merges with the vision of hell as a place which is traditionally beyond both the body and the marketplace. The Faust story, in placing the price-less soul within the realm of economic exchange, collapses the boundaries between the religious and secular. The city setting, by the mid-nineteenth century a familiar trope for both extreme economic contradictions and corruption, becomes a space which Folle-Farine traverses, in frantic wanderings as Arslan lies dying, in a quest which transforms her from a melodramatic victim to a tragic hero:

[H]er bloodless face had the horror in it that Greek sculptors gave to the faces of those whom a relentless destiny pursued... She went on through the sulphurous yellow glare, and the poisonous steam of these human styes, shuddering from the hands that grasped, the voices that wooed her, the looks that ravished her, the laughs that mocked her. It was the hell of the Christians; it was a city at midnight. (vol. iii, p. 309)

Paradoxically, it is her acceptance that "all the gods are dead" and her decision to sell her body that deprives hell of its power over her and removes her from the marketplace, in its specific geography of the city, into the domestic non-space of the prince's palace. Because she accepts that gold is the "one God" of the Christians (vol. iii, p. 310) she offers herself up as an economic sacrifice for Arslan, thus becoming the vehicle by which the antagonistic spheres of the sacred and profane intersect. Religion is sacred, outside the realms of both sex and exchange. Whereas the Faust story debases religion in its blending of the two, Folle-Farine's substitution of a narrative of sacrifice for one of sale transforms Sartorian's "sensualist's palace" into a temple and its and her "innermost recesses" into holies of holies.

As Schroeder points out, his indebtedness to her leaves Folle-Farine, in her death, more powerful than the living Arslan. Although her gift indeed places her in the superior position to Arslan, it is paradoxically even more powerful because unacknowledged. The acknowledgment would place it in the public realm, back into the realm of the social and commercial exchange. Should Arslan find out, she should accrue a certain amount of socially acknowledged power over him. Once socially acknowledged, that power becomes capital, with an exact monetary value which can be repaid and spent again, i.e., interpreted in different ways. Curiously, however, that power would be Folle-Farine's undoing; should she accrue that power, it would place her in the subject position, and her subjectivity would be the object of the prince's purchase and violation. It would also vitiate the price-less value of her silent suffering, bringing Folle-Farine's sacrifice into the realm of the merely commercial. Again, it is in her abjection that she is invulnerable.

The actual "climax" of the seduction plot, Folle-Farine's loss of chastity, takes place off-stage, marked by a chapter consisting of a dramatically set-off single page containing the continued dialogue of the

Red Mouse and the sun, which both explains what has happened to Folle-Farine and evaluates its results. The sun congratulates the Mouse on his victory, but the Mouse answers "'Nay, not so. For the soul is still closed against me; and the soul still is pure" (vol. III, p. 318). Within the year, both Arslan and Sartorian's mistress are famous; "One day the man whom the nations at last had crowned, saw the woman whom it was a tyrant's pleasure to place beside him now and then, in the public ways... 'So soon?' he murmured... He had his heart's desire. He was great. He only smiled to think – all women were alike" (vol. III, p. 320). Arslan has, in fact, misread everything. His blindness is all the more culpable because of his role as seer, truth-teller – artist. If he is not capable of seeing Folle-Farine for what she is, rather than for what he and others want her to represent, then the "terrible Truth" that his paintings supposedly represent is at best a partial, cynical truth, at worst an outright lie – and in any case a mere reflection of his (and our) desires. The analogy is clear: Folle-Farine, as she is, not as she appears, is the Christ; the much feted Arslan is Barabbas.

Lest we harbor confusion about the state of Folle-Farine's soul – or body – the last chapter spells it out for us. She returns to the gods sketched out in the granary and falls down dead at their feet "free, even in base bondage; pure, even though every hand had cast defilement... incorrupt, amidst corruption; – for love's sake. The Red Mouse sat without, and was afraid, and said: 'To the end she hath escaped me'" (vol. III, p. 328). And to the end she has escaped her readers, who are denied any account of erotic surrender to Sartorian, which is what the novel appeared to be building toward. The Red Mouse never enters her perpetually closed lips: "Thanatos, in answer, laid his hand upon her lips, and sealed them ... mute for evermore" (vol. III, p. 327), and the final "violation" of her body, by reapers who strip her corpse and "dragged her naked body to the air, and thrust it down there, into its nameless grave" (vol. III, p. 331) is less evocative of eroticism than horror. Like Faust, Folle-Farine's body is given to the devils and her "immortal part" goes to the gods. Since the readers are left with the disposal of the former, there is little doubt with whom we are aligned.

Folle-Farine's identity as waste material, what Julia Kristeva calls the abject, makes possible her invulnerability. Kristeva notes that the revulsion caused by waste materials, what we reject and throw away, particularly from the body, exists not merely because they remind us of "the other side of the border," death which defines and forever encroaches on our lives, but because they signify the nullity of identity, the seed of death within us which we cannot "reject" and which will one day consume us and replace identity: "The corpse, seen without God and outside of science, is the utmost of abjection... It is something rejected from which one does not part, from which one does not protect oneself as from an object... It is thus not lack of cleanliness or health but what disturbs identity, system, order. What does not respect borders, positions, rules."[28] Kristeva's observation yields interesting results when applied to Folle-Farine. Folle-Farine is "always already" thrown away, the already rejected product of a grotesque, because illicit, coupling. Because death is therefore not a boundary set against her, but is itself integral to her identity, she is invulnerable to boundaries so long as her anti-identity as abject is not threatened with desire. (As when she wakens from a nightmare that the Red Mouse is claiming her away from Thanatos.) If the Red Mouse represents the seed of the abject, of revulsion in every object of desire, of death in life, her imperviousness to it rests in her non-recognition of desire. Her upbringing reinforces her "outsideness"; she is defined by the villagers as death, she is supernatural, she is the plague. As she remarks of her relationship with these villagers in retrospect, "If I had loved them, and they me, I might have become a liar, and have thieved, and have let men kiss me" (*Folle-Farine*, vol. III, p. 311), equating sex with other forms of illicit exchange.

Death has no power to define her so long as her life has no meaning, as demonstrated in her casual offer to Arslan to kill herself if he would rather sketch her dead than alive. Because the mill-dust is "valueless," she is able, consistently, to set no price on herself. Sartorian's temptation of her is often based on the attempt to change her identity:

Well – be Folle-Farine still. Why not? But let Folle-Farine no longer be a beggar, an outcast, a leper, a thing attainted, proscribed, and for ever suspected, but let it mean on the ear of every man that hears it the name of the most famous, most imperious ... woman of her time ... homeless, tribeless, nationless, though you stand there now, Folle-Farine. (vol. III, p. 211)

Yet the name Folle-Farine "meant that she was a thing utterly useless, absolutely worthless; the very refuse of the winnowings of the flail of fate" (vol. I, p. 3). Her ability for self-sacrifice is based on her abject identity; she is already "dead." Deciding to sell herself to Sartorian, she reasons, "For her – what could it matter – a thing baser than the dust, – whether the feet of men trampled her in scorn a little more, a little less" (vol. III, p. 317). Sartorian attempts to reconstruct her identity within the realm of the living by reinterpreting the "waste material" of Folle-

Farine as something of value, an object of desire rather than rejection, thus subjecting her, as a living subjectivity motivated by the rejection of death, to what Kristeva calls order – the social and economic laws of patriarchy in which women are objects of exchange.

Because Folle-Farine is largely denied a human subjectivity, the reader is asked to have pity for her rather than sympathy; the reader is invited to align her or himself with the other educated adults in the novel who are able to "read" Folle-Farine, both character and novel, with the full appreciation of the social and narrative complexities which she lacks for her own situation. Those characters are Arslan, Sartorian (and his *alter ego*, the Red Mouse). The two principal genres of the novel, melodramatic seduction story and the sermonizing social satire, laden with parable and analogy, are antagonistic. The melodrama is heavily invested in traditional social practice; the heroine clings to her physical chastity like a life raft, and when it goes, however blameless she is, she must die to retain the reader's favor. It will not bear overt irony, which would both question the rules by which melodrama is played and distance the reader and protagonist from the immediacy of physical and emotional suffering through the mediation of an intellectual commentary on its dubious worth and/or necessity. The social satire, on the other hand, is heavily invested in irony, cynical about traditional social practice, and relies on emotional distance from the events described in the plot, often through the invocation of the author and reader's sense of shared intellectual superiority to the protagonists. Folle-Farine "suffers dumbly" entirely in the realm of melodrama; her pain is real and immediate, and despite her status as outsider, she is subject to a very traditional fate. Sartorian, who intellectualizes even his pleasures and surveys Folle-Farine's suffering with humorous cynicism, aligns himself with the decadents. It is his voice combined with the authorial voice, which invokes the non-traditional moral code that Sartorian lacks, which together create social satire. The reader is shuttled between three levels: in the consciousness of Folle-Farine, there is never any ironic awareness, only pain; in that of Sartorian or Arslan, we see the anguish of a specific melodrama in the larger context of an implacable social aesthetic which demands that pain for its greater pleasure; in the "authorial" consciousness we are called upon to understand that tragedy lies in the choice of the reader to participate in an aesthetic which requires that this be so. It is the reader–consumer who, in her or his relentless demand, requires the subjugation of a speaking subjectivity to the mute object–commodity. On one of the rare occasions when Folle-

Farine speaks from her lived experience to answer the goading of Sartorian, and challenges him to do the same, Sartorian immediately disregards the substance of her response, transforming her pain into aesthetic appeal:

"Do I know? [the pain of poverty]" her voice ... rang loud ... "Do *you?* The empty dish ... the mud floors, with the rats fighting to get first at your bed, the bitter black months ... whose holy days are feasted by fresh diseases. Do *I* know? Do *you?*"

He did not answer her; he was absorbed in his study of her face; he was thinking how she would look in Paris in some theatre's spectacle of Egypt, with anclets of dull gold and a cymar of dead white, and behind her a sea of palms and a red and sullen sky ... He watched her with a musing smile, a dreamy calm content; all this tempest of her scorn ... all this whirlwind of her passion and her suffering, seemed but to beguile him more ... "She would be a great creature to show to the world," he thought. (vol. III, p. 207–213)

Her pain is transformed for his own aesthetic pleasure and for the pleasure of display, the conspicuous consumption of a valuable object made more valuable by its capacity for displaying anguish. It is not incidental that the content of her disregarded message is what he calls "unlovely things": i.e., her experiences of the poverty and disease which are the hidden face of nineteenth-century commodity capitalism. The unlovely things make possible the "loveliness" he appreciates, which is based not merely on her "natural" beauty, but on her powerlessness. She is a "chained whirlwind" because she is in his monetary debt, and her physical strength contrasts against his frailty to underscore the power that gold gives him, to buy Arslan's paintings of her and to transform her into the visual representation of his desires. As he tells her in Paris, "gold" has "a million eyes" (vol. III, p. 258) to transform her into the object of his gaze. Whereas the appeal of her beauty is "natural," the sadistic appeal of her pain is a cultivated taste, and has less to do with sexuality than a commercial sensuality wherein the pleasure is to be had in the exertion of power over nature. Sartorian tells her frankly, "I do not speak of passion. I use no amorous phrase. I am old and ill-favoured; and I know that, anyway, you will for ever hate me. But the rage of the desert beast is more beautiful than the weak submission of the animal timid and tame. It is the lioness in you that I care to chain.... Name your price" (vol. III, p. 263).

Sartorian desires her, though, precisely because she is not for sale. Melodrama demands that she die or at least be raped rather than submit to the economy of an exchange; it is in this sense that melodrama is a characteristically feminine genre, in that, like the virtuous Victorian wife, even as it presents itself as a commodity (in popular novels and plays), it claims to be outside the realm of the commercial. It makes that claim resting on the back of capitalism, the existence of which it requires in order to define its "separate sphere." (Consider the archetypal melodramatic situation: the evil landlord attempting to coerce the impoverished daughter of the house into a simple commercial exchange of sex for shelter.) Tragedy, like social satire, recognizes that inexorable logic, and demands that the character submit to it. But for tragedy, that logic is not absolute, but conditional and therefore subject to critique. Melodrama, as it allows no mercy for the woman once she loses the "privileged" position of pursued victim by becoming a caught victim, allows for no critique of the values on which it depends. Social satire, while allowing some critique, also depends on traditional values for much the same reasons. Classical tragedy sets up an alternative and usually absolutist value system (in *Folle-Farine*, that of Greek tragic myth) from which to critique the social values which result in the character's fall. That this value system is also, in its sources, social and traditional, matters less here than that it serves to provide some critical distance from the assumptions which drive the plot, thus rendering them vulnerable to examination and questioning. (It is also profoundly anti-critical, as it naturalizes the absolutist values which it invokes at a level supposedly "beyond" the social, endowing them with the legitimacy of the natural.) It is in this sense and at this level that Folle-Farine, like Faust, is "saved" – for all the opening of her body, her soul remains "closed" against the Red Mouse, outside the realm of exchange.

The reader, on the other hand, finds herself implicated in her acceptance of Sartorian's assumption that as long as Folle-Farine lives, her subjectivity can be equated with her body, which, if it can be seen, can be bought. Folle-Farine manages to remain outside the realm of the commodity by allowing her body to become a conduit for an exchange in which she is not *essentially* involved. It is telling that Arslan is the one who has been contaminated by fever in the end; in every other scene which has hinted at violation of Folle-Farine's chastity, she has experienced fever and ill-health. Yet when she gives her body to Sartorian, it is to save Arslan from his fever, and although all who see her assume she is contaminated with his fever, her health remains intact. Even though her body is given in order to pay for Arslan's life, his success, and the reader's pleasure, her selflessness prevents corruption; in short, while her empty subjectivity cannot be commodified or penetrated, Sartorian penetrates Arslan, proving that even the genius-god can be "had" by a Barabbas who cares to make an offer, and incidentally he "has" the reader as well. Arslan, Sartorian and the reader, voyeurs together, gaze upon Folle-Farine, objectifying her beauty and in so doing implicitly consenting to the logic established by the assumption that possession of the body, already defined as a commodity by social practice, is tantamount to purchase of subjectivity. Once Sartorian actually touches this beautiful object, however, we find there is nothing there, except, perhaps, the reflection of our own desires. Meanwhile, Folle-Farine disappears into the intersection of melodrama and tragedy, leaving us alone with a corpse and a red mouse, in a picture that we now understand was never really of Folle-Farine at all.

Ouida's conclusion is transgressive in that it undermines – spectacularly – the equation of the woman's body with her subjectivity. However, it fails to rescue the surrender of physical chastity outside of the romantic relation from its status as a fate worse than death, and makes woman's highest purpose self-immolation on the altar of romantic love. In seeking to redefine female purity and closure, Ouida does nothing to displace purity and closure as tropes of feminine goodness, but reinscribes them beyond the personal and political level at which the plot moves, in the mythic and eternal level of the tragedy wherein Folle-Farine's purity remains intact. Perhaps Ouida's most telling act of revolt against a Romanticism which turns women into aesthetic objects of inspiration at the expense of their humanity is her rewriting of Goethe. (Oddly, this is a credo which Ouida herself espoused, asking "who would not give the lives of a hundred ordinary women?" to make the poet Shelley happy for a moment.) Whereas his Gretchen is saved only by her turning away from Faust and Mephistopheles and back toward God, Folle-Farine remains true to her love throughout. Whereas Gretchen is tricked into her fall, Folle-Farine makes her own decisions and takes responsibility for them. And whereas Gretchen's sacrifice is incidental to Faust's ambition, Folle-Farine's is integral to Arslan's. Finally, while Faust is Goethe's protagonist whom the reader follows through life into death and beyond, Arslan's career and fate fall from importance in the novel with Folle-Farine's demise. Ouida takes the "dust" of an incidental scene, and transforms it into the vital substance of a Victorian tragedy.

# Afterword: the other Victorians

Examining the construction of popular, potentially "decadent" genres allows us to see something of the attitudes that shaped Victorians' perceptions of gender and reading in relation to beliefs about the body. The development of a discourse of a somatized popular culture with the rise of mass literacy in the nineteenth century evolved to account for and include debates on national and international politics, the "science" of race, the "nature" of gender, and the "ethics" of health. However, as stated in the Introduction, every history is an exercise in analysis of the culture and historical moment that produces that history as well as of the subject at hand. The workings of Victorian metaphors of cultural production and consumption and physical and political health are "readable" by us and important to us in part because those discursive structures remain present today. Obviously, these constructions have been bequeathed to different cultures in different configurations and have been reshaped by varying circumstances. They have had to encompass new national and international relationships, a host of new media, and a changing set of aesthetic standards. Yet some similarity of structure remains in the construction of the healthy, appropriate, "epic" body of culture in its relations to its representation and the representation of its consumers. My purpose here is not to give a survey of these differences or even to discuss a single example in detail, but to indicate a couple of broad connections with examples from my own late twentieth-century US American cultural environment, and raise some salient questions.

Victorian attitudes about genre shaped and continue to shape the canon today. One obvious result, of course, was to exclude authors like M. E. Braddon or Rhoda Broughton from consideration as canonical, thus allowing them to go out of print and be forgotten. This affects the canon of Victorian literature as it is, or can, be taught today. It also masks and perpetuates the assumptions that shaped that canon by excluding the opportunity for critical comparison of "canonical" Victorian works with "marginal" ones. Another, less obvious way that Victorian attitudes continue to influence us is evidenced in our continued distinction between "high" and "popular" forms, not only in Victorian studies, but in contemporary culture. Even when popular (in particular, "mass") cultural forms are accorded critical interest, they are perceived by (generally liberal) academic critics as having a different relationship to culture than "high" or avant-garde forms. Often, the critical assumption is that popular forms are rarely directly critical of the dominant ideology, and are therefore somehow more "representative" of a commonly perceived reality – often in a naively mimetic sense. Additionally, the habit of thinking of popular forms as market-determined commodities versus "art" as non-market-determined remains depressingly current. Finally, the tendency to categorize popular culture according to its epic, pedagogic function is very much with us.

Popular culture, when critical "policing" comes into play, in rating systems, political debates and so forth, is still seen as a way to represent a social "body" to itself and to others, and in so doing, to reinforce "desirable" qualities in the individuals who are supposed to be interpellated within the construct it represents. The assumptions of (generally conservative) politicians and journalists today mirror Victorian attitudes most closely in their conception of "good" and "bad" popular culture. Conceptualizing the mass public (above which the critic is always elevated by his or her own rhetoric) as uncritically responsive to the "moralities" set forth in popular representations, the would-be censor distinguishes between "healthy" popular culture supportive of the dominant ideology and dangerous, "unhealthy" popular culture which subverts the social order.

Earlier attitudes toward disease and the body have also remained remarkably current, just as the structural association of the body of culture and the body of the individual "consumer" continues. Just as the archetypal "low" forms of television and print are the feminine forms of the soap opera and the Harlequin-type romance novel respectively, disease is still linked to the feminine, foreign, impoverished, immoral Other. This is an association which antedates the Victorian period considerably; what was new in the Victorian period was the application of this discourse to an emergent mass culture and its incorporation in turn in and of the new "scientific" discourses of race, gender, class, health, and nation. In our own era, the disease which symbolizes all the "evils" of the Other is of course AIDS (and to the extent that the two are conflated, HIV). AIDS's metaphorical descent from syphilis is well documented and has become a critical commonplace.[1] To the extent that syphilis was associated with the feminine or feminized and racial Other, this correlation holds. However, there are complications in this simple identification. The perception of syphilis underwent a change in the late nineteenth century; as it became more and more widespread, it was stripped of some of the negative moral implications associated with it earlier and began to share kinship with a very different disease, tuberculosis, in its romantic associations with creativity.[2] Additionally, syphilis was traditionally associated with excessive, but essentially "normal" or acceptable masculine sexuality. Although female prostitutes were blamed (and duly policed) as vectors for the spread of disease, male syphilitic patients were not, by the end of the Victorian period, seen so much as perverse as incautious.

AIDS, however, is, despite all medical evidence to the contrary, still often perceived as a disease of perversity – to some extent, a filth disease. Despite its early identification as a largely male disease in the United States, it is associated with a feminized grotesque body. I refer here, not to the body of the prostitute, but to the body of the homosexual male and the drug user, both "addicted" to "unnatural" stimuli, both representing the "grotesque" penetration of the (passive) male body, whether penile or hypodermic. In its association with the anal region, with the impoverished drug user, with the third world (in its feminized, passive relationship to the first world powers) and with the specifically Black body, whether American, Haitian, or African, we see the same old associations with filth, foreignness, beastliness (and bestiality), femininity, and the (post)colonial body. The notion of Africa as the "cradle of AIDS" and the rumor, at one time given some currency, that the virus first developed in a simian species and then, through African intermediaries, was passed to "degenerates" such as male homosexuals, has nineteenth-century Darwinist roots too painfully obvious to require detailed explication. At one point, it was argued that heterosexual American women would not get AIDS because of the toughness of the vagina, and that African women's AIDS could be explained in terms of degenerate vaginal conditions resulting from the prevalence of venereal diseases there.[3]

The white male homosexual, then, has been aligned with both femininity and Blackness on the margin of society. The fear of this "filth disease" infiltrating the upper (white, moral, heterosexual) classes, should it become "endemic" (hence US restrictions on immigration and the granting of visas) is, precisely, the descendent of cholera anxiety. The alignment of AIDS to the urban, and the economic relationship of the third and first world mirror the nineteenth-century relationship of cholera to urban industrialism and the colonial to the imperial nations. Finally, the rhetoric of "plague" that surrounds AIDS not only, as Susan Sontag points out, identifies it as the "punishment from God" that syphilis (and, indeed cholera) were supposed, in their times, to be, but also with the rapid devastation of the Black or bubonic plague – or cholera – in contrast with the actual slow onset and extended progress of the AIDS pathologies. Like Black plague, cholera killed quickly, within hours or days. AIDS kills over several years, like certain kinds of cancers or systemic infections. Yet the rhetoric of early journalistic and political discourse on AIDS was of the Plague – catastrophic, even Apocalyptic, at direct variance with the protracted process we know living with AIDS to be. This catastrophic Plague association – which in fact refers to the disease's capacity for rapid spread rather than rapid progress within the individual body – allows for a much less measured response. In short, a catastrophic model allows for a militaristic solution, just as we declare martial law in the wake of natural catastrophe, and has led to the "war" metaphor that Sontag so deplores. The impulse to subsume the individual beneath the sign of disease, and to make that individual and disease Other is still overwhelming.

Examining the popular presentation of AIDS, Sander Gilman observes that through the mid-1980s – the crucial early period of media coverage in which lasting impressions of the disease were formed and the terms of debate were set – "the male black homosexual [was] still the archetype of the individual suffering from AIDS" even in the context of an official effort to stress the spread of the disease across categories.[4] In short, AIDS occurs outside the "normal" nuclear family. Cultural critic Henry Abelove, surveying materials on AIDS in the newspapers as well as "preventive" informational literature given out by the Yale–New Haven Hospital, argues compellingly that this literature is less about the prevention of death than the need to "reassert and reinforce both racism and conventional, regulative positions about sex and the family."[5]

The "family values" debate surrounding the policing of popular culture, particularly film and television, today reflects the fear of the "sex and violence" associated with metaphors of AIDS. The rhetoric associated with US film at the site of its production is particularly interesting, given US economic primacy in the world film market. This rhetoric often uses the models of environmental pollution and toxicity to elaborate the dangers violent entertainment poses to the minds of viewers. These models, with their connections to physical health, down-play the voluntary nature of viewers' consumption of entertainment by comparing it with environmental poisoning (e.g. passive smoking). As self-pollution, viewing violent entertainment ranks with active smoking (and, of course, Victorian self-pollution – masturbation). The violence we fear is the violence of the Other – the criminal, the lower class, who is always dirty, monstrous, ugly, and often aligned with the drug-world. The persistent pairing of sex and violence in discourses on censorship of popular culture continues its relatively long tradition without much scrutiny and with ever increasing vigor. Most oddly, this sex and violence is formulated in the US in terms of an attack on the American nuclear family, another construction which continues in its perceived importance without much scrutiny. And popular culture again is seen as a degraded art that life will come to imitate, or as a warped "magic mirror" that, in supposedly simply re-presenting the social body, actual-ly distorts and injures it. Commercialism and the appeal to "popular" tastes is, even now, charged with the responsibility for the degradation and dangerousness of popular culture.

Film violence is generally attacked on a couple of different bases. The first is the exposure of children to violence, premised on the notion that children can be "infected" by television violence, reproducing it on their own bodies and the bodies of others. The second is the notion of violence as a drug or unhealthy stimulus to which adults become addicted, or at least habituated, with unspecified, but negative effects. The concern with television violence in its connection with children has led to serious "scientific" investigation since the 1950s and has been a topic of recurring debate.[6] The emphasis on the child, as a genderless, classless, raceless cultural icon of innocence and vulnerability masks more complex and less innocent interests. Whereas the middle-class woman, as wife, represented the avenue of infection in the Victorian British family, here the American family is invaded through the children, especially of the lower, ethnically or racially marginal classes. Through those "diseased" individuals, violence "infects" the upper classes, as those children grow up to be criminals preying on society. In the statistics presented on violence in society as support for the assump-tion that TV violence is dangerous, it is clear that researchers are concerned with adult criminal violence, mostly perpetrated by (and, although this is not stressed, upon) minorities. Yet, in most literature on violence, the gender- and class-neutral icon of the ubiquitously threatened "child" cloaks these racist and classist concerns. The rhetoric of media violence is rife with metaphors of disease, sex, and the grotesque body. In the interest of brevity, I shall give only a few examples, taken from speeches before the US Congress as reported in the December 1993 *Congressional Digest*, under the assumption that such speeches represent attitudes of at least a significant minority of the population. Senator Ernest F. Hollings notes that "The National Institute of Mental Health and the Centers for Disease Control conclude that violence on television *breeds* violent behavior" (italics mine) and proposes a bill that "treats violence like indecency."[7] Doctor Robert E. Gould, President of the National Coalition on Violence, flatly states "Violence is contagious and infectious."[8] He continues to explain that this "epidemic" is a danger to the "health of all who are exposed to the poisonous doses of violence that TV sends into our homes... An antidote to this poison" would be Legislation analogous to that restricting pollution and drug and alcohol "ingestion":

and so, when the air in our living rooms is polluted by programs glorifying and sanitizing violence and promoting it ... we must act to protect those most vulnerable, the children, from being infected by the virus of violence which they will only spread. This may be deemed as one of the most important public health measures our government can institute... Adults who may need their violence fix can still obtain it at other hours.[9]

Representation of violence is repeatedly described as and made indistinguishable from substances that actually enter the body – smoke, air pollution, drugs, alcohol, poison, and, of course, viruses. The argument is not merely that representation of violence (and sex) is *like* these substances, but that it *is* one of them. The anti-regulation arguments indicate a recognition of the basis of the discussion as the body's continuity with its environment.

My concern in sketching out this homology is not to refute researchers' connections between television violence and viewers' violent acts, nor is it to elide the differences between the two very different historical situations; it is simply to show how the rhetoric of AIDS and of censorship in popular culture coincide, and reflect attitudes about popular culture and the body which are rooted in Victorian concerns about and constructs of gender, class, and national (here racial/ethnic) identity. I do not suggest that the anxieties they encode arise from the same circumstances or should be addressed in the same way. I do suggest, however, that, on the level of popular political discourse, modes of discussing the body, of using the body as a metaphor uncritically, and of homogenizing the consumership of popular culture into an undifferentiated, unintelligent, naive, and potentially dangerous corporative *lumpen* have not signally evolved since the inception of a mass-consumed popular culture. The stereotype of the naive consumer of a diseased popular culture is a non-innocent historical construction based on the need to maintain boundaries which, supposedly, a liberal humanistic society is committed to eradicating. The structures developed to somatize and contain early mass culture are still vital, still operating with remarkably similar metaphors. Those metaphors generally figure forth representation in bodily terms – a gesture which seeks to naturalize them and artificially unify diverse individuals and groups into one homogenous "body" with one set of needs, goals, and enemies. In the policing of popular culture, we reveal our persistent anxieties about the tenuous fictions from which we construct identities and garner a sense of security. The trope of the body, unregenerately bestial but inscribed by culture, passively penetrated yet actively consuming, remains as central to our understanding of cultural production and consumption, as elusively resistant to analysis, and as suasively potent as it was a hundred years ago.

# Notes

INTRODUCTION

1 Hayden White, "Historicism, History and the Figurative Imagination," *History and Theory: Studies in the Philosophy of History* 14 (1975), pp. 48–67.
2 Peter Stallybrass and Allon White, *The Politics and Poetics of Transgression* (Ithaca, NY: Cornell University Press, 1986); Donna Haraway, "A Manifesto for Cyborgs: Science, Technology and Socialist Feminism in the 1980s," in Elizabeth Weed (ed.), *Coming to Terms: Feminism, Theory, Politics* (New York: Routledge, 1989).
3 Stallybrass and White, *The Politics and Poetics of Transgression*, p. 135.
4 Elaine Showalter, *A Literature of Their Own: British Women Novelists from Brontë to Lessing* (Princeton, NJ: Princeton University Press, 1977).
5 Mary Elizabeth Braddon, *Lady Audley's Secret*, ed. David Skilton (New York: Oxford University Press, 1987).
6 Mary Elizabeth Braddon, *The Doctor's Wife* (London: Ward, Lock and Tyler [no date, 1864?]).
7 Rhoda Broughton, *Cometh Up As A Flower: An Autobiography* (London: Richard Bentley and Son, 1878); *Not Wisely But Too Well* (Leipzig: Tauchnitz edition, 1867).
8 Rhoda Broughton, *A Beginner* (London: Macmillan, Two-Shilling Library Series, 1899).
9 Ouida [pseud. Marie Louise de la Ramée], *Under Two Flags* (Chicago and New York: Rand, McNally and Co., [no date, 1917?]).
10 Ouida, *Folle-Farine*, In Three Volumes (London: Chapman and Hall, 1871).

1 "IN THE BODY OF THE TEXT": METAPHORS OF READING AND THE BODY

1 Peter Stallybrass and Allon White, *The Politics and Poetics of Transgression* (Ithaca, NY: Cornell University Press, 1986), pp. 134–135.
2 Elizabeth Grosz, *Volatile Bodies: Toward a Corporeal Feminism* (Bloomington: Indiana University Press, 1994).
3 Luce Irigaray, "Women on the Market," in *This Sex Which is Not One*, trans. Catherine Porter with Carolyn Burke (Ithaca: Cornell University Press,

1985), pp. 170–191.

4   Mary Poovey, *Making a Social Body: British Cultural Formation, 1830–1864* (Chicago: University of Chicago Press), 1995.

5   Mikhail Bakhtin, *Rabelais and His World*, trans. Hélène Iswolsky (Bloomington: Indiana University Press, 1984), p. 317.

6   Catherine Sheldrick Ross, "Metaphors of Reading," *Journal of Library History, Philosophy and Comparative Librarianship* 22 (1987), pp. 147–163.

7   Noah Porter, 1877, in *ibid.*, p. 149.

8   "Literary Voluptuaries," *Blackwood's* 142 (1887), p. 805.

9   Maggie Kilgour, *From Communion to Cannibalism: An Anatomy of Metaphors of Incorporation* (Princeton: Princeton University Press, 1990), p. 9.

10  Author's emphasis, "The Vice of Reading," *Temple Bar* 42 (1874), p. 256.

11  "Literary Exhaustion," *Cornhill Magazine* 22 (1870), p. 290.

12  "The Vice of Reading," p. 251.

13  "English Realism and Romance," *Quarterly Review* 173 (1891), pp. 486–488.

14  *Ibid.*, p. 470.

15  Catherine Gallagher, "George Eliot and Daniel Deronda: The Prostitute and the Jewish Question," in Ruth Bernard Yeazell (ed.), *Sex, Politics and Science in the Nineteenth-Century Novel. Selected Papers from the English Institute, 1983–1984*, New Series 10 (Baltimore: Johns Hopkins University Press, 1986).

16  Gaye Tuchman with Nina E. Fortin, *Edging Women Out: Victorian Novelists, Publishers, and Social Change* (New Haven: Yale University Press, 1989), p. 60.

17  Sandra Gilbert and Susan Gubar, *The Madwoman in the Attic: The Woman Writer and the Nineteenth Century Literary Imagination* (New Haven: Yale University Press, 1979).

18  Gallagher, "George Eliot and Daniel Deronda," pp. 40–41.

19  Susan Stanford Friedman, "Creativity and the Childbirth Metaphor: Gender Difference in Literary Discourse," in Elaine Showalter (ed.), *Speaking of Gender* (New York: Routledge, 1989).

20  Frederic Harrison, "On the Choice of Books," *Fortnightly Review* 31 (1879), p. 491.

21  As Susan Griffin discusses at length in *Woman and Nature: The Roaring Inside Her* (New York: Harper and Row, 1978).

22  See Lee Erickson, "The Economy of Novel Reading: Jane Austen and the Circulating Library," *Studies in English Literature* 30 (1990), pp. 573–585.

23  A. Strahan, "Bad Literature for the Young," *Contemporary Review* 26 (1875), p. 981.

24  "Contemporary Literature," *Blackwood's* 125 (1879), p. 323.

25  *Ibid.*

26  *Ibid.*, p. 325.

27  "Class Criticism," *Temple Bar* 8 (1863), pp. 238–239.

28  "Penny Fiction," *Quarterly Review* 171 (1890), p. 169.

29  "English Realism and Romance," p. 469.

30  "The Novels of Miss Broughton," *Temple Bar* 41 (1874) pp. 198–199.

31  "On the Reading of Books," *Temple Bar* 72 (1884), pp. 178–186.

32  "The Novels of Miss Broughton," pp. 199–201.

33  Harrison, "On the Choice of Books," p. 497.

34  Ouida, *Views and Opinions*, 2nd edition (London: Methuen, 1896), p. 82.

35  Mark Pattison, "Books and Critics," *Fortnightly Review* 28 (1877), pp. 660–661.

36  Guinevere Griest, *Mudie's Circulating Library and the Victorian Novel* (Bloomington: Indiana University Press, 1970), p. 56.

37  George Moore, *Literature at Nurse or Circulating Morals: A Polemic on Victorian Censorship*, edited and with an Introduction by Pierre Coustillas (Brighton: Harvester Press, 1976).

38  Griest, *Mudie's*, p. 55.

39  *Ibid.*, p. 52.

40  Vincent E. H. Murray, "Ouida's Novels," *Contemporary Review* 22 (1873), p. 935.

41  "Sensation Novels," *Quarterly Review* 113 (1863), p. 512.

42  Strahan, "Bad Literature for the Young," p. 986.

43  "Penny Fiction," p. 154.

44  "The Literature of the Streets," *Edinburgh Review* 165 (1887), pp. 55–57.

45  *Ibid.*, pp. 63, 65.

46  *Ibid.*, p. 61.

47  A. Susan Williams, *The Rich Man and the Diseased Poor in Early Victorian Literature* (London: Macmillan, 1987).

48  Charles Kingsley, *Cheap Clothes and Nasty* (London: W. Pickering, 1850).

49  Cyrus Edson, "The Microbe as Social Leveller," *The North American Review* 161 (1895), p. 421.

50  See Judith Walkowitz, *Prostitution and Victorian Society: Women, Class and the State* (Cambridge and New York: Cambridge University Press, 1980).

51  Charles Kingsley, "Great Cities and their Influence for Good or Evil," in *Sanitary and Social Essays* (London: Macmillan, 1889), pp. 195–205.

52  *Parliamentary Papers: Health/Infectious Diseases*, volume IV. Irish University Press Series of *British Parliamentary Papers* (Shannon, Ireland: Irish University Press, 1970), p. 727.

53  Ibid., p. 750.

54  Jessica Benjamin, *The Bonds of Love: Psychoanalysis, Feminism and the Problem of Domination* (New York: Pantheon, 1988).

55  Jacques Sarano, *The Meaning of the Body*, trans. James H. Farley (Philadelphia: Westminster Press, 1966), pp. 53–54.

56  George Lakoff and Mark Johnson, *Metaphors We Live By* (Chicago: Chicago University Press, 1980).

57  Stallybrass and White, *Politics and Poetics of Transgression*, p. 2.

58  D. A. Miller, *The Novel and the Police* (Berkeley: University of California Press, 1988), pp. 162–163.

59  Nancy Aycock Metz, "Discovering a World of Suffering: Fiction and the Rhetoric of Sanitary Reform – 1840–1860," *Nineteenth Century Contexts* 15.1

(1991), p. 65.
60 Eve Kosofsky Sedgwick, *Between Men: English Literature and Male Homosocial Desire* (New York: Columbia University Press, 1985), p. 184.
61 Dickens, in *ibid.*, p. 184.
62 George R. Humphery, "The Reading of the Working Classes," *The Nineteenth Century* 33 (1893), p. 692.
63 *Ibid.*
64 "Penny Fiction," p. 170.
65 Thomas Wright, "Concerning the Unknown Public," *The Nineteenth Century* 13 (1883), p. 283.
66 Andrew McClary, "Beware the Deadly Books: A Forgotten Episode in Library History," *Journal of Library History, Philosophy and Comparative Librarianship* 20 (1985), p. 431.
67 J. K. Crellin, "The Dawn of the Germ Theory: Particles, Infection and Biology," in F. N. L. Poynter (ed.), *Medicine and Science in the 1860s* (London: Wellcome Institute of the History of Medicine, 1968).
68 Robson Roose (psued.), "Infection and Disinfection," *Fortnightly Review* 47 (1887), p. 253.
69 Benjamin Ward Richardson, "The Health of the Mind," *Longman's Magazine* 14 (1889), pp. 148–149.
70 Kate Flint, *The Woman Reader, 1837–1914* (Oxford: Clarendon Press, 1993), p. 55.
71 *Ibid.*, pp. 50–51.
72 *Ibid.*, p. 64.
73 W. F. Poole, "The Spread of Contagious Diseases by Library Books," *The Library Journal* 4 (1879), pp. 258–262.
74 Gerald S. Greenberg, "Books as Disease Carriers, 1880–1920," *Libraries and Culture* 23 (1988), p. 283.
75 Gardner Maynard Jones, "Contagious Diseases and Public Libraries," *The Library Journal* 16 (1891), p. 37.
76 Jacques Boyer, "The Disinfection of School Books," *Scientific American* (July 24, 1909), pp. 60–61.
77 "No Infection in Library Books," *The Literary Digest* 51 (1915), p. 1348.
78 Boyer, "The Disinfection of School Books," pp. 60–61.
79 Greenberg, "Books as Disease Carriers," p. 288.

2 GENRE: THE SOCIAL CONSTRUCTION OF SENSATION

1 Fredric Jameson, *The Political Unconscious: Narrative as a Socially Symbolic Act* (Ithaca: Cornell University Press, 1981), p. 105.
2 Author's emphasis, Julia Kristeva, *Desire in Language: A Semiotic Approach to Literature and Art*, trans. Thomas Gora, Alice Jardine, and Leon S. Roudiez; ed. Leon S. Roudiez (New York: Columbia University Press, 1980), p. 36.
3 Tzvetan Todorov, *Genres in Discourse*, trans. Catherine Porter (Cambridge: Cambridge University Press, 1990), pp. 18–20.

4 Tzvetan Todorov, *Mikhail Bakhtin: The Dialogical Principle*, trans. Wlad Godzich, Theory and History of Literature 13 (Minneapolis, MN: University of Minneapolis Press, 1984).

5 Review of *Not Wisely But Too Well* ("New Novels"), *The Athenaeum* 2088 (1867), p. 569.

6 *Ibid.*

7 *Ibid.*

8 *Ibid.*

9 Margaret Oliphant, "Novels," *Blackwood's* 102 (1867), p. 274.

10 Peter Brooks, *Body Work: Objects of Desire in Modern Narrative* (London and Cambridge, MA: Harvard University Press, 1993).

11 See especially Michel Foucault, *The Birth of the Clinic: An Archaeology of Medical Perception*, trans. A. M. Sheridan Smith (New York: Random, 1973); and *The History of Sexuality*, volume 1, trans. Robert Hurley, (New York: Vintage, 1980).

12 Athena Vrettos, *Somatic Fictions: Imagining Illness in Victorian Culture* (Stanford: Stanford University Press, 1995), p. 3.

13 Peter Brooks, *Body Work*; Helena Michie, *The Flesh Made Word: Female Figures and Women's Bodies* (New York and Oxford: Oxford University Press, 1987); Elaine Scarry, *The Body in Pain* (New York and Oxford: Oxford University Press, 1985).

14 Thomas Laqueur, *Making Sex: Body and Gender from the Greeks to Freud* (Cambridge, MA: Harvard University Press, 1990); Londa Schiebinger, *Nature's Body: Gender in the Making of Modern Science* (Boston: Beacon Press, 1993).

15 Winifred Hughes, *The Maniac in the Cellar: Sensation Novels in the 1860s* (Princeton: Princeton University Press, 1980), pp. 16, 18.

16 Thomas Boyle, *Black Swine in the Sewers of Hampstead: Beneath the Surface of Victorian Sensationalism* (New York: Viking, 1989), p. 3.

17 Hughes, *Maniac*, p. 42.

18 Northrop Frye, *Anatomy of Criticism* (Princeton: Princeton University Press, 1957).

19 Jenny Bourne Taylor, *In the Secret Theater of Home: Wilkie Collins, Sensation Narrative and Nineteenth Century Psychology* (London: Routledge, 1988), p. 4.

20 Boyle, *Black Swine*, p. 225.

21 Hughes, *Maniac*, p. 242.

22 "The Cholera Conference," *Quarterly Review* 122 (1867), p. 30.

23 *Ibid.*, p. 43.

24 *Ibid.*, p. 50.

25 "The Novels of Miss Broughton," *Temple Bar* 41 (1874), pp. 198–199.

26 "The Literature of the Streets," *Edinburgh Review* 165 (1887), p. 61.

27 Mark Pattison, "Books and Critics," *Fortnightly Review* 28 (1877), pp. 677–679.

28 "Sensation Novels," *Quarterly Review* 113 (1863), p. 487.

29 *Ibid.*, p. 487.

30 Hughes, *Maniac*, p. 30.

31 Oliphant, "Novels," p. 280.
32 Flint, *The Woman Reader, 1837–1914* (Oxford: Clarendon Press, 1993), p. 274.
33 "Contemporary Literature," *Blackwood's* 125 (1879), pp. 322–344.
34 Jonathan Loesberg, "The Ideology of Narrative Form in Sensation Fiction," *Representations* 13 (1986), p. 118.
35 Nancy K. Miller, "Emphasis Added: Plots and Plausibilities in Women's Fiction," *PMLA* 96 (1981), pp. 36–48.
36 "Sensation Novels," pp. 483, 502, 505–506.
37 *Ibid.*, p. 483.
38 Natalie Schroeder, "Feminine Sensationalism, Eroticism, and Self-Assertion: M. E. Braddon and Ouida," *Tulsa Studies in Women's Literature* 7 (1988), pp. 87–103.
39 Boyle, *Black Swine*, p. 137.
40 Lyn Pykett, *The "Improper" Feminine: The Women's Sensation Novel and the New Woman Writing* (London and New York: Routledge, 1995), p. 80.
41 Patrocinio P. Schweickart, "Reading Ourselves: Toward a Feminist Theory of Reading," in Elizabeth A. Flynn and Patrocinio P. Schweickart (eds.), *Gender and Reading: Essays on Readers, Texts and Contexts* (Baltimore and London: Johns Hopkins University Press, 1986); Judith Fetterly, *The Resisting Reader: A Feminist Approach to American Fiction* (Bloomington: Indiana University Press, 1978).
42 Ann Cvetkovich, *Mixed Feelings: Feminism, Mass Culture and Victorian Sensationalism* (New Brunswick: Rutgers, 1992), p. 23.
43 Thomas Wright, "Concerning the Unknown Public," *The Nineteenth Century* 13 (1883), p. 290.
44 Vincent E. H. Murray, "Ouida's Novels," *Contemporary Review* 22 (1873), p. 935.
45 "Contemporary Literature," p. 335.
46 *Ibid.*
47 *Ibid.*
48 See Phillip Thurmond Smith, *Policing Victorian London: Political Policing, Public Order and the London Metropolitan Police* (Westport, CT: Greenwood Press, 1985).
49 S. J. Davies, "Classes and Police in Manchester 1829–1880." in Alan J. Kidd and K. W. Roberts (eds), *City, Class and Culture: Studies of Social Policy and Cultural Production in Victorian Manchester* (Manchester, Manchester University Press, 1985), p. 38.
50 Smith, *Policing Victorian London*, pp. 11–12.
51 *Ibid.*, p. 42.
52 Review of *The Massarenes*, *The Spectator* 78 (1897), p. 595.
53 G. S. Street, "An Appreciation of Ouida," *Yellow Book* 6 (1895), pp. 167–175.
54 John G. Cawelti, *Adventure, Mystery and Romance: Formula Stories as Art and Popular Culture* (Chicago: University of Chicago Press, 1976), p. 263.
55 "Miss Broughton's Novels," *Temple Bar* 80 (1887), p. 206.
56 Oliphant, "Novels," p. 259.

57 *Ibid.*, pp. 260–261.
58 *Ibid.*, p. 275.
59 *Ibid.*, p. 275.

### 3 M. E. BRADDON: SENSATIONAL REALISM

1 M. E. (Mary Elizabeth) Braddon, *Lady Audley's Secret*, ed. David Skilton (New York: Oxford University Press, 1987). All further references will be included parenthetically in the text.
2 See especially Elaine Showalter, *A Literature of Their Own: British Women Novelists from Brontë to Lessing* (Princeton, NJ: Princeton University Press, 1977).
3 M. E. Braddon, *The Doctor's Wife* (London: Ward, Lock and Tyler [no date, 1864?]. All further references will be included parenthetically in the text.
4 Quoted in Robert Lee Wolff, *Sensational Victorian: The Life and Fiction of Mary Elizabeth Braddon* (New York: Garland Publishing, 1979), p. 165.
5 Kate Flint, *The Woman Reader, 1837–1914* (Oxford: Clarendon Press, 1993), pp. 181, 291.
6 M. E. Braddon, *The Lady's Mile* (London: Simpkin, Marshalls, Hamilton and Kent, 1900).

### 4 RHODA BROUGHTON: ANYTHING BUT LOVE

1 Marilyn Wood, *Rhoda Broughton (1840–1920): Profile of a Novelist* (Stamford, Lincolnshire: Paul Watkins, 1993).
2 Rhoda Broughton, *Not Wisely But Too Well* (Leipzig: Tauchnitz edition, 1867). All further references will be included parenthetically in the text.
3 Rhoda Broughton, *Cometh Up As A Flower: An Autobiography* (London: Richard Bentley and Son, 1878).
4 Rhoda Broughton, *A Beginner* (London: Macmillan, Two-Shilling Library Series, 1899). All further references will be included parenthetically in the text.
5 Margaret Oliphant, "Novels," *Blackwood's* 102 (1867), p. 269.
6 *Ibid.*, p. 267.
7 Henry Norman, "Theories and Practice of Modern Fiction," *Fortnightly Review* 40 (1883), p. 878.
8 "Miss Broughton's Novels," *Temple Bar* 80 (1887), p. 209.
9 *Ibid.*, p. 196.
10 Review of *A Beginner*, *The Athenaeum* 3471 (1894), p. 574.
11 Oliphant, "Novels," p. 260.
12 "Miss Broughton's Novels," p. 203.

### 5 OUIDA: ROMANTIC EXCHANGE

1 Monica Stirling, *The Fine and the Wicked: The Life and Times of Ouida* (London:

Victor Gollancz, 1957), p. 97.

2 Jeff Nunokawa, *The Afterlife of Property: Domestic Security in the Victorian Novel* (Princeton: Princeton University Press, 1994).

3 Ouida (pseud., Marie Louise de la Ramée), *Under Two Flags* (Chicago and New York: Rand, McNally and Co., [no date 1917?]). All further references will be included parenthetically in the text.

4 Stirling, *The Fine and the Wicked*, p. 109.

5 *Ibid.*, p. 65.

6 Review of *Under Two Flags*, *The Athenaeum*. 2103 (1868), p. 249.

7 Ouida, *Puck*, In Three Volumes (London: Chapman and Hall, 1870), p. 62.

8 Ouida, *Views and Opinions*, 2nd edition (London: Methuen, 1896), p. 4.

9 "The Cantinières and Vivandières of the French Army," *Illustrated Times* (July 16, 1859), p. 44.

10 Vincent E. H. Murray, "Ouida's Novels," *Contemporary Review* 22 (1873), p. 935.

11 Ouida, *Views*, p. 324.

12 Stirling, *The Fine and the Wicked*, p. 66.

13 Ouida, *Views*, p. 219.

14 *Ibid.*, p. 209.

15 *Ibid.*, p. 215.

16 Ouida, *Granville de Vigne; or, Held in Bondage. A Tale of the Day* (Philadelphia: J. B. Lippincott Co., 1867).

17 Ouida, *Views*, p. 30.

18 For extensive discussion of the cultural dynamics of gift-giving, see Marcel Mauss, *The Gift*, trans. Ian Cunnison (New York and London: W. W. Norton and Co., 1967).

19 Emphasis mine, Ouida, *Folle-Farine*, In Three Volumes (London: Chapman and Hall, 1971), vol. III, p. 56. All further references will be included parenthetically in the text.

20 See Stirling, *The Fine and the Wicked*.

21 In *Ibid.*, p. 11.

22 See Johann Wolfgang von Goethe, *Faust: A Tragedy*, trans. Walter Arndt, ed. Cyrus Hamilton (New York: Norton, 1976).

23 Stirling, *The Fine and the Wicked*, p. 75.

24 "Ouida's Novels," *Westminster Review* 105 (1876), p. 374.

25 Ouida, *Two Little Wooden Shoes: A Sketch* (London: Chapman and Hall, 1874); Rhoda Broughton, *Dear Faustina* (London: Richard Bentley and Son, 1897); M. E. Braddon, *Gerard; or, The World, The Flesh and The Devil* (London: Simpkin, Marshalls, Hamilton and Kent, 1891).

26 Natalie Schroeder, "Feminine Sensationalism, Eroticism and Self-Assertion: M. E. Braddon and Ouida," *Tulsa Studies in Women's Literature* 7 (1988), pp. 96–97.

27 *Ibid.*, p. 94.

28 Julia Kristeva, *The Powers of Horror: An Essay on Abjection*, trans. Leon S. Roudiez, (New York: Columbia University Press, 1982), pp. 3–4.

AFTERWORD: THE OTHER VICTORIANS

1 See Sander L. Gilman, *Disease and Representation: Images of Illness from Madness to AIDS* (Ithaca: Cornell University Press, 1988); Susan Sontag, *Illness as Metaphor and AIDS and its Metaphors*, (reprints) (New York: Doubleday, Anchor Books, 1990); Roy Porter and Lesley Hall, *The Facts of Life: The Creation of Sexual Knowledge in Britain, 1650–1950* (New Haven: Yale University Press, 1995).

2 Sontag, *Illness*, p. 111.

3 Henry Abelove, "The Politics of the 'Gay Plague': AIDS as a US Ideology," in Michael Gordon and Avery Ryan (eds.), *Body Politics: Disease, Desire and the Family*. (Boulder, San Francisco and Oxford: Westview Press, 1994), pp. 3–5.

4 Gilman, *Disease and Representation*, p. 269.

5 Abelove, "Politics of the 'Gay Plague'," p. 4.

6 Charles S. Clark, "TV Violence," *CQ Researcher*. 3.12 (1993), p. 174.

7 Ernest F. Hollings, "Should Congress Pass Legislation Regulating TV Violence? PRO," *Congressional Digest* 72.12 (1993), pp. 300, 301.

8 Robert E. Gould MD, "Should Congress Pass Legislation Regulating TV Violence? PRO," *Congressional Digest* 72.12 (1993), p. 303.

9 *Ibid.*, p. 306.

# Bibliography

Abelove, Henry, "The Politics of the 'Gay Plague': AIDS as a US Ideology," in Michael Gordon and Avery Ryan (eds.), *Body Politics: Disease, Desire and the Family* (Boulder, San Francisco and Oxford: Westview Press, 1994), pp. 3–17.

Acton, William, *Prostitution, Considered in its Moral, Social, and Sanitary Aspects, in London and Other Large Cities and Garrison Towns, with Proposals for the Control and Prevention of its Attendant Evils*, second edition (London: J. Churchill and Sons, 1870).

Altick, Richard D., *The English Common Reader: A Social History of the Mass Reading Public, 1800–1900* (Chicago: University of Chicago Press, 1957).

Arens, W., *The Man-Eating Myth: Anthropology and Anthropophagy* (New York: Oxford University Press, 1979).

Bakhtin, Mikhail, *Rabelais and His World*, trans. Hélène Iswolsky (Bloomington: Indiana University Press, 1984).

*The Dialogic Imagination: Four Essays*, trans. C. Emerson and Michael Holquist, ed. Michael Holquist (Austin: University of Texas Press, 1981).

Benjamin, Jessica, *The Bonds of Love: Psychoanalysis, Feminism and the Problem of Domination* (New York: Pantheon, 1988).

Bourdieu, Pierre, *Distinction: A Social Critique of the Judgment of Taste*, trans. by Richard Nice (Cambridge, MA: Harvard University Press, 1984).

Boyer, Jacques. "The Disinfection of School Books," *Scientific American* (July 24, 1909), pp. 60–61.

Boyle, Thomas, *Black Swine in the Sewers of Hampstead: Beneath the Surface of Victorian Sensationalism* (New York: Viking, 1989).

Braddon, Mary Elizabeth, *Aurora Floyd*, with an Introduction by Jennifer Uglow (London: Virago, 1984).

*Gerard; or, The World, The Flesh and The Devil* (London: Simpkin, Marshalls, Hamilton and Kent, 1891).

*Joshua Haggard* (London: Ward, Lock and Tyler, 1877).

*Lady Audley's Secret*, ed. David Skilton. (New York: Oxford University Press, 1987).

*The Doctor's Wife* (London: Ward, Lock and Tyler, [no date, 1864?]).

*The Lady's Mile* (London: Simpkin, Marshalls, Hamilton and Kent, 1900).
*The Trail of the Serpent* (London: Ward, Lock and Tyler, 1867).
Brantlinger, Patrick. *Rule of Darkness: British Literature and Imperialism, 1830–1914* (Ithaca: Cornell University Press, 1988).
Brooks, Peter, *Body Work: Objects of Desire in Modern Narrative* (London and Cambridge, MA: Harvard University Press, 1993).
Broughton, Rhoda, *A Beginner* (London: Macmillan, Two-Shilling Library Series, 1899).
*Cometh Up As A Flower: An Autobiography* (London: Richard Bentley and Son, 1878).
*Dear Faustina* (London: Richard Bentley and Son, 1897).
*Not Wisely But Too Well* (Leipzig: Tauchnitz edition, 1867).
Butler, Samuel, *Erewhon: or, Over the Range*, ed. Hans-Peter Breuer and Daniel F. Howard (Newark, NJ: University of Delaware Press; London: Associated University Presses, 1981).
Casey, Ellen Miller. "Other People's Prudery," in Don Richard Cox (ed.), *Sexuality and Victorian Literature* (Knoxville: University of Tennessee Press, 1984), pp. 72–82.
Cawelti, John G., *Adventure, Mystery and Romance: Formula Stories as Art and Popular Culture* (Chicago: University of Chicago Press, 1976).
Chadwick, Edwin, *The Health of Nations: A Review of the Works of Edwin Chadwick with a Biographical Dissertation by Benjamin Ward Richardson* (London: Longman's, 1887).
Clark, Charles S., "TV Violence," *CQ Researcher* 3.12 (1993), pp. 167–180ff.
Crellin, J. K. "The Dawn of the Germ Theory: Particles, Infection and Biology," in F. N. L. Poynter (ed.), *Medicine and Science in the 1860s* (London: Wellcome Institute of the History of Medicine, 1968).
Cvetkovich, Ann, *Mixed Feelings: Feminism, Mass Culture and Victorian Sensationalism* (New Brunswick: Rutgers, 1992).
Davies, S. J. "Classes and Police in Manchester 1829–1880." in Alan J. Kidd and K. W. Roberts (eds.), *City, Class and Culture: Studies of Social Policy and Cultural Production in Victorian Manchester* (Manchester, Manchester University Press, 1985).
Dickens, Charles, *Bleak House* (Oxford: Oxford University Press, 1948).
*Oliver Twist* (Oxford: Oxford University Press, 1949).
*Our Mutual Friend*, ed. Stephen Gill (New York: Viking, 1971).
Dijkstra, Bram, *Idols of Perversity: Fantasies of Feminine Evil in Fin de Siècle Culture* (New York: Oxford University Press, 1986).
Edson, Cyrus. "The Microbe as Social Leveller," *The North American Review* 161 (1895), pp. 421–426.
Eliot, George, *Adam Bede* (New York: Harcourt, Brace and World, 1962).
*Scenes of Clerical Life* (Boston: Little, Brown, 1900).
Eliot, Simon. "Public Libraries and Popular Authors, 1883–1912," *The Library* 8 (1986), pp. 322–350.
Erickson, Lee, "The Economy of Novel Reading: Jane Austen and the Circula-

ting Library," *Studies in English Literature* 30 (1990), pp. 573–585.

Fetterley, Judith. *The Resisting Reader: A Feminist Approach to American Fiction* (Bloomington: Indiana University Press, 1978).

Flaubert, Gustave, *Madame Bovary*, trans. William Blaydes (New York: Collier, 1902).

Flint, Kate, *The Woman Reader, 1837–1914* (Oxford: Clarendon Press, 1993).

Foucault, Michel, *The Birth of the Clinic: An Archaeology of Medical Perception*, trans. A. M. Sheridan Smith (New York: Random, 1973).

*The History of Sexuality*, volume I, trans. Robert Hurley (New York: Vintage, 1980).

*The Order of Things: An Archaeology of the Human Sciences* (New York: Random House, 1970).

Friedman, Susan Stanford, "Creativity and the Childbirth Metaphor: Gender Difference in Literary Discourse," in Elaine Showalter (ed.), *Speaking of Gender* (New York: Routledge, 1989), pp. 73–100.

Frye, Northrop, *Anatomy of Criticism* (Princeton: Princeton University Press, 1957).

Gallagher, Catherine, "George Eliot and Daniel Deronda: The Prostitute and the Jewish Question," in Ruth Bernard Yeazell (ed.), *Sex, Politics and Science in the Nineteenth-Century Novel. Selected Papers from the English Institute, 1983–1984*, new series 10 (Baltimore: Johns Hopkins University Press, 1986).

Gavin, Hector, *Sanitary Ramblings, Being Sketches and Illustrations of Bethnal Green, a Type of the Condition of the Metropolis and Other Large Cities*, facsimile edition of the London 1848 edition (London: F. Cass, 1971).

Gilbert, Sandra and Susan Gubar, *The Madwoman in the Attic: The Woman Writer and the Nineteenth Century Literary Imagination* (New Haven: Yale University Press, 1979).

Gilman, Sander L. *Disease and Representation: Images of Illness from Madness to AIDS* (Ithaca: Cornell University Press, 1988).

Goethe, Johann Wolfgang von, *Faust: A Tragedy*, trans. Walter Arndt, ed. Cyrus Hamilton (New York: Norton, 1976).

Gould, Robert E, MD, "Should Congress Pass Legislation Regulating TV Violence? PRO," *Congressional Digest* 72.12 (1993), pp. 300–306.

Greenberg, Gerald S., "Books as Disease Carriers, 1880–1920," *Libraries and Culture* 23 (1988), pp. 281–292.

Griest, Guinevere, *Mudie's Circulating Library and the Victorian Novel* (Bloomington: Indiana University Press, 1970).

Griffin, Susan, *Woman and Nature: The Roaring Inside Her* (New York: Harper and Row, 1978).

Grosz, Elizabeth, *Volatile Bodies: Toward a Corporeal Feminism* (Bloomington: Indiana University Press, 1994).

Haraway, Donna, "A Manifesto for Cyborgs: Science, Technology and Socialist Feminism in the 1980s," in Elizabeth Weed (ed.), *Coming to Terms: Feminism, Theory, Politics* (New York: Routledge, 1989).

Hardy, Thomas, *Tess of the D'Urbervilles: A Pure Woman* (New York: New American Library, 1980).

Harrison, Frederic, "On the Choice of Books," *Fortnightly Review* 31 (1879), pp. 491–512.

Hollings, Ernest F., "Should Congress Pass Legislation Regulating TV Violence? PRO," *Congressional Digest* 72.12 (1993), pp. 300–302.

Homer, *The Odyssey of Homer*, trans. Richard Lattimore (New York: Harper and Row, 1965).

Hughes, Winifred, *The Maniac in the Cellar: Sensation Novels in the 1860s* (Princeton: Princeton University Press, 1980).

Humphery, George R., "The Reading of the Working Classes," *The Nineteenth Century* 33 (1893), pp. 690–701.

Irigaray, Luce, "Women on the Market," in *This Sex Which is Not One*, trans. Catherine Porter with Carolyn Burke (Ithaca: Cornell University Press, 1985), pp. 170–191.

Jameson, Fredric, *The Political Unconscious: Narrative as a Socially Symbolic Act* (Ithaca: Cornell University Press, 1981).

Jones, Gardner Maynard, "Contagious Diseases and Public Libraries," *The Library Journal* 16 (1891), pp. 35–38.

Kilgour, Maggie, *From Communion to Cannibalism: An Anatomy of Metaphors of Incorporation* (Princeton: Princeton University Press, 1990).

Kingsley, Charles, *Cheap Clothes and Nasty* (London: W. Pickering, 1850).

"Great Cities and their Influence for Good or Evil," in *Sanitary and Social Essays* (London: Macmillan, 1889), pp. 187–222.

Kristeva, Julia, *Desire in Language: A Semiotic Approach to Literature and Art*, trans. Thomas Gora, Alice Jardine, and Leon S. Roudiez, ed. Leon S. Roudiez (New York: Columbia University Press, 1980).

*The Powers of Horror: An Essay on Abjection*, trans. Leon S. Roudiez (New York: Columbia University Press, 1982).

Laqueur, Thomas. *Making Sex: Body and Gender from the Greeks to Freud* (Cambridge, MA: Harvard University Press, 1990).

Lakoff, George and Mark Johnson, *Metaphors We Live By* (Chicago: Chicago University Press, 1980).

Loesberg, Jonathan, "The Ideology of Narrative Form in Sensation Fiction," *Representations* 13 (1986), pp. 115–138.

Marcus, Steven, *The Other Victorians: A Study of Sexuality and Pornography in Mid-Nineteenth Century England* (New York: Basic Books, 1964).

Mauss, Marcel, *The Gift*, trans. Ian Cunnison (New York and London: W. W. Norton and Co., 1967).

Mayhew, Henry, *London Labour and the London Poor; Cyclopaedia of the Condition and Earnings of Those That Will Work, Those That Cannot Work, and Those That Will Not Work*, reprint of the 1861–1862 edition (New York: Dover, 1968).

McClary, Andrew, "Beware the Deadly Books: A Forgotten Episode in Library History," *Journal of Library History, Philosophy and Comparative Librarianship* 20 (1985), pp. 427–433.

"Germs are Everywhere: The Germ Threat as Seen in Magazine Articles 1890–1920," *Journal of American Culture* 3 (1980), pp. 33–46.

Metz, Nancy Aycock, "Discovering a World of Suffering: Fiction and the Rhetoric of Sanitary Reform – 1840–1860," *Nineteenth Century Contexts* 15.1 (1991), pp. 65–81.

Michie, Helena, *The Flesh Made Word: Female Figures and Women's Bodies* (New York and Oxford: Oxford University Press, 1987).

Miller, D. A., *The Novel and the Police* (Berkeley: University of California Press, 1988).

Miller, Nancy K., "Emphasis Added: Plots and Plausibilities in Women's Fiction," *PMLA* 96 (1981), pp. 36–48.

Modleski, Tania, *Loving With A Vengeance: Mass-Produced Fantasies for Women* (Hamden, CT: Archon Books, 1982).

Moore, George, *Literature at Nurse or Circulating Morals: A Polemic on Victorian Censorship*, edited and with an Introduction by Pierre Coustillas (Brighton: Harvester Press, 1976).

Murray, Vincent E. H., "Ouida's Novels," *Contemporary Review* 22 (1873), pp. 921–935.

Norman, Henry, "Theories and Practice of Modern Fiction," *Fortnightly Review* 40 (1883), pp. 870–886.

Nunokawa, Jeff, *The Afterlife of Property: Domestic Security in the Victorian Novel* (Princeton: Princeton University Press, 1994).

Oliphant, Margaret, "Novels," *Blackwood's* 102 (1867), pp. 257–280.

Ouida (pseudonym for De La Rame or Ramée, Morie Louise), *Folle-Farine*, In Three Volumes (London: Chapman and Hall, 1971).

*Granville de Vigne; or, Held in Bondage. A Tale of the Day* (Philadelphia: J. B. Lippincott Co., 1867).

*Puck*, In Three Volumes (London: Chapman and Hall, 1870).

*Strathmore; or, Wrought by His Own Hand, a Life Romance* (London: Chapman and Hall [no date, 1865?]).

*The Tower of Taddeo*, In Three Volumes (London: William Heinemann, 1892).

*Two Little Wooden Shoes: A Sketch* (London: Chapman and Hall, 1874).

*Under Two Flags* (Chicago and New York: Rand, McNally and Co., [no date, 1917?]).

*Views and Opinions*, second edition (London: Methuen, 1896).

*Parliamentary Papers: Health/Infectious Diseases*, volume IV (Irish University Press Series of *British Parliamentary Papers* (Shannon, Ireland: Irish University Press, 1970).

Pattison, Mark, "Books and Critics," *Fortnightly Review* 28 (1877), pp. 659–679.

Poole, W. F., "The Spread of Contagious Diseases by Library Books," *The Library Journal* 4 (1879), pp. 258–262.

Poovey, Mary, *Making a Social Body: British Cultural Formation, 1830–1864* (Chicago: University of Chicago Press, 1995).

Porter, Roy and Lesley Hall, *The Facts of Life: The Creation of Sexual Knowledge in Britain, 1650–1950* (New Haven: Yale University Press, 1995).

Pykett, Lyn, *The "Improper" Feminine: The Women's Sensation Novel and the New Woman Writing* (London and New York: Routledge, 1995).

Reade, Charles, *Hard Cash: A Matter of Fact Romance*, second edition (London: Sampson Low, Son, and Marston, 1864).

Richardson, Benjamin Ward, "The Health of the Mind," *Longman's Magazine* 14 (1889), pp. 145–163.

Richardson, Samuel, *Clarissa: or, The History of a Young Lady*, ed. and with an Introduction by John Angus Burrell (New York: The Modern Library, 1950).

   *Pamela*, Introduction by M. Kinkead-Weekes (New York: Dutton, 1966).

Rogers, Robert, *Metaphor: A Psychoanalytic View* (Los Angeles; Berkeley: University of California Press, 1978).

Roose, Robson (psuedonym), "Infection and Disinfection," *Fortnightly Review* 47 (1887), pp. 249–261.

Ross, Catherine Sheldrick, "Metaphors of Reading," *Journal of Library History, Philosophy and Comparative Librarianship* 22 (1987), pp. 147–163.

Rushdie, Salman, *The Satanic Verses* (New York: Viking, 1989).

Said, Edward, *Culture and Imperialism* (New York: Vintage, 1994).

Sarano, Jacques, *The Meaning of the Body*, trans. James H. Farley (Philadelphia: Westminster Press, 1966).

Scarry, Elaine, *The Body in Pain* (New York and Oxford: Oxford University Press, 1985).

Schiebinger, Londa, *Nature's Body: Gender in the Making of Modern Science* (Boston: Beacon Press, 1993).

Schroeder, Natalie, "Feminine Sensationalism, Eroticism, and Self-Assertion: M. E. Braddon and Ouida," *Tulsa Studies in Women's Literature* 7 (1988), pp. 87–103.

Schweickart, Patrocinio P. "Reading Ourselves: Toward a Feminist Theory of Reading," in Elizabeth A. Flynn and Patrocinio P. Schweickart (eds.), *Gender and Reading: Essays on Readers, Texts and Contexts* (Baltimore and London: Johns Hopkins University Press, 1986).

Sedgwick, Eve Kosofsky, *Between Men: English Literature and Male Homosocial Desire* (New York: Columbia University Press, 1985).

Showalter, Elaine, *A Literature of Their Own: British Women Novelists from Brontë to Lessing* (Princeton, NJ: Princeton University Press, 1977).

Smith, Phillip Thurmond, *Policing Victorian London: Political Policing, Public Order and the London Metropolitan Police* (Westport, CT: Greenwood Press, 1985).

Sontag, Susan, *Illness as Metaphor and AIDS and its Metaphors*, reprints (New York: Doubleday, Anchor Books, 1990).

Stallybrass, Peter and Allon White, *The Politics and Poetics of Transgression* (Ithaca, NY: Cornell University Press, 1986).

Stirling, Monica, *The Fine and the Wicked: The Life and Times of Ouida* (London: Victor Gollancz, 1957).

Strahan, A., "Bad Literature for the Young." *Contemporary Review* 26 (1875), pp. 981–991.

Street, G. S., "An Appreciation of Ouida," *Yellow Book* 6 (1895), pp. 167–176.

Taylor, Jenny Bourne, *In the Secret Theatre of Home: Wilkie Collins, Sensation Narrative and Nineteenth Century Psychology* (London: Routledge, 1988).

Todorov, Tzvetan, *Genres in Discourse*, trans. Catherine Porter (Cambridge: Cambridge University Press, 1990).

  *Mikhail Bakhtin: The Dialogical Principle*, trans. Wlad Godzich. Theory and History of Literature 13 (Minneapolis, MN: University of Minneapolis Press, 1984).

Tuchman, Gaye with Nina E. Fortin, *Edging Women Out: Victorian Novelists, Publishers, and Social Change* (New Haven: Yale University Press, 1989).

Vrettos, Athena, *Somatic Fictions: Imagining Illness in Victorian Culture* (Stanford: Stanford University Press, 1995).

Walker, George Alfred, *Gatherings from Graveyards*, reprinted from the 1839 edition (New York: Arno, 1977).

Walkowitz, Judith, *City of Dreadful Delight: Narratives of Sexual Danger in Late-Victorian London* (Chicago: University of Chicago Press, 1992).

  *Prostitution and Victorian Society: Women, Class and the State* (Cambridge and New York: Cambridge University Press, 1980).

White, Hayden, "Historicism, History and the Figurative Imagination," *History and Theory: Studies in the Philosophy of History* 14 (1975), pp. 48–67.

Williams, A. Susan, *The Rich Man and the Diseased Poor in Early Victorian Literature* (London: Macmillan, 1987).

Wolff, Robert Lee, *Sensational Victorian: The Life and Fiction of Mary Elizabeth Braddon* (New York: Garland Publishing, 1979).

Wood, Mrs. Henry, *East Lynne*, ed. Sally Mitchell, (New Brunswick, NJ: Rutgers University Press, 1984).

Wood, Marilyn, *Rhoda Broughton (1840–1920): Profile of a Novelist* (Stamford, Lincolnshire: Paul Watkins, 1993).

Wright, Thomas, "Concerning the Unknown Public," *The Nineteenth Century* 13 (1883), pp. 279–296.


ANONYMOUS

"Class Criticism," *Temple Bar* 8 (1863), pp. 236–239.

"Contemporary Literature," *Blackwood's* 125 (1879), pp. 322–344.

"Do Books Carry Infection?" *Library Journal* 49 (1924), p. 416.

"English Realism and Romance," *Quarterly Review* 173 (1891), pp. 468–494.

"Literary Exhaustion," *Cornhill Magazine* 22 (1870), pp. 285–296.

"Literary Voluptuaries," *Blackwood's* 142 (1887), pp. 805–817.

"Miss Broughton's Novels," *Temple Bar* 80 (1887), pp. 196–209.

"No Infection in Library Books," *The Literary Digest* 51 (1915), p. 1348.

"On the Reading of Books," *Temple Bar* 72 (1884), pp. 178–186.

"Ouida's Novels," *Westminster Review* 105 (1876), pp. 360–386.

"Penny Fiction," *Quarterly Review* 171 (1890), pp. 149–171.

Review of *A Beginner*, *The Athenaeum* 3471 (1894), p. 574.

Review of *Not Wisely But Too Well* ("New Novels"), *The Athenaeum* 2088 (1867), p. 569.

Review of *The Doctor's Wife* ("Recent Novels"), *The Spectator* 71 (1893), pp. 146–147.

Review of *The Massarenes*, *The Athenaeum* 109 (1897), p. 536.

Review of *The Massarenes*, *The Spectator* 78 (1897), p. 596.

Review of *Under Two Flags*, *The Athenaeum* 2103 (1868), pp. 248–249.

"Sensation Novels," *Quarterly Review* 113 (1863), pp. 481–515.

"The Cantinières and Vivandières of the French Army," *Illustrated Times* (July 16, 1859), p. 44.

"The Cholera Conference," *Quarterly Review* 122 (1867), pp. 29–55.

"The Literature of the Streets," *Edinburgh Review* 165 (1887), pp. 40–65.

"The Novels of Miss Broughton," *Temple Bar* 41 (1874), pp. 197–209.

"The Vice of Reading," *Temple Bar* 42 (1874), pp. 251–257.

# Index

CAMBRIDGE STUDIES IN NINETEENTH-CENTURY
LITERATURE AND CULTURE

General editors
Gillian Beer, *University of Cambridge*
Catherine Gallagher, *University of California, Berkeley*

Titles published

1. The Sickroom in Victorian Fiction: The Art of Being Ill
   by Miriam Bailin, *Washington University*

2. Muscular Christianity: Embodying the Victorian Age
   edited by Donald E. Hall, *California State University, Northridge*

3. Victorian Masculinites: Manhood and Masculine Poetics
   in Early Victorian Literature and Art
   by Herbert Sussman, *Northeastern University*

4. Byron and the Victorians
   by Andrew Elfenbein, *University of Minnesota*

5. Literature in the Marketplace: Nineteenth-Century British
   Publishing and the Circulation of Books
   edited by John O. Jordon, *University of California, Santa Cruz*
   and Robert L. Patten, *Rice University*

6. Victorian Photography, Painting and Poetry:
   The Enigma of Visibility in Ruskin, Morris and the Pre-Raphaelites
   by Lindsay Smith, *University of Sussex*

7. Charlotte Brontë and Victorian Psychology
   by Sally Shuttleworth, *University of Sheffield*

8. The Gothic Body
   Sexuality, Materialism, and Degeneration at the *Fin de Siècle*
   Kelly Hurley, *University of Colorado at Boulder*

9. Rereading Walter Pater
   by William F. Shuter, *Eastern Michigan University*

DH

823.
809
928
7
GIL

Printed in the United Kingdom
by Lightning Source UK Ltd.
129123UK00002B/241-243/A